HONOR
THE
BRAVE

HONOR THE BRAVE

America's Wars and Warriors

Victor Brooks

THE MILITARY BOOK CLUB
New York

Published by
BOOKSPAN
Department GB
401 Franklin Avenue
Garden City, New York 11530

ISBN 0-7394-1570-0

Prepared and designed by Combined Publishing, Pennsylvania.

Printed in the United States of America.

Contents

This engraving entitled simply '76 was published in Harper's Weekly *in July of 1876, for the 100th anniversary of the start of the American Revolution.*

CHAPTER I

Liberty or Death

On the balmy spring evening of April 18, 1775, the simmering hostility between the government of His Majesty King George III and his American colonists was about to erupt into open warfare. General Thomas Gage, royal governor of the province of Massachusetts and commander in chief of British forces in North America, had just issued orders for 21 companies of elite troops, about 700 men, to march out of Boston and launch a predawn raid on the town of Concord, 21 miles away. Gage's spies had informed him that rebel militia units had stored large quantities of cannons, muskets, and gunpowder in the small Middlesex community, and the British general was determined to confiscate the weapons before they could be used against the 3,500 men of his garrison.

A little more than a decade earlier, American colonists had toasted their king as "that wisest of monarchs" and considered themselves fortunate to be members of the mighty and prosperous British Empire. However, during the next 10 years, a series of tariffs, taxes, and trade restrictions culminating in the Boston Tea Party had turned Massachusetts Bay into a virtual occupied province with Royal Navy ships blockading the harbor and red-coated soldiers patrolling the streets of Boston. The alarmed and outraged colonists had begun organizing a provincial army of militiamen to protect themselves against an expected attack by the British Regulars, and by the spring of 1775 their predictions of open warfare were about to come true. A few days before this climactic Tuesday evening, Lord

Paul Revere's famous ride alerted the countryside around Boston that the revolution was at hand.

Dartmouth, the British secretary of state for the Colonies, had in effect ordered his field commander to initiate open warfare against the colonists as he insisted, "the people of Massachusetts are conducting proceedings that amount to an actual revolt and the King's dignity and the honour and safety of the Empire require that in such a situation, force should be repelled with force."

Almost as soon as preparations for the march were begun, sharp-eyed patriot residents of Boston relayed their information to Dr. Joseph Warren, the most prominent member of the Sons of Liberty who still remained in the city. Warren hurried over to the home of his friend and fellow patriot leader, Paul Revere, and asked him to begin a prearranged series of alarms designed to warn the countryside of this threat. Revere, a prosperous silversmith and engraver and one of the best horsemen in the town, immediately headed for Old North Church, and accompanied by the church sexton, climbed the creaking stairs high into the tower, drew out a flint, and lit two lanterns that he held out of the topmost window of the steeple. Across the Charles River, a group of Charlestown patriots was keeping a careful watch for just such a signal and suddenly saw the two flashes of light in the darkness. The signal of two lights meant that the British troops were expected to come "by sea," that is, to row across Back Bay to the mainland town of Cambridge and begin their march westward from that point. A short time later, a small boat manned by two volunteer sailors reached the Charlestown ferry terminus and Revere himself disembarked to greet the patriots waiting for him. These colonists had prepared one of the fastest horses in the town, owned by Deacon John Larkin, and the patriot silversmith quickly mounted and began to spread the alarm through a series of villages and towns.

When Revere arrived in the small crossroads village of Lexington, about six miles from Concord, he alerted the commander of the town's single militia company,

Stand your ground! Don't fire unless fired upon! But if they want to have a war, let it begin here!

— Captain John Parker to his men on Lexington Common, April 19, 1775.

Captain John Parker. Parker was a well-known, 46-year-old local farmer who had served in the French and Indian War and was now ill with tuberculosis, a condition that would kill him before the end of that summer. Revere informed Parker that "the regulars are coming out," and the militia captain began making plans for deploying his small force. Just before dawn on Wednesday, April 19, 1775, the advance force of six companies of British troops, under the immediate command of Major John Pitcairn, emerged from the tree-lined road on the outskirts of Lexington and, in the grayish light, could just make out a force of men deployed in two lines on the far end of Lexington Common. Pitcairn, an officer in the Royal Marines, urged his horse forward and closed on the militiamen who had between 75 and 80 men deployed along the village green. Pitcairn belligerently yelled, "Lay down your arms you damned rebels!" and ordered his men to line up in battle formation and fix bayonets for a charge.

Captain Parker's initial inclination was to accept the British challenge to fight and he yelled to his men, "Stand your ground! Don't fire unless fired upon! But if they want to have a war, let it begin here!" However, as he rapidly counted off a British force that was almost four times the size of his own

This Earle and Doolittle engraving, made shortly after the action at Lexington, April 19, 1775, is believed to be the most accurate. British troops are firing at colonists who are dispersing, but who have not laid down their arms as ordered. The Royal Marine officer Major Pitcairn is mounted at right.

Henry Knox's men bring Fort Ticonderoga's artillery to Boston, a 300-mile journey in the dead of winter that caught the British by surprise. The colonists besieging Boston now out-gunned their British opponents.

company, he accepted the informal advice of many of his men that "there are too many of them and too few of us" and reluctantly ordered his men to disperse to their homes, although none of the colonists dropped their weapons as Pitcairn had ordered. As the militiamen began to turn and walk away from the village green, a single shot exploded into the morning air and pandemonium quickly followed.

Over two centuries later, historians still debate whether this first shot was fired by a redcoat, a militiaman, a bystander, or was merely a misfire, but one thing is certain, this "shot heard round the world" produced deadly consequences. Only seconds after the shot was fired, the redcoats, without orders, began to open fire on the dispersing militiamen and within minutes seven colonists were lying dead or dying on or near the Lexington Common. While most of the patriots who were killed or wounded in this action were shot or bayoneted as they tried to leave the field, at least one man, Jonas Parker, refused to leave his position on the village green. According to one witness, Parker, a cousin of the militia commander "was standing with his balls and flints in his hat on the ground between his feet and he declared he would never run." Parker got off a single shot against the charging

> *The balls flew so thick, I thought there was not chance for escape, and that I might as well fire my gun as stand still and do nothing.*
>
> — COLONIST EBENEZER MUNROE ON THE BRITISH CHARGE AT LEXINGTON.

Regulars. While he was reloading he was shot by a redcoat and "as he lay on the ground, they ran him through with the bayonet." A second patriot, Ebenezer Munroe, was equally determined to hold his place in the face of the terrifying British charge. He recalled afterward, "The balls flew so thick, I thought there was not chance for escape, and that I might as well fire my gun as stand still and do nothing." He insisted that the biggest challenge was to get a clear shot at the Regulars as smoke was already covering the field and it was difficult to locate a target.

Most of the militiamen, however, did not return the redcoats' fire and local minister Reverend Jonas Clarke insisted, "Far from firing first upon the King's troops; upon the most careful enquiry, it appears that but very few of our people fired at all." Thus when the commander of the entire British column, Lieutenant Colonel Francis Smith, finally arrived on the scene he saw a virtually out of control advance unit running wild as they attempted to shoot or bayonet anyone in sight, including innocent bystanders. Smith ordered a drummer to beat a recall but the tactic did not fully work. As one officer noted, "We then formed on the Common but the men were so wild they could hear no orders." Another lieutenant admitted, "We formed on the Common, but with some difficulty," while Smith himself noted his initial frustration at the slow response of his troops as "I was desirous of putting a stop to all further slaughter of those deluded people."

——————★ ★ ★——————

June 28.—Several scouting parties sent out, who having captured the officers of the Tories, swore them to be true to Congress, and then dismissed them.

June 29.—At 4 P.M. we embarked for Marcus Hook, and having a favorable wind, we reached our desired haven July 1, at 10 A.M.

July 4.—Marched from Marcus Hook at Reveille, proceeded through Chester, Derby and over Schuylkill and arrived at Philadelphia at 2 P.M.

July 6.—At 2 o'clock P.M. marched from our quarters to Stamper's Wharf [between Dock and Spruce Streets] where we embarked for Bordentown.

July 7.—Arrived at Bordentown at sunrise, and were ordered to proceed to Amboy. At 2 P.M. we marched. When near to Allentown, Capt. Farmer's gun went off accidentally and shot a soldier of his own company. Reached Allentown at 6 P.M. and encamped.

July 8.—At 6 A.M. resumed our march—passed thro' Cranberry at noon, and reached Brunswick at dusk.

July 11.—Left Brunswick and reached Perth Amboy at noon, where we discovered the enemy on Staten Island. The inhabitants seem to be friends to our present struggle.

July 17.—At Reveille were informed that the enemy had landed at Elizabethtown, which caused us to be marched there. On arrival at 2 o'clock, we found the alarm was a false one. We determined to cross to Staten Island that night to visit the troops of Gen. Howe, but a hurricane arose which prevented our embarkation. We afterward ascertained that we would have been cut off, had we landed.

— DIARY OF LIEUTENANT JAMES McMICHAEL, 1776-1778

——————★ ★ ★——————

Israel Putnam was plowing a field in Connecticut when he heard the news of Lexington and Concord. Immediately mounting a horse he was at the scene of the action within a few hours. Because of his French and Indian War experience, Putnam was quickly made second in command of the patriot forces converging on Boston.

Colonel Smith had been able to restore some semblance of order, but few colonists would soon forget the orgy of bloodshed on Lexington Green and the redcoats would return to the town in very different circumstances than they entered the community. The march toward Concord was resumed and by midmorning the redcoats had arrived in that town. However, the colonists had removed or hidden most of the precious military supplies and, other than three small cannons, almost nothing of military value was found. One British observer noted sarcastically of the modest gains of this bloody raid, "The Grenadiers spoiled some flour, knocked the trunions off several iron guns, burned a heap of wooden spoons and cut down a liberty pole," hardly a satisfying accomplishment for a major assault force.

As Smith ordered his men to re-form for the march back to Boston, hundreds and then thousands of militiamen were forming in the hills around Concord to contest the British withdrawal. Colonial snipers concealed themselves behind every available stone wall and tree along the road back toward Boston, and began picking off large numbers of redcoats. One British officer insisted, "The countryside was an amazing strong one, covered with trees and fences and, on all the hills on each side of us were covered with rebels." The British companies of grenadiers and light infantrymen were being rapidly whittled down to skeleton units and by midafternoon almost half of the officers were dead or wounded. By the time the red-coat column had returned to the outskirts of Lexington the British forces were on the verge of collapse. One participant noted, "we began to run rather than retreat in order," while another redcoat admitted, "we must have laid down our arms or been picked off by the rebels at their pleasure." Only the prov-idential arrival of a British relief force under General Hugh Percy saved Smith's column from annihilation on the first day of the War of Independence.

As the reinforced column rested in Lexington and then began the final stage of the march, American patriots who fell outside the traditional definition of frontline soldiers were swept up in the confrontation. When rebel snipers fired from buildings in towns between Lexington and Cambridge, British flanking par-ties swept in from behind and often killed every adult male in the structure. When the redcoat column approached the town of Menotomy, a badly crippled resident named Samuel Whittmore refused to be evacuated and remained in his own home which was right in the line of the British march. Whittmore barricaded the door to his bedroom and then armed himself with a musket, two pistols, and a cavalry saber to challenge any redcoat invaders. When a British flanking party burst into the house and then smashed through the bar-ricade, the senior citizen shot the first man through with his musket, killed two more with his pistols, and hacked several others with his saber before being left for dead with 14 bayo-net wounds through his body. After the enemy column passed through the town, neighbors discovered the old man still breathing and nursed him well enough to live until the ripe old age of 96.

A number of other older patriots contributed their own ener-gies to the confrontation with the ministerial troops. David Lamson, a late-middle-aged, gray-haired mulatto who lived near Menotomy, was elected commander of a force of overaged residents who were designated as an alarm company, a unit that was only expected to be used in extreme emergencies. A colonial scout informed Lamson that a wagon train of reserve ammunition was moving west from Boston to reinforce the British column and there were no regular militia companies

readily available to confront the enemy force. Lamson carefully set up an ambush along the road by concealing most of his
men while he stood in the middle of the road and challenged
the wagon train's drivers and guards to surrender. When the
lead wagon attempted to run Lamson down, the concealed

*If one old Yankee
woman can take six
redcoats, how many
soldiers will it take to
conquer America?*

— MOTHER BOTHERICK AFTER SHE SINGLE-
HANDEDLY CAPTURED SIX BRITISH SOLDIERS

"alarm" men opened fire, killing or wounding nearly
half the enemy force and capturing the wagons. A half-
dozen grenadiers ran panic-stricken into the woods
and when they came upon an old woman digging for
vegetables they promptly begged her for protection.
The woman, named Mother Botherick, quickly led the
men to the home of a local militia officer and supervised their surrender. As she left the redcoats she
warned, "If you ever live to get back, you tell King
George that an old woman took six of his grenadiers
prisoner. If one old Yankee woman can take six redcoats, how
many soldiers will it take to conquer America?"

The intervention of Percy's reinforcements allowed the
British raiding force to return to Boston somewhat intact, but
almost 300 redcoats, nearly half the original column, had been
killed or wounded compared to a loss of about 90 patriots. The
alarms that had spread across the New England countryside
as the British Regulars approached Concord had produced an
outpouring of militiamen from as far away as Connecticut, and
when Thomas Gage awoke the morning after the battle, he was
startled by the presence of over 20,000 armed and determined
colonists encircling Boston. While Sir Thomas attempted to
explain away the battle to his superiors in London as "a minor
affair," the power of His Majesty's government in Massachusetts now reached only as far as the outer picket lines
around Boston.

As General Gage fumed at the embarrassment of being effectively besieged by men that he disparagingly referred to as
"country people," reinforcements were on their way from
England. Several regiments of redcoats and three influential
generals, John Burgoyne, Henry Clinton, and William Howe,
arrived in May and the three new generals immediately convinced Gage to order an offensive against the patriot headquarters in Cambridge. However, the commander of the patriot
army, General Artemus Ward, was almost immediately warned

of Gage's intentions and on the humid, sultry evening of June 16, 1775, Colonel William Prescott and three regiments of Massachusetts soldiers were ordered to march onto Charlestown Peninsula and fortify the largest hill in the area, Bunker Hill. Once the column had marched past Charlestown Neck onto the peninsula, Prescott decided to leave only a small covering force on Bunker Hill and erect his main fortifications on Breed's Hill which was both lower and closer to Boston. All during the night, the colonial troops worked furiously with spades and picks, and the next morning the officer of the watch on a British warship stared in amazement at a redoubt that stood where an empty field had been observed the previous evening.

Shortly after noon on the sunny, hot day of June 17, 28 Royal Navy barges pushed off from Long Wharf in Boston and began to glide toward the far side of the Charles River. The vessels were formed up into two parallel lines of 14 barges each and the passengers in these vessels represented General Gage's response to the rebel fortification of Breed's Hill. Sir William Howe was leading over 2,000 redcoat infantrymen and several batteries of cannons into a massive assault against the colonists on Charlestown Peninsula. While the British field commander waited for additional units to arrive, the HMS *Falcon* and several other Royal Navy vessels moved in close to the shoreline and swept the parapets of the American redoubt as Colonel Prescott walked along the walls defying the British guns to hit him. Captain William Linsey, master of the *Falcon*, admitted that he greatly admired the bravery of his rebel adversary, having not the slightest inkling that in one of the ironies of the war, his granddaughter would marry Prescott's grandson and the newly married couple would place the crossed swords of

─────── ★ ★ ★ ───────

September 22.—The Fifth Battalion marched from Mount Mifflin at 10 A.M., and arrived at Mount Washington at noon.

September 23.—At 11 o'clock the whole army at Mount Washington met on the grand parade in order to see a man shot, who had left his post in the battle of 16th inst.—but he was reprieved by his Excellency Gen. Washington.

September 29.—We received intelligence at midnight, that the enemy were advancing. We all paraded immediately and man'd the lines. The alarm proved false and at day-break we returned to our encampment.

October 9.—At 8 o'clock three men-of-war and three Tenders came up Hudson's River, which brought on a heavy cannonade from all our forts and batteries near the shore. They, however, passed by. We were all paraded and man'd the lines, but had no engagement. We are now situate on the banks of Hudson's River, ten miles from New York, two miles from Fort Washington, with our lines advantageous and well fortified, both by nature and art.

October 10.—A party of 120 men with wagons, were detached from our brigade to take forage from the enemies lines, with the intent to bring on an attack, but they would not come out.

— DIARY OF LIEUTENANT JAMES MCMICHAEL, 1776-1778

─────── ★ ★ ★ ───────

John Stark's ambush on Mystic Beach not only covered Bunker Hill's open flank but also wiped out an elite British light infantry battalion. Although Stark was already 48 at the time of the Boston campaign, he was to outlive all the other generals of the Revolution.

their contending grandparents over the mantlepiece of their first home.

At nearly 3:00, as the temperature soared to almost 95 degrees, the heavily perspiring, wool-coated British Regulars were ordered to form ranks and advance toward the rebel positions. Contrary to popular belief, Howe had no initial intention of simply throwing his men against the colonists in a straight frontal assault. British scouts had discovered a small beach on the Mystic River side of the peninsula about eight feet below the broad meadows where the Americans had built their fortifications. Sir William planned to send an elite strike force of light infantry charging up the narrow beach, at which point they would climb up to the fields well behind the patriot defenses and smash the rebels from behind just as the main force of redcoats advanced from the front. Unfortunately for Howe, Colonel John Stark, the dynamic leader of a regiment of New Hampshiremen, was preparing for just such a contingency. Stark ordered several units of his best sharpshooters to drag rocks from the adjoining fields down onto the narrow beach and then fashioned crude stone barricades that held three lines of riflemen. When the improvised walls were finished, Stark sprang over the most forward fortification and hammered a stake into the sand 40 yards ahead. He then ordered, "not a man is to fire until the first regular crosses that stake. When you can see their garters clear, that's when to shoot."

A few minutes later a long column of redcoats rounded a curve on the beach and immediately noticed the crude stone walls facing the attack force. Each company was ordered to shift from marching order to attack formation and spread out in lines about 15 men abreast. The captain of the lead company, the light infantry of the Royal Welsh Fusiliers, gave the order for his men to advance, but as they marched past Stark's markers, the rebel colonel lowered his arm in a dramatic gesture and a wall of flame erupted from the barricade. Within seconds, only three or four of the 35 men in the company were still standing. A moment later, the light infantry of the second company, the King's Own Regiment, took the place of their fallen comrades, confident that they could rush the colonial position before the patriots could reload. However, Stark had hidden three lines of sharpshooters behind the stone wall and the second rank of colonials stepped to the front and virtually annihilated the approaching redcoats. As perhaps five survivors staggered to the rear, the third British company, the men of the 10th Regiment of Foot, surged forward just in time to encounter Stark's third firing line. Almost every member of this company was dead or wounded a few seconds later and the pitiful few survivors retreated in a daze back toward the seven companies of men who had not yet gone into action. Despite the annihilation of three companies of redcoats about 200 Regulars were still on their feet, and they now thrust forward in a barely controllable mob. Stark's rotation of men kept alternating between firing and loading, and dozens of British soldiers spun around and fell as surviving officers screamed and smashed at the panic-stricken men with their swords. By the time the senior officer with the column called a withdrawal, a staggering total of 96 of the most elite troops in the British army had been killed and several dozen more were writhing in agony on the narrow beach. "I never saw sheep lie as thick in the fold," was Stark's grim description of the scene in front of him.

The failure of the flank attack along Mystic Beach essentially unraveled Sir William Howe's entire attack plan and the main force of redcoats would now be advancing against a rebel force that was focused totally on the enemy in front of them. A long line of scarlet-coated Regulars moved against American militiamen protected by a redoubt and a series of fence rails and stone embankments. The perspiring, cursing men were carrying packs weighing more than 60 pounds and the 95 degree heat caused some of the men to pass out with heatstroke. When the force closed on the patriot lines, colonial officers gave almost simultaneous orders to fire and a wall of flame tore gaping holes in the redcoat line. A blood-spattered Howe watched every one of his staff drop from the colonial musket fire, stunned that a ragged force of amateurs was anni-

Charlestown burns after the Royal Navy's bombardment on the morning of the Bunker Hill assault. Civilian buildings were not usually fired upon in 18th-century warfare and the action was controversial even in England.

hilating such an impressive British force. As the dazed survivors staggered back out of range Sir William immediately organized a second assault.

The grim men holding the colonial defense line were exuberant about their spectacular showing and when they observed the redcoats advancing a second time, one officer shouted, "You drove them back once. You can do it again. Hold your fire until you get the order and don't shoot until you have a target." The only ominous development was that ammunition was beginning to run out and no new supplies had arrived.

You drove them back once. You can do it again. Hold your fire until you get the order and don't shoot until you have a target.

— A COLONIAL OFFICER TO TROOPS HOLDING A DEFENSE LINE AGAINST ADVANCING REDCOATS.

However, when the scarlet line approached a second time, the result was much the same as the first encounter. Israel Putnam, the colorful commander of Connecticut forces, directed a deadly fire from a colonial breastwork and then was startled to see that the officer commanding this part of the British assault was Colonel John Small, one of his closest friends from the French and Indian War. Virtually all of Small's force had retreated from behind him and he was standing alone, a perfect solitary target for rebel snipers. As one colonial rifleman shouted, "There's an officer, let's get him," Small refused to run or duck and later admitted, "I then prepared myself for death." However, Putnam desperately knocked aside the American musket shouting, "For God's sake, spare that man, I love him as a brother." Small bowed his thanks to his now-recognized friend and followed his men down the hill.

> ## For God's sake, spare that man, I love him as a brother.
>
> — COLONIALIST ISRAEL PUTNAM, SAVING THE LIFE OF BRITISH COLONEL JOHN SMALL.

Howe was incredulous at the disaster spread out in front of him and admitted that "this was a moment that I never felt before," a British army was being slaughtered by amateurs. Sir William determined to launch one final assault, but this time the Regulars were ordered to remove their cumbersome packs and many officers even permitted their men to remove their famous red coats in order to provide more mobility. The British commander did not realize it, but the Royal Navy gunfire had largely prevented the arrival of reinforcements or fresh ammunition for the patriots as the narrow Charlestown Neck was pounded by cannonfire. Therefore when the final assault began, the British assault force had far more men than the rebels and an even larger edge in ammunition. The result was one last, bloody confrontation. Major Pitcairn, the officer who had faced the militia on Lexington Green, climbed on top of the wall of the American redoubt and shouted for his men to follow. An instant later the major lay dying as Peter Salem, the black servant of a Connecticut officer, used his last bullet to shoot the redcoat leader. A few minutes later, as redcoats swarmed over the walls, Dr. Joseph Warren, now a major general in the provincial army, sprinted toward Bunker Hill and was killed almost instantly by a British rifleman. Colonel Prescott, the last living rebel inside the redoubt, parried the bayonets of several redcoats with his sword and withdrew from the fort with his long coat shredded from enemy thrusts. Sir William Howe had captured his hill, but more than 1,000 of his men were dead or seriously wounded, and as one appalled British official in London exclaimed of the "victory" at Bunker Hill, "Six more such victories and there will be no one left alive to bring us news of the triumph."

Israel Putnam was the senior officer present when the British launched their attack on Bunker Hill on June 17, 1775. He ordered his own Connecticut troops and other nearby militiamen not to fire at the British until they could see the "whites of their eyes."

The next time that Americans and British met in battle around Boston, the patriot forces would be commanded by a man who would ultimately become the personification of the American Revolution. Only hours before Prescott's men had begun digging their entrenchments on Breed's Hill, the Continental Congress in Philadelphia had appointed Colonel George Washington as the commander in chief of the "Grand American Army." Washington was a Virginia planter with a commanding presence, a notable record of service in the French and Indian War, and perhaps most important for the men who nominated him, a fellow delegate to the Congress. Washington was initially less than enthused about his new soldiers, sending letters back to fellow Southern planters that the New Englanders were "an exceedingly dirty and nasty people." However, by March of 1776 his opinion of his men had improved and he was prepared to initiate an operation that would turn the first campaign of the war into a significant American victory.

Six more such victories and there will be no one left alive to bring us news of the triumph.

— BRITISH OFFICER IN LONDON AFTER HE HEARD OF THE PRICE IN LIVES LOST TO WIN THE BATTLE OF BUNKER HILL.

During the predawn hours of March 2, colonial troops had secretly erected massive artillery batteries on Dorchester Heights above the city of Boston, and a few hours later shattered the late winter calm in the British camp. Abigail Adams, sitting in her bedroom 10 miles away in Braintree, provided her husband John, who was in Philadelphia as a delegate of the Continental Congress, with a dramatic account of the American artillery offensive. "The house this instant shakes with the roar of cannon. I have been to the door and I find it a cannonade from our army. No sleep for me tonight!" The next day, as the bombardment began again, she insisted to her husband, "the sound, I think, is one of the grandest in nature and is one of the true species of the sublime. I could no more sleep than if I had been in the engagement; the rattling of the windows, the jar of the house, the constant roar of the twenty-four pounders and the bursting of the shells gives us such ideas and we realize a scene of which we could scarcely form any conception." Sir William Howe, who had taken over command of the British army after Thomas Gage was relieved, could also "scarcely form any conception" of what the rebels were capa-

George Washington was appointed commander of the Continental Army on June 19, 1775, and arrived in Boston on July 2. Ironically, both his first and last victories over the British, at Boston and Yorktown, were won by siegecraft and skilled placing of artillery, rather than on a battlefield.

ble of doing to his army. Two weeks later, on the morning of St. Patrick's Day, the British army evacuated Boston. Three thousand miles away, when word of the evacuation reached Britain, the Duke of Manchester rose in the House of Lords and noted, "The army of Britain, equipped with every possible essential of war; a chosen army with chosen officers, backed by the power of a mighty fleet, has now been forced to quit a town that was the first object of the war, a place of arms which has cost this nation more than a million pounds to defend." The colonial rebels had won the first round of their confrontation with Britain, but before King George finally acknowledged the independence of his colonies, dozens of battles, many of them disasters for the American cause, would have to be fought.

The house this instant shakes with the roar of cannon. I have been to the door and I find it a cannonade from our army. No sleep for me tonight!

— ABIGAIL ADAMS ON THE AMERICAN ASSAULT AGAINST THE BRITISH CAMP IN BOSTON.

The British evacuation of Boston helped accelerate the process of declaring full independence from England, and on July 2, 1776, the Continental Congress approved a motion accepting Thomas Jefferson's preliminary draft of the Declaration of Independence. An enthusiastic John Adams wrote in his diary: "The second day of July will be the most memorable epoch in the history of America. It ought to be solemnized with pomp and parades, with shows, games, sports,

Peter Salem

Born into slavery in 1750 in Framington, Massachusetts, and freed in 1774, Peter Salem was one of an estimated 5,000 black Americans who served in the Revolution. All were volunteers, and some were slaves who accepted freedom in exchange for enlisting.

Later described by several officers as "an excellent soldier," Salem enrolled in the local militia and was one of thousands of men who turned out on April 19, 1775, to confront the British at Concord Bridge and pursue them back to Boston. He took part in the Patriots' campaign on British-occupied Boston and fought at Bunker Hill, where an uncertain tradition has it that he killed Royal Marine Major John Pitcairn (famed for yelling "Disperse ye rebels" to the minutemen on Lexington Common). Salem's enlistment expired at the end of 1775, but early the following year he enlisted in the Continental Army.

Salem went on to serve in various Massachusetts regiments. He fought at White Plains, took part in the Saratoga campaign, and endured the hardships of Valley Forge. In 1779, Salem joined the 4th (Massachusetts) Regiment of Brigadier General "Mad" Anthony Wayne's Light Infantry Brigade and took part in the storming of Stoney Point, New York.

By then, the focus of the war had shifted to the South, and like most of the men of the Northern Army, Salem spent the remaining years of the war on outpost duty, keeping the British bottled up in New York City, and countering enemy raids. Discharged in 1782, he returned to Framington, where he engaged in farming and business until his death in 1816. There is a statue of Salem in Framington, and he is among the soldiers depicted in John Trumbull's famous painting *The Battle of Bunker's Hill*.

bells, bonfires and illuminations from one end of this continent to the other, from this time forward for evermore." However, at the moment that Adams was writing those words, a flotilla of over 100 British warships was screening the disembarkation of almost 35,000 British and German troops on Staten Island, a tangible reminder that His Majesty's government had no intention of allowing its colonies to merely walk away from the British Empire without a struggle.

George Washington commanded only 19,000 largely untrained men and had virtually no naval support, so his first inclination was to abandon New York City to the British and confront General Howe in a more defendable location. But Congress insisted that the general should make some attempt to hold the city, and the Virginian, rather unwisely, divided his army in two, deploying 7,000 men on the eastern tip of Long Island while the rest of the army was assigned to cover Manhattan. While Washington concentrated on organizing the main army, General John Sullivan was placed in command of the defenses around Brooklyn Heights on the Long Island side of the East River. Washington and Sullivan were hoping that Howe would oblige them with a replay of Bunker Hill, a direct frontal assault into the mouth of American guns, but Sir William had no intention of repeating that earlier disaster. In the early hours of August 26, 1776, Howe landed 24,000 troops

Washington made a difficult retreat across the East River after losing the battle of Long Island on August 27, 1776. The escape of the Continental Army was made possible by Maryland and Delaware troops who sacrificed themselves in one of the most desperate battles in American history.

at Gravesend at the extreme tip of Long Island and set in motion a huge flanking operation which, if fully implemented, might have ended the war that evening. While half the force attracted the attention of the Americans manning the front lines, over 10,000 men slipped through virtually undefended Jamaica Pass and marched in the humid summer night down Jamaica Road which came out behind the rebel lines. Shortly after dawn, while a large force of green-coated jaegers and blue-coated grenadiers of the Hessian Corps advanced toward the American defenses, an elite force of Scottish Highlanders swept in from behind and caught the startled patriot defenders in a huge pincers.

Good God! What brave fellows this day I must lose!

— GEORGE WASHINGTON WATCHING THE BRAVERY OF HIS OUTNUMBERED MEN ON LONG ISLAND.

The trapped Americans suffered enormous casualties and entire units began to surrender. However, just as it seemed that the redcoats would bag the whole American army, a crack brigade of 1,700 Maryland and Delaware Continentals, commanded by General William Alexander, formed a huge V formation on the high ground and exchanged volleys with 5,000 redcoats. General Alexander, better known as Lord Stirling, kept the door open for most of the rest of the defenders to escape while British generals quickly threw in 2,000 Royal Marines and an additional 4,000 Regulars to deal with the American bluecoats. As the British lines closed in on the badly outnumbered Continentals, Stirling ordered the majority of his men to break out while he remained behind with Major Mordecai Gist and 250 of his elite Maryland regulars. Stirling and Gist shocked the British officers when they began swinging their swords and led their small force in a downhill bayonet charge against nearly 11,000 startled redcoats. Washington, who was watching the action a short distance away, marveled at the bravery of this tiny force as it attempted to slash its way through an overwhelming force of enemy soldiers; the Virginian remarked emotionally, "Good God! What brave fellows this day I must lose!" During the ensuing melee, Gist and exactly eight Continentals managed to slip through the scarlet lines while Stirling and a few other wounded survivors surrendered to a reluctantly admiring General Charles Cornwallis.

When Howe decided to besiege the remaining Americans on

Long Island rather than launch a final frontal assault on the last patriot positions, Washington staged a dramatic evacuation of his men across the East River during a providential onset of fog and haze. Less than three weeks later, the British assault on Manhattan itself would almost end the War of Independence and with it, George Washington's life. On the morning of September 15, 1776, an advance force of 4,000 British and Hessian soldiers landed on a series of beaches near Kip's Bay. The 900 defending Americans fled the field within 10 minutes, leaving 120 men behind dead, wounded, or captured. When Washington arrived later with nine newly recruited regiments intending to throw the redcoats into the water, the entire colonial force began to unravel alarmingly. At one point a force of 2,500 virtually untrained patriots was being chased over nearby fields by only 70 British light infantrymen who followed their adversaries through

their trail of discarded knapsacks, canteens, and muskets. As the American force disintegrated, Washington's emotions changed from anger to near suicidal resignation, and the general spurred his horse toward an advancing company of redcoats intending to charge them alone with his sword. As General Nathanael Greene noted, "General Washington was so vexed at the infamous conduct of his troops that he sought death rather than life." Only the quick action of an aide who grabbed Washington's horse and led him to safety with British bullets spattering around him saved the general from probable death. By nightfall on September 15, the British were pushing rapidly across Manhattan Island at a trivial cost of 12 men slightly wounded while the American army had lost nearly 400 men with hundreds of others missing or merely deserted.

The humiliation of that afternoon was rammed home even more dramatically by the British the following morning.

Nathanael Greene served throughout the Revolution, from Boston to Valley Forge to the final battles in the south. His campaign of 1780-1782 in the southern colonies is still studied by military strategists.

★ ★

"Molly Pitcher"

It's a well-known legend of the Revolutionary War: Molly Pitcher, the soldier's wife, helped load and fire a weapon at the battle of Monmouth on June 28, 1778. In fact, there was no Molly Pitcher. But the story is not a complete fabrication. And, as it turns out, the truth is even more interesting than the tale.

Until the early part of the 19th century, it was common for troops to be accompanied by groups of women, and they often did lend a hand with the fighting when things got tough. In later times, these women would generally be dismissed as mere "camp followers." Some were, but there were women who served with the troops as well. The Continental Army regularly enlisted women for a variety of duties, as nurses, laundresses, and as auxiliaries to artillery units. Unlike camp followers, these women were paid, subject to military discipline, and sometimes granted pensions.

Women took part in every important operation of the war, even accompanying Benedict Arnold's heroic expedition from Massachusetts to Quebec through the frozen wilderness of Maine in late 1775. They helped fire the guns at Monmouth, defending forts and frontier posts, and taking part in raids. Most are—and will forever remain—nameless.

One of the most notable army women was Margaret Corbin. Born in Pennsylvania in 1751, from the age of four Margaret Cochran was raised by an uncle, her father having been killed and her mother kidnapped by Indians. Married to John Corbin in 1772, she accompanied him into the 1st Company of Pennsylvania Artillery when he enlisted three years later.

When her husband was mortally wounded at Fort Washington in Upper Manhattan in November 1776, Corbin stepped forward to assume his post, helping to load, lay, and fire the guns. During the fight, she was severely wounded, taking a burst of grape shot—one-inch metal balls—that shattered an arm and mangled a breast. Taken prisoner when the fort surrendered, she was later paroled, returning to duty with the Invalid Corps. She was awarded a pension in 1779 and formally discharged four years later.

As she grew old, she was referred to as "Captain Molly." Corbin settled in Westchester County, New York, as an honored veteran of the war, before she died in 1800. In 1926 her body was moved to West Point.

★ ★

Washington was concerned about the extent of the British penetration of Manhattan Island and he dispatched a force of 120 elite rangers under Colonel Thomas Knowlton to attempt a reconnaissance of the British lines. Soon after the American troops moved into the woods and hollows separating the contending armies, they were attacked by over 400 British light infantrymen who were in the process of carrying out the same mission for General Howe. The rangers fought well, but were forced to retreat, and as they fell back toward the American lines the redcoats blasted a series of taunting bugle calls. Washington, who was an accomplished fox hunter, quickly recognized the calls as those made when the fox has skulked into his hole, a supreme insult against the American soldiers. The Virginian was furious at this extremely unchivalrous taunt and immediately dispatched three rifle companies to support Knowlton with orders to counterattack if at all possible. As the American sharpshooters began picking off large numbers of redcoats, the British column began a slow withdrawal that came to a sudden halt with the arrival of the famed Black Watch Regiment of Scotsmen, who arrived on the scene with bagpipes playing and swinging huge claymore broadswords. The colonials pitched into the overconfident Scots, and in a battle with rifle butts and tomahawks against bayonets and broadswords, Knowlton went down with a fatal wound. Just as the American line was about to break, the timely arrival of 800 Continentals turned the course of the battle as the newly arrived rebels slipped through a wooded area and slammed the redcoats in the flank.

A reinforcement of several regiments of Hessians was not enough to stem the American drive, and when a regiment of Maryland Continentals managed to get into the rear of the British column, the redcoats began to panic and sprint back toward their own camp. Now, whooping and cheering rebel soldiers were chasing the British and Germans through a series of fields and orchards, and the redcoats were in serious danger of being cut off from the main army. Only the last minute arrival of two elite infantry regiments and two grapeshooting cannons was able to keep the charging

Born in poverty in the West Indies, Alexander Hamilton served as both an artillery officer and military aide to George Washington. As the nation's first secretary of the treasury he laid the groundwork for much of America's later banking and finance system.

Stylized depiction of the Hessian surrender at Trenton. The Grenadier Regiment von Rall at right is accurately rendered, as is Washington's Philadelphia Light Horse bodyguard in plumed helmet, but other details are fanciful.

Americans at bay long enough to allow Howe's men to retreat to the safety of the British fleet, while the battle of Harlem Heights had become a major morale boost to a faltering American cause. Slightly more than 2,000 rebels had essentially routed almost 5,000 elite British and Hessian troops during a battle in which 130 Americans and 170 redcoats were killed or wounded. Even Howe was forced to admit that the battle was "an unfortunate business" which "caused a good deal of concern." For the first of several times during the War of Independence, a dying American cause was invigorated by a dramatic, one-sided rebel victory.

While the battle of Harlem Heights demonstrated that American troops could challenge the best units in the British army, Washington was forced to evacuate New York in a campaign that produced few bright spots for the patriot cause. The final insult occurred when Washington allowed himself to be talked into maintaining a presence in New York after the rest of the army had been evacuated to New Jersey. Almost 3,000 men were deployed in Fort Washington, a post that was a disaster waiting to happen as the fort had no well, no bombproof

Washington Crossing the Delaware *was painted in Germany many years after the actual crossing of December 24, 1776. Although the boat is inaccurate, the demeanor and build of the men and the black oarsman, third from left, reflect the reality of the time.*

rooms to store ammunition, and few facilities for utilizing cannons. General Howe took advantage of these weaknesses and on the morning of November 16, 1776, 8,000 British and Hessian troops overwhelmed the fort and captured 3,000 Americans while Washington watched in helpless frustration on the other side of the Hudson River.

By the middle of December, the American army had retreated across New Jersey and was forced to cross the Delaware River into Pennsylvania with the advance units of the British army snapping at its heels. Since most of the army was due to go home on January 1, 1777, and few men could be enticed to serve in an apparently doomed cause, even Washington admitted to his cousin just before Christmas, "I think the game will be pretty much up." However, the Virginia planter was also an enthusiastic gambler, and he finally decided to risk everything on one final roll of the dice. Fortunately for the American commander, his adversary's next move made the upcoming gamble far less risky than it might have been. Rather than push the British army across the Delaware River and attack Washington in Pennsylvania, Howe concluded that the rebel cause was virtually doomed and, with any luck, would merely wither away during the upcoming winter. Therefore, he ordered most of his

★ ★

Daniel Morgan

A cousin of Daniel Boone, Daniel Morgan engineered an amazing victory at a place called the Cowpens in South Carolina.

Shortly after the American disaster at Camden, South Carolina, he had assumed command of the light infantry of the Army of the South, and Congress rewarded him with a brigadier's commission. Morgan took part in Nathanael Greene's Southern campaign, a merry chase across most of the South that saw the British lured deeper and deeper into the American territory.

During this campaign, Morgan distinguished himself at the Cowpens in South Carolina. There, on January 17, 1781, he skillfully combined his poorly trained militia and his skilled regulars, together no more than 1,000 men, to defeat an even larger Tory force.

It was a simple plan. The militia absorbed the initial assault of the Tories and then withdrew to the flanks. As the enemy became entangled with the greatly outnumbered Continentals, Morgan rallied the militia. As the Continentals fell back, Morgan sent the militia to envelop the enemy's right flank, and his handful of cavalry against their left. The resulting "double envelopment" was a huge success, with only a few of the enemy making their escape. Although outnumbered by Tories, he had crushed them with the "double envelopment," resulting in one of the most perfect victories in American history, one which is still studied today.

Although he had attained the rank of general by 1780, the brilliant strategist Daniel Morgan seems to have continued wearing the hunting shirt and leggings of his frontier origins.

★ ★

army back to comfortable winter quarters in New York, leaving a series of unsupported garrisons in key points in New Jersey. One of these bases was the town of Trenton and this was George Washington's target for a planned Christmas attack.

At 2:00 on a cold, clear Christmas afternoon, 2,400 Continental soldiers began forming up in front of their tents and marched down to an embarkation point on the Delaware River. By the time the men were being loaded into a small fleet of large Durham boats, a light snow had begun to fall and as the vessels pushed out into the ice clogged Delaware the snow reached near blizzard proportions. The huge chunks of ice in the water slowed the progress of Colonel Glover's Marblehead contingent of Massachusetts mariners and the boats didn't reach the New Jersey side until 3 A.M. on December 26, far too late to initiate a dawn attack since Trenton was still nine miles distant. The supply situation for the American army had reached a particular low point unmatched until Valley Forge, and large numbers of men were without shoes. Thus dozens of men, reduced to tying strips of cloth around their feet, shuffled through the piercingly cold night along roads covered with a combination of snow and ice. As hundreds of bloody footprints were left in the newly fallen snow, the small army pushed toward an enemy stronghold that was garrisoned by three regiments of Hessians under Colonel Johann Rall. Contrary to popular accounts, Rall had actually been warned by a Loyalist sympathizer that the Americans were planning a dawn attack on Trenton, but the colonel simply stuffed the message in his pocket and continued his all-night celebration of card playing and drinking.

At 7:30 A.M. an advance force of 60 American riflemen crept silently through the snow into the outskirts of the town and, after silencing a number of Hessian sentries, took positions behind the windows of several strategically located buildings. A few minutes later, Washington's main force arrived, supported by a battery of six cannons commanded by Captain Alexander Hamilton. As the patriots spread across the main intersection in the town, Rall stumbled out of his headquarters and tried to organize a counterattack. However, the blue-coated men of Rall's own regiment and the accompanying

Horatio Gates won the key American victory at Saratoga, which proved to be the high point of his career. Efforts by a faction in the Continental Congress to replace Washington as supreme commander with Gates came to nothing, and he was unsuccessful in his command of troops in the final southern campaign of the Revolutionary War.

Knyphausen Regiment were rapidly torn to pieces by the combination of American musket fire, Hamilton's guns, and the riflemen concealed in the nearby houses. When Rall ordered his own artillerymen to deploy for a countering fire, a company of elite infantrymen under Captain William Washington and Lieutenant James Monroe sloshed through the snowy drifts along King Street and smashed into the Hessian gunners before they could open fire. Washington and Monroe both went down with wounds, but the Hessian infantry were now near collapse. At this point, a force of riflemen under Colonel John Stark of Bunker Hill fame charged up the street from behind the German lines and fired a volley that dropped Rall from his horse with a mortal wound. The panic-stricken survivors, who had been told by the British that the rebels didn't take prisoners, began throwing down their weapons, probably fearing almost immediate execution, and breathed a sigh of relief when it became evident that the Americans had no intention of slaughtering them. At the cost of four men wounded, including future President Monroe, the ragged colonial army had captured over 1,000 Hessian soldiers, inflicted more than a hundred casualties, and breathed new life into a dying cause.

A few days later Washington's army attacked the British garrison at Princeton and eliminated another three regiments from the chessboard of the war. In a campaign that had lasted less than two weeks, the patriot army had inflicted more than 2,000 casualties on Howe's army, recovered most of New Jersey for the American cause, and encouraged thousands of wavering citizens back into the ranks of the Congressional cause. Frederick the Great of Prussia was so fascinated by this lightning turnabout in the war that he wrote, "The achievements of Washington and his little band of compatriots between the 25th of December and the 4th of January were the most brilliant of any recorded in the history of military affairs." The dying embers of the Revolution had been rekindled and the upcoming year would prove decisive for the cause of American independence.

The campaigning season of 1777 began with two rival British generals each receiving permission to initiate campaigns that were essentially at cross purposes to one another. Sir William Howe had received permission from Lord George Germain, the secretary of state for the Colonies, who had replaced Lord Dartmouth, to leave a small screening force in New York City and launch a shipborne expedition against the colonial capital of Philadelphia from its theoretically vulnerable south side. On the other hand, General John Burgoyne had received the king's blessing to march an invasion force down from Canada to capture Albany and cut off New England from the rest of the colonies. Much of Burgoyne's planning was based on the assumption that General Howe had been ordered to move his army up the Hudson River in order to link up with the Canadian-based army to crush any rebel forces between them. Obviously, Howe could not be in two places at the same time, and the patriot cause would enormously benefit from this fantastic error in British strategy.

On the crystal clear, warm morning of June 11, 1777, Burgoyne's 7,000 redcoats, Hessians, Tories, and Indian auxiliaries embarked in a colorful assortment of canoes and bateaux with dozens of regimental flags and banners flapping in the breeze. By early July the army had brushed aside an undermanned American garrison at Fort Ticonderoga and was preparing to move southward toward the Hudson. However, at this moment of apparent triumph, Burgoyne made a fatal mistake. Local Tories and Indian scouts informed him that if he made a slight retrograde move to the north, he could utilize a number of interconnected streams and rivers to push down within sight of the Hudson almost entirely by water. Burgoyne

The achievements of Washington and his little band of compatriots between the 25th of December and the 4th of January were the most brilliant of any recorded in the history of military affairs.

— FREDERICK THE GREAT OF PRUSSIA, JANUARY 1777.

was livid at even the hint of a supposedly "morale shattering" retreat and in order to maintain the appearance of constant forward momentum, ordered an advance through the wilderness roads. These "roads" were generally little more than narrow trails that were usable for small groups of men on foot but

The defeat of Burgoyne's troops at Bemis Heights, October 7, 1777, led directly to the surrender of the British a few days later at Saratoga. Benedict Arnold played a major role in the fighting before being wounded, at center; the last honorable event of his career.

enormously insufficient for a huge army with a large wagon train and dozens of artillery pieces. As the redcoats lurched forward, American ax-men chopped down trees faster than British engineers could remove them and the advance slowed to an agonizing one mile a day with the relatively short campaigning season rapidly drawing to a close.

Meanwhile Horatio Gates, who had been appointed commander of the Northern Army of the United States, welcomed thousands of short-term militiamen into his camp and utilized them to build an impressive series of fortifications around Bemis Heights, a ridge of high ground three miles north of the Hudson's confluence with the Mohawk River. The English-born Gates, who had served with Burgoyne for a number of years before he emigrated to America, had selected an impressive position that featured a left flank protected by thick, hilly forests and a right flank that extended to the Hudson River. By the time that Burgoyne approached these fortifications, Gates commanded an imposing army of over 12,000 men while nearly 7,000 other volunteers would swarm into camp before the campaign was over.

On the morning of September 19, 1777, a thick fog enveloped Bemis Heights as Burgoyne ordered his army to advance in three columns to try to locate a gap in the American lines that might allow the British to pour through all the way to Albany. When Burgoyne found both the American left and right flanks too strong to penetrate, he concentrated his forces on the center of the rebel line which was deployed around a local landmark known as Freeman's Farm. When the redcoats threatened to penetrate the patriot line, a furious counterattack was organized by Gates's senior division commander, General Benedict Arnold. A combination of Continentals and Daniel Morgan's elite riflemen opened a level of fire that few British veterans had ever experienced. One American officer marveled at the firepower his men displayed writing: "there was one continual blaze, such an explosion of fire I never had any idea of before and the heavy artillery joining in concert like great peals of thunder, assisted by the echoes of the woods almost deafened us with the noise." Arnold, who largely disagreed with Gates's determination to hold the American army in its fortifications, personally led a number of charges across the fields of Freeman's Farm. A patriot colonel later noted, "Arnold rushed into the thickest of the fight with his usual recklessness and at times acted like a madman," while Burgoyne took personal command of the most advanced units of redcoats and according to one of his aides "through it all shunned no danger, his presence and conduct animated the troops for they greatly loved the general." By 4:30 in the afternoon three British regiments had been decimated, several Royal artillery batteries had been virtually annihilated, and the whole line was beginning to falter. At this point Gates recalled Arnold's units back to the main fortification, fearful that during a night engagement the less well-organized American militiamen might lose all that had been gained all day.

The British army held the ground at Freeman's Farm at the end of the day, but they had suffered grievously. Over 160 redcoats were dead, another 400 wounded or captured, while the Americans lost only 63 killed and 212 wounded. British Lieutenant Thomas Anburry was astonished at the fighting

John Burgoyne offers his sword to Horatio Gates at Saratoga, October 17, 1777. Daniel Morgan stands at right in his customary hunting dress. As with his earlier Bunker Hill painting, the artist John Trumbull actually served in this campaign.

abilities of opponents who wore mostly civilian clothing and waved few regimental emblems. "The courage and obstinacy with which the Americans fought were the astonishment of everyone and we now became fully convinced that they are not that contemptible enemy we had hitherto imagined them."

The badly battered British army now found itself under a virtual siege as additional, newly arriving American militia units were utilized to cut off Burgoyne's avenue of retreat back north, and when the British general ordered a breakout attempt on October 7, the redcoats lost nearly a thousand men without even denting the American fortifications. Ten days later "Gentlemen Johnny" agreed to Gates's fairly generous capitulation terms and almost 6,000 British and German troops passed into captivity. In return for a disaster that would soon bring France into the war as an American ally, the British strategy for 1777 produced only the hollow triumph of Howe's capture of the colonial capital of Philadelphia after he defeated, but hardly annihilated, Washington's army in a battle along Brandywine Creek in southern Pennsylvania. When an American attempt to recapture Philadelphia unraveled in a fog-bound battle in the city's Germantown suburbs, the colonial army went into winter quarters at Valley Forge and the focal point of the war began to shift southward.

The surrender of the British army at Saratoga and the subsequent American alliance with France shocked IIis Majesty's government into a far more modest strategic plan for the next phase of the war. George III and his advisors believed that the strongest feelings of loyalism among the colonists were in the southern provinces and the monarch authorized the transfer of much of Britain's military power to an attempted reconquest of the Carolinas and Georgia. At first, the southern strategy worked even beyond Britain's wildest expectations as in rapid succession Savannah was captured, Charleston surrendered to the British army, and a badly bungled American counterattack under Horatio Gates was annihilated at the battle of Camden. The only bright spot during most of 1779 and 1780 for the southern patriots occurred when an army of frontiersmen from Kentucky crossed the mountains and destroyed a Tory army at King's Mountain, South Carolina. However, Washington's appointment of two of his most talented generals to command the remnants of the patriot army in the south soon began to turn this tide.

The courage and obstinacy with which the Americans fought were the astonishment of everyone and we now became fully convinced that they are not that contemptible enemy we had hitherto imagined them.

— British Lieutenant Thomas Anburry after fighting the colonists at Freeman's Farm.

In the fall of 1780, Nathanael Greene and Daniel Morgan were transferred from Washington's main army to take charge of operations in the southern states. Greene temporarily divided his small army into two commands, one under his personal direction and one under the colorful rifleman Morgan. During the bitterly cold month of January 1781, a large wing of the British army under Colonel Banastre Tarleton drove rapidly against Morgan's column and pushed it back toward the Broad River near King's Mountain. Rather than risk a British attack while his largely untrained army tried to cross a major river, Morgan chose to make a stand against an army that outnumbered his regulars more than two to one.

During the afternoon of January 16, 1781, Morgan began to deploy his small army of 1,100 men along a series of meadows and low ridges called the Cowpens by local residents. The grizzled veteran of a number of Indian wars was affectionately known as the "Old Waggoner," and held a quite personal grudge against a British army that had sentenced him to a near fatal punishment of 500 lashes when he struck a British

Published in Harper's Weekly *on the hundredth anniversary of the Revolution, this illustration was entitled "Dangerous Ground."*

officer during a dispute. Now Morgan was determined to exact revenge. He was convinced that the British leaders were so accustomed to watching colonial militia units turn and flee in panic at the first sign of a bayonet charge that he intended to use this tactic to suck the redcoats into a trap. Therefore, he deployed his army in a three-tiered defense. First, 150 picked sharpshooters were deployed behind a line of trees that fronted the main American position. These men were ordered to pop up from behind cover when the redcoats closed to within 50 yards, pick off every officer they could identify, and then fallback to the ridge behind. A second force of 300 of the most raw militiamen was placed in a line 150 yards behind the riflemen. Morgan emphasized that these men were not expected to stand their ground, but had to merely fire two well-aimed volleys, pick off as many redcoats as possible, and then fall back behind the ridge to form an emergency reserve. The Old

Waggoner lauded the men's courage and insisted, "Just hold up your heads boys, and then when you return to your homes, how the old folks will bless you, and the girls will kiss you for your gallant conduct. Two shots, and you are home free."

The main battle line would be placed on the crest of a ridge about 150 yards further back and would be anchored by a small force of Maryland and Delaware Continentals in the center with the more reliable militiamen on the flanks. Morgan's ace in the hole was a force of 150 mounted riflemen, under the command of Colonel William Washington, who would be concealed on the far side of the ridge and emerge only when Tarleton was convinced he was winning the battle. As Morgan insisted, "the whole idea is to lead Tarleton into a trap as they come up the slopes. When they've been cut down to size by our fire, we'll attack *him*!"

On the bitterly cold morning of January 17, 1781, with the temperature hovering in the teens, the combined army of redcoats, Scotsmen, Tories, and Royal Artillerymen marched out from its camps and advanced toward the Cowpens.

> *Just hold up your heads boys, and then when you return to your homes, how the old folks will bless you, and the girls will kiss you for your gallant conduct. Two shots, and you are home free.*
>
> — DANIEL MORGAN TO HIS MEN ABOUT TO FACE A BRITISH ASSAULT.

One American officer described the advance: "a brilliant army of scarlet, green, blue and white with glittering rows of bayonets and drums rolling with regimental colors rippling in the wind marched inexorably forward." Suddenly, 50 yards from a narrow line of trees, British officers began dropping to the ground and the organization of the advancing column began to unravel. Then as the army closed in on the second American line, two consecutive volleys of musket fire began tearing gaping holes in the lines. Almost half of the British officers were now out of action, but when Tarleton saw the American militiamen running toward the rear, he was convinced that the rebels were now on the verge of panic and would disintegrate with one more spirited bayonet charge.

Tarleton now unleashed his most potent weapon, the elite regiment of Scottish Highlanders, and the kilted warriors streamed up the side of the ridge and slashed through Virginia militiamen with bayonets and claymore swords, threatening to roll up the main American line. At this point, the Delaware and Maryland Continentals, who had been busy shooting at the redcoats launching an assault up the front of the ridge, suddenly swung around in a new perpendicular line and blasted the oncoming Highlanders. At the same time, Colonel Washington unleashed his cavalrymen, who caught the already disorganized Scots from behind and opened a withering fire from horseback. At this point Tarleton, chased personally by Washington, spurred his horse forward and abandoned his army as he rode from the field with a handful of British cavalrymen. In less than an hour, at a cost of only 12 men killed, Daniel Morgan and his largely untrained army of militiamen had killed 100 redcoats, including 39 officers, wounded 229 men, and captured over 600 uninjured British survivors. The final march to Yorktown had now begun.

The disaster at the Cowpens forced the commander of the British southern army, Lord Charles Cornwallis, to spend most of the next seven months engaging in a fruitless, and often bloody, attempt to trap Nathanael Greene's army and consolidate his position in the southern provinces. A series of advances and counteradvances which resulted in at least one bloody encounter at Guilford Court House, North Carolina, resulted in the British army marching into Tidewater, Virginia, during the summer of 1781. The senior British general in America, Sir Henry Clinton, finally ordered Cornwallis to select a defensible position near the Virginia coast and sit tight until the Royal Navy could send him reinforcements and supplies. However, at this point, Washington, who had been engaged in a frustrating series of skirmishes around New York City, received word that the French allies could supply a large fleet and a substantial number of troops in the vicinity of Virginia during September and early October. The American general quickly left a screening force to distract Clinton's army, and set off with the majority of his men in a fast-paced march to the south.

By late September an American army of almost 20,000 men had surrounded Cornwallis's 7,000 redcoats in the Virginia village of Yorktown while the French navy prevented Clinton from sending in the promised reinforcements. As French and

American siege guns blew Cornwallis's fortifications to bits, daring infantry raids captured the key positions in the British defense system, and prompted the English general to ask for terms. On October 19, 1781, as British bands played a variety of tunes that probably included the ironic "The World Turned Upside Down," 7,000 scarlet-coated Regulars marched out from their battered entrenchments and surrendered 24 regimental standards to George Washington. The British surrender at Yorktown ultimately convinced His Majesty's government to recognize the United States as an independent nation, and as Thomas Jefferson stated, "a new age has now begun."

> *A new age has now begun.*
> — THOMAS JEFFERSON

General Andrew Jackson won the battle of New Orleans on January 8, 1815, at the end of the War of 1812. The strategic port city now remained in American hands. Unbeknown to those in the battle a peace treaty with the British had already been signed on December 24, 1814.

CHAPTER II

Defending a Young Republic

O n May 11, 1812, Sir Spencer Perceval, the prime minister of Great Britain, ended a short stroll along the Thames River and entered Parliament for the upcoming session of the House of Commons. Perceval was a decidedly mediocre leader but had one single saving grace among many conservative landowners—he viewed the young United States of America as a nation beneath the serious attention of significant leaders of His Majesty's government. This contempt for the new republic led the prime minister to authorize continuation of the policy of forcibly removing former British sailors from American sailing vessels and the enforcement of the Orders in Council which essentially forbade the United States from trading with any country that was friendly to Napoleonic France.

These policies had pushed Britain and America to the brink of war and bankrupted many British merchants who needed free trade with the United States to maintain themselves in business. Now, as Perceval strolled through the lobby of the House of Commons to defend his policies in the next debate, a disgruntled British merchant stepped out from behind a pillar, pulled out a pistol, and mortally wounded the king's first minister. John Bellingham's desperate act created a crisis in the British government that resulted in the appointment of Robert Jenkinson, Lord Liverpool, as the new prime minister, and one of Jenkinson's first acts was to initiate a review of British rela-

Stephen Van Rensselaer

Scion of a Hudson Valley Dutch landowning family, Stephen Van Rensselaer was raised in wealth with an obligation to perform public service. He became one of the finest militia officers in American history, although his first and only exposure to active battle was a brief campaign along the Niagara River.

With the outbreak of the War of 1812, Van Rensselaer was assigned the defense of the Niagara Frontier in cooperation with regular army Major General Alexander Smyth. By October of 1812, Van Rensselaer had about 900 U.S. regulars and 2,300 New York militiamen camped out along the Niagara River. On October 13, he planned a surprise crossing of the river, but 1,900 of his militiamen refused to cooperate on the grounds that they were only obliged to serve in defense of New York. Despite this and the fact that the jealous Smyth denied him the use of additional regulars, Van Rensselaer persevered, attacking with his 900 regulars and his remaining 400 militiamen.

The assault was a surprise and also a considerable success. Van Rensselaer was able to capture Queenstown Heights. With only about 1,300 men, however, his position was precarious. A counterattack by British Regulars and Canadian militia was beaten off, during which British commander Major General Isaac Brock was killed. But Brock's successor brought in additional forces and a good deal of artillery. A second counterattack several days later overwhelmed Van Rensselaer's little force, with only 300 managing to escape back across the Niagara to the safety of U.S. soil.

A thousand of Van Rensselaer's men had become prisoners, some 100 had been killed. Disgusted with the lack of courage displayed by many of the militiamen and Smyth's unprofessional behavior, Van Rensselaer resigned his commission and never again took up arms.

Van Rensselaer spent the rest of his life pursuing his business and political interests, becoming a major promoter of the Erie Canal and serving as a regent and, for a time, chancellor of the University of the State of New York. He also founded what is now Rensselaer Polytechnic Institute. He died in 1813.

tions with America with the ultimate objective of rescinding the hated Orders in Council. On June 23, 1812, Lord Liverpool announced the repeal of the Orders and the *London Times* noted enthusiastically, "May all the expected good follow this act." Unfortunately, the British pull back from the brink was too little, too late; five days earlier, President James Madison had formally signed a bill declaring that a state of war existed between Great Britain and the United States.

The War of 1812, America's second conflict with the British mother country, found the United States about as unprepared for war as at any point in the nation's history. The American regular army of 5,000 men was dwarfed by a British military establishment 60 times as large. The United States Navy, although well-led and energetic, had only 12 significant warships to challenge Britain's 1,000 fighting vessels, 180 of which were powerful ships of the line, a category of ship that the Americans did not even possess. However, when the United States declared war, Britain was engaged in a struggle to the death with Napoleon, and, until that war was concluded, most of His Majesty's forces would be tied up confronting the French. The American political and military leaders generally agreed that the greatest opportunity for the United States was to invade the thinly defended British province of Canada, occupy most of the country, and then offer to trade some or all of it back to Britain in return for the end of impressment and the Orders in Council. If the young republic could conquer Canada quickly, while Britain was still fully distracted by Napoleon, there was a real possibility that the United States might gain the "free trade and sailors' rights" that ignited the war, while also adding large stretches of northern land to a rapidly expanding nation. Almost everyone's hopes rode on the success of a complex, three-pronged invasion of Canada, a northern thrust that would prove to be one of the most disastrous military offensives in American history.

The basic American operational plan devised by General Henry Dearborn was for a western column under the Michigan

Although Henry Dearborn had been a gallant junior officer in the Revolutionary War, his campaign on the Canadian border early in the War of 1812 was a disaster.

American losses in land battles during the War of 1812 were partially offset by naval victories. Oliver Hazard Perry defeated a British flotilla at the battle of Lake Erie, September 10, 1813. In addition to the capture and destruction of British vessels, Perry's victory helped secure American possession of Detroit.

governor, General William Hull, to invade Ontario from Fort Detroit, a central column under General Stephen Van Rensselaer to penetrate eastern Ontario in the vicinity of the Niagara River, and an eastern column under Dearborn himself to push into Quebec from upper New York State. A combination of much of the regular army and huge levies of state militia would overwhelm the limited British and Canadian forces and capture most of the territory in one campaign season.

Unfortunately for the hopes of the "War Hawks" in Congress, three essentially incompetent, elderly generals led three unco-ordinated offensives that resulted in total disaster. Hull, a hard-drinking, silver-haired Revolutionary War veteran in his sixties, led off the succession of horrors by making a tentative thrust into Canada from Fort Detroit, quickly pulling his army back to the American side of the river, and allowing his 2,300-man army to be besieged by a British force about a third as large as his own. In the middle of a drunken stupor, he surrendered the

entire garrison and 33 invaluable artillery pieces to General Isaac Brock, who at that moment had only four companies of British Regulars supplemented by a few Canadian woodsmen and a party of Indian allies under the legendary war chief Tecumseh. After pulling off a monumental bluff, the American flag over Fort Detroit was hauled down and a large part of Michigan was occupied by the British.

The second offensive, the thrust from the Niagara frontier, proved almost as embarrassing. When Von Rensselaer tried to invade Canada from New York, most of his militia units refused to cross the river, a British sympathizer stole the oars to the invasion barges, and the invasion force could not push beyond the opposite shore. Brock, rushing back from his triumph in Michigan, organized a successful defense with a badly outnumbered British army and then was killed at the moment of triumph. Only the heroic stand of young Colonel Winfield Scott and a handful of regulars prevented the entire invasion force from being annihilated. Finally, the elderly and sickly Dearborn, in command of an impressive 8,000 man column, pushed a short distance into Quebec, panicked at the sight of one fourth as many redcoats and Canadian woodsmen, and declared the campaign of 1812 officially over.

Americans were stunned at this long string of embarrassing defeats that were only partially ameliorated by the impressive naval victories of the *Constitution*, the *United States,* and the *Wasp* in dramatic maritime clashes with the Royal Navy. The second year of the war, unfortunately, proved only to be a little more palatable to the United States. Commodore Oliver Hazard Perry scored a spectacular naval triumph on Lake Erie, William Henry Harrison defeated and killed the legendary Tecumseh at the battle of the Thames, and minor footholds were maintained on Canadian soil. However, an American militia army was annihilated at the battle of the River Raisin, several New York communities includ-

Although many Indians sided with the British during the War of 1812, representatives of the Iroquois Six Nations met at the Onandaga Reservation to offer peace. As their letter shows, the modern world was already encroaching upon these fearsome warriors:

"Brother, You must not suppose from what we have now told you that we are unfriendly to you or your people. We are your decided friends. We reside among your people. Your friends are our friends, and your enemies are our enemies. In the former war between your people and the British some of us took up the Tomahawk on their side. When the peace took place we buried it deep, and it shall never again be raised against you and your people.
"Brother, We are few in number, and can do but little, but our hearts are good. We are willing to do what we can, and if you want our assistance say so, and we will go with your people to battle. We are anxious to know your wishes respecting us as soon as possible because some of our young are uneasy, and we fear they may disperse among different Tribes and be hostile to you. Pray direct your communication to the chiefs and warriors or our respective Tribes to be left at Onondaga Post Office."

ing Buffalo were burned to the ground by British offensives, and the Royal Navy imposed a naval blockade that rendered most of the tiny American navy useless in port. Even worse, Napoleon's empire was unraveling rapidly, and few observers expected France to continue fighting Britain through the coming year. By the spring of 1814, Napoleon had abdicated, many of the Duke of Wellington's best regiments were embarking for America, and Admiral Sir Alexander Cochrane echoed the feelings of many Britons when he insisted, "I have it much to heart to give America a complete drubbing before any peace is made." The crisis period of the War of 1812 had now begun, and only a spectacular turnaround from the generally dismal showing of the American forces up to this point could prevent large swaths of the new republic from being gobbled up by a rapacious and vengeful Great Britain.

You will have a battle, General Scott!

— GENERAL JACOB BROWN, ON SEEING THE APPROACHING BRITISH ARMY.

Before Wellington's crack regiments could be transported to North America, United States forces made one final attempt to expand their shrinking bridgehead in Canada to better resist the expected British counteroffensive. The basic American operational plan was for energetic, young Major General Jacob Brown's mixed force of regulars and militia to push from the Niagara frontier to capture the provincial capital of York (now Toronto) in concert with a naval assault by Commodore Isaac Chauncey's squadron. On July 13, 1814, the American offensive got underway and the Yankees quickly captured the important British post at Fort Erie. Brown then ordered his brigade of regulars under General Winfield Scott and a brigade of New York and Pennsylvania militia under General Eleazor Ripley to march to the Chippewa River as a first stop on the way to link up with Chauncey's fleet for an assault on York. However, Brown's counterpart, Lieutenant General Sir Gordon Drummond, was rapidly assembling detachments from all over Ontario to overwhelm the American invasion force of about 2,400 men while he dispatched his deputy, Major General Phineas Riall, with about 2,000 Regulars to hold the Americans in place on the Chippewa.

Brown's scouts observed the redcoats filing into defensive positions on the far side of the river on the morning of July 4, but when it appeared that Riall had no intention of launching an immediate attack, everyone in the American camp relaxed and, near evening, Scott authorized his brigade to conduct an Independence Day grand review which he had promised them earlier. However, Riall had no intention of simply staying in place until the Americans attacked him; he had already ordered an early evening assault. The sun was a red ball low in the western sky when the 1,300 men of Winfield Scott's 1st Brigade lined up by companies for a dress parade. Despite the still oppressive heat of this Independence Day on foreign soil, Scott's men were elated at their obvious professionalism, with the only element to mar the occasion the fact that they were wearing uniforms of militia gray since a promised consignments of new blue coats had been diverted to the garrison of Sackett's Harbor. But in the middle of the grand review, General Brown rode over to the brigade commander and yelled, "You will have a battle, General Scott!" and pointed to the columns of redcoats splashing across the water and already closing in on the American militia brigade. A spirited bayonet charge drove off Ripley's volunteers and now 2,000 British Regulars were closing in on an American force that was only two-thirds as large as the redcoats. A young officer in Scott's command insisted, "This was now no dress parade, no stage play for effect, it was a single and sublime reality, it was War!"

Scott assumed that Riall would expect him to retreat under the pressure of superior numbers and perhaps held a glimmer of hope that the redcoats would assume that their gray-clad

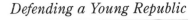

A veteran of nearly 20 years of frontier warfare, William Henry Harrison defeated the British and their Indian allies under Tecumseh at the battle of the Thames, in Ontario on October 5, 1813. He was elected president of the United States in 1841 but died a month after taking office.

opponents were merely untrained militia who would quickly break and run. Therefore, the towering Virginian used reverse psychology and ordered his men to charge the oncoming British column. The men ran at a fast trot, guns at the ready, and at a given command halted and opened a withering volley on the redcoats, then, just as quickly, the regiments formed in a shallow V formation and caught Riall's men in a deadly crossfire. At this point the excited

This was now no dress parade, no stage play for effect, it was a single and sublime reality, it was War!

— YOUNG OFFICER IN COLONEL WINFIELD SCOTT'S COMMAND.

★ ☆ ★ ☆ ★ ☆ ★ ☆ ★ ☆ ★ ☆ ★ ☆ ★ ☆ ★ ☆ ★ ☆ ★ ☆ ★ ☆ ★

William Henry Allen

Beginning his Navy career as a midshipman at the age of 15, William Henry Allen became a modern-day pirate for the American government, seizing more enemy ships than any other Navy captain and holding that record for nearly a century until the submarine campaign against Japan in World War II.

Appointed first lieutenant of the frigate United States in 1809, Allen found his ship had a skipper much to his liking, the aggressive Stephen Decatur, who had acquired an impressive reputation in the Barbary Wars. When the War of 1812 broke out, Decatur took the *United States* on a lengthy cruise against British shipping.

On October 25, 1812, the *United States* fell in with the newly commissioned British frigate *Macedonian*, and there ensued one of the most notable ship-to-ship actions ever, one in which Allen played an important role. By the end of the bloody affair, the British vessel was virtually dismasted and struck her colors, one of three first-class British frigates taken by Americans in the opening months of the war. Assuming command of the prize vessel, Allen directed a number of hasty repairs and then brought her safely to port, where the heavily damaged ship was overhauled and entered U.S. service.

In recognition of his services during the *United States-Macedonian* fight and his impressive seamanship in bringing the captured vessel to safety, Allen was promoted to commander. Given command of the 20-gun brig *Argus* in the spring of 1813, Allen transported a new American minister to France and then cruised in British waters to raid enemy shipping.

The voyage was enormously successful, with 27 British ships taken in about three weeks, driving British maritime insurance rates up by 25 percent. While sailing off St. David's Head in St. George's Channel, however, the *Argus* fell in with the British brig *Pelican*, a larger, sturdier vessel with about 25 percent more firepower.

Although the *Argus* was the faster vessel, Allen decided to fight. The action commenced at 6 A.M. At about 6:05, Allen's leg was blown off by a cannonball. He refused to leave the deck until loss of blood caused him to pass out. Within minutes, his second-in-command was wounded, and the ship's third officer took over.

Although a gallant fight was made, the *Argus* was soon overwhelmed and forced to strike her colors. Mortally wounded, Allen died several days later in British captivity and was buried with military honors in St. Andrew's Churchyard in Plymouth, England.

★ ☆ ★ ☆ ★ ☆ ★ ☆ ★ ☆ ★ ☆ ★ ☆ ★ ☆ ★ ☆ ★ ☆ ★ ☆ ★ ☆ ★

British commander turned to his aides and exclaimed in shock, "Those are regulars by God!", a stark admission that these Yankees were not about to run. American flanking fire was now devastating the British line and Riall decided to call off the battle while he still had an army to command. The red-coats pulled back across the Chippewa with losses of 148 killed, 221 wounded, and 41 captured, compared to an American loss of only 44 killed and 224 wounded. The first conventional slugging match between two relatively equal forces of regulars on an open field had produced a clear-cut American victory, but lack of follow-up support nearly turned the triumph into a disaster.

Brown's victorious army spent the next three weeks cautiously moving toward York while waiting for confirmation that Commodore Chauncey's squadron had arrived to provide naval support for the assault. However, Chauncey essentially called off the naval part of the combined operation and the American land force now found itself in hostile territory with at least three separate British columns closing in to trap the army on the wrong side of the Niagara River. General Brown immediately dispatched Scott with his brigade to secure an open road back to New York, but on the sultry afternoon of July 25, the startled Americans came face to face with a British column that was heading for the vital crossroads of Lundy's Lane in order to cut off any possible American retreat. British and American units now raced to occupy the crossroads and the adjacent ridges that dominated the road. The redcoats won the race and put 2,000 men on a hill that would dominate the upcoming battle.

The energetic Scott dispatched a messenger requesting that Brown bring up the rest of the army while the Virginian tried to find a way to push the redcoats off the ridge line. Lundy's Lane was essentially a country road that ran westward from the intersection of the main river road, and was dominated by a large, narrow ridge that was heavily wooded with a small graveyard near the center. Scott decided to employ his crack regiment of Connecticut rangers to slip through the dense woods and hit the British line from behind while the remainder of the brigade distracted the redcoats with a frontal charge. The charge turned into a bloody slugging match as

———— ★ ★ ★ ————

My first impressions of the American service were very favorable. The treatment in the Syren *was more lenient and favorable than in the* Macedonian. *The captain and officers were kind, while there was a total exemption from that petty tyranny exercised by the upstart midshipmen in the British service. As a necessary effect, our crew were as comfortable and as happy as men ever are in a man of war.*
While we lay in Boston harbor, thanksgiving-day arrived. Some of our Salem men inquired if I was not going home to keep thanksgiving, for they all supposed I belonged to Salem. What they meant by "thanksgiving," was a mystery to me, but, dissembling my ignorance, I obtained leave, determined to learn what it meant. The result of my visit was the idea that thanksgiving-day, was one in which people crammed themselves with turkeys, geese, pumpkin-pies, &c; for, certainly, that was the chief business of the day, so far as I could perceive. With too many people, I believe that this is the leading idea associated with the day even now.

—SAMUEL LEECH, A BRITISH SAILOR CAPTURED
BY THE U.S. NAVY

———— ★ ★ ★ ————

one young American officer later asserted, "Our young soldiers, who had so gallantly subdued the enemy on the open field at Chippewa, now burned with ardor to prove their valor on a new scene, in the daring peril of an escapade."

The plan almost worked, Colonel Thomas Jessup's Connecticut men crashed through the woods, annihilated a battalion of Canadian militiamen, and captured General Riall who was deploying his Regulars for a counterattack against Scott's main force. However, the attack went on without the general and as American Colonel Henry Leavenworth noted, "the enemy was again advancing, and their approach was greeted by a sheet of flame from both armies, who were not to exceed 30 yards from each other and nearly in parallel lines." At this point, Brown arrived with the rest of the army but it was now twilight and British reinforcements were streaming up the opposite side of the ridge.

Brown decided on a rare night assault in which Scott's brigade was able to capture the ridge in some of the bloodiest fighting of the war. An American captain noted proudly, "Our men fought like bulldogs, so close did they charge that the fire from British muskets' discharge seemed to strike us in the face." However, during the wild melee in the dense wooded ridge, leaders on both sides dropped rapidly. Sir Gordon Drummond was carried from the field with a severe leg wound, and a few minutes later Brown was hit by the staff of a misfired British rocket and had to be carried from the ridge. Almost simultaneously, Scott went down with a severe shoulder wound, and the two decimated armies, almost by mutual agreement, temporarily halted the confrontation as the moonlit field was now covered with both writhing and still bodies.

The battered American army was able to hold the ridge above Lundy's Lane for the remainder of the night, but the painfully injured Brown could not afford to simply sit tight on the hill and allow several converging British columns to surround him. Therefore, he reluctantly ordered his men to pull back from the hill under cover of darkness and then quietly sidle around the British flank until they reached the cover of the guns of newly captured Fort Erie. The battle of Lundy's Lane was the last major American offensive of the war and it produced a confused and disputed outcome. The British army was ultimately able to regain Lundy's Lane when the Americans circled around them, but the Yankees had actually held the crucial ridge during the climax of the battle. The Americans had lost 171 killed, 573 wounded, and 117 captured which was overall about the same loss as the British 87 killed, 562 wounded, and 233 captured, but far more of Brown's men had died in the battle than Drummond's. Brown and Scott had emerged as outstanding combat generals, but as this battered army licked its wounds on the frontier, the focal point of the war shifted to the very heart of the American republic.

Our men fought like bulldogs.

— AN AMERICAN CAPTAIN AT THE BATTLE OF LUNDY'S LANE.

While many of the Duke of Wellington's victorious regiments were designated for deployment for an offensive into the United States from Canada, the British government was also anxious to at least temporarily carry the war to the center of population in America. President Madison and most of his military advisors were convinced that the most likely target would be Baltimore with its enormous harbor and bulging dockyards. Few of them believed that the much less heavily populated national capital would be of interest to an enemy assault force. Thus while Baltimore had been filled with troops and artillery batteries, fewer than 400 regulars had been assigned to guard the region around the District of Columbia when a huge fleet under Sir Alexander Cochrane dropped anchor near the head of Chesapeake Bay and rendezvoused with a powerful assault force under Admiral Sir George Cockburn and Major General Robert Ross.

As a torrid late summer sun rose above the Maryland countryside on August 24, 1814, five British infantry regiments, a brigade of Royal Marines, and a Royal Artillery rocket regiment trudged inland toward the important crossroads town of Bladensburg. The 4,400 redcoats were about to clash with a

Memoirs of Polly Kemp

Polly Kemp was a resident of Washington, D.C. at the time of the British occupation:

"It was an almost suffocating day in August, the 24th, when the sound of guns reached our ears. We were all tuned up to a high pitch of excitement from early morn until afternoon when our flying soldiers from the battle-field at Bladensburg told us that our army had been completely routed and that the enemy was marching rapidly on to Washington.

"Uncle John, who, as you know, was in the city militia, came to us immediately and all was bustle. While the carriage was coming we got together all of our valuables and soon we were in the midst of a great cavalcade of teams of all descriptions, moving as rapidly as possible into Maryland, and it was near midnight before we reached a tavern. Before that it began to rain in great torrents, the lightning and thunder adding to the terrors of a dark night. Our man walked ahead with a lantern. The outhouses and stable were full so that our poor tired rain-beaten horse had to be tied to the trees and remain out in the rain for hours.

"We were made as comfortable as was possible in our wet garments, and had been seated scarcely an hour when there was a loud rap upon the door and the great rough tavern keeper made it known to us in an angry voice that the intruder was Dolly Madison. As he attempted to push her away from the door, father indignantly sprang to the door and pushing aside the angry keeper, went out in the rain to find that lady walking away in that terrible rain. Taking her by the arm he led her back into the house.

"The keeper began denouncing the President as the cause of the war and the destruction of the capital; many of the occupants murmured against admitting her, but father was determined that she should remain and remain she did: we took her under our special protection. We sat silently until 3 or 4 o'clock in the morning, when a rap came upon the door. One of our party opened the door and who should walk in but President Madison himself and several gentlemen, but the President did not remain long.

"An hour later a messenger announced to the President that the enemy was coming that way. He quickly drew on his great cloak and kissing his wife went out again into the storm followed by his faithful followers.

"By daybreak, Mrs. Madison became restless and could not stand the suspense any longer and started out with her coachman to find Mr. Madison. After they had gone, some of the people in the tavern, who were under the influence of liquor, were very angry with father for admitting them. Yet how very sorry we were for 'Queen Dolly,' as she was called sometimes."

6,000-strong force of American militia under General William Winder in an engagement that would go down in the annals of American history as the "Bladensburg Races."

Winder had plenty of men, but very little else. His own deployment of his forces was hardly brilliant, but then President Madison and his cabinet arrived on the scene to watch the impending battle and acting Secretary of War James Monroe promptly shifted most of the defenders into even worse positions. The redcoats formed ranks on the far side of a small stream, rocket batteries started launching their terrifying, if often inaccurate, projectiles, and the scarlet ranks began their, inexorable advance. Private Henry Sulford of the Maryland militia noted with astonishment, "the British took no notice of our fire, their men moved like clockwork, the instant a part of a platoon was cut down, it was filled up by the men in the rear without the least noise and confusion whatever. I was lucky to have escaped alive." In turn, as the untrained American militiamen began to melt away from their firing positions, a British officer noted sarcastically, "most of the American troops seemed like country people who would have been more appropriately employed in attending their agricultural occupations than in standing with muskets in their hands."

The only serious resistance to this tide of scarlet was a group of marines and naval gunners under Commodore Joshua

After defeating American forces at Bladensburg, Maryland, on August 24, 1814, British troops occupied Washington, DC, and burned many public buildings. Although American land and naval forces remained intact, this was a blow to the prestige of the young nation.

Barney. Five hundred men and a battery of big guns essentially challenged almost 10 times as many British and actually inflicted fairly severe casualties on the redcoats until the line was overwhelmed and Barney went down with several bullet and bayonet wounds. As Barney dropped to the ground, still clutching his sword, Admiral Cockburn, in a surprising act of chivalry, saved his fellow mariner from redcoat bayonets, paroled him on the spot, and ordered British sailors to carry him to the rear for medical attention while congratulating him on his courage. By late that evening, Cockburn would be performing a much less chivalrous act as he ordered his men to set fire to the White House, Capitol, and several other public buildings.

The burning of the nation's capital was one of the lowest points of the War of 1812 for the United States, but a remarkably short time later an event that was more uplifting would occur less than 40 miles north of the ruined president's mansion. The British assault force was now intent on attacking Baltimore but this time a much different reception awaited them.

Francis Scott Key, who had been negotiating for the release of American prisoners, was held captive during the British bombardment of Fort McHenry on September 13, 1814. In addition to inspiring the national anthem, the British failure to take Fort McHenry prevented them from occupying Baltimore.

On Monday, September 12, the British fleet anchored off North Point, Maryland, and 3,700 soldiers and 1,000 marines and naval infantry moved inland toward the Baltimore city center 14 miles away. General Samuel Smith, a far more competent citizen-soldier than General Winder, had crammed over 12,000 men in excellent defensive positions astride the main road to the city. When American scouts reported the British column stopping for lunch at Gorsuch's Farm about halfway to the city, Smith sent General John Stricker with a brigade of militiamen, several rifle companies, and a battery of six cannons to impede the redcoats until the main American line was completed. Admiral Cockburn and General Ross were the unwelcome guests for lunch at the Gorsuch home, and when Mrs. Gorsuch inquired if the general would be also requiring dinner, he responded, "I'll eat in Baltimore tonight or in hell!" Ross and Cockburn then heard an exchange of gunfire in the woods ahead of them and unwisely rode forward to investigate without an escort. When the admiral finally convinced the general to pull back to get assistance, Ross slumped from his horse with a mortal chest wound. As a belated rescue party arrived on the scene, a British officer noted "a groan came from the column as the army had lost its mainspring."

The column's second in command, Colonel Arthur Brooke, now decided to postpone an advance until the next day, when, presumably, the Royal Navy would be available to provide naval support to an army offensive. However, in order for the navy to provide significant help, the fleet would first have to face the surrender of the most powerful bastion in Baltimore harbor, Fort McHenry. This citadel would hardly be a pushover for the British as the fort's commander, Major George Armistead, had crammed over 1,000 men and 57 heavy guns into the structure. Just to make sure that the British knew he was there, Armistead had hired a widowed flagmaker, Mrs. Mary Pickersgill, to make an enormous national flag with stripes that were two feet wide and an overall size that was so enormous that the widow had to borrow the malthouse of a local brewer to spread the entire flag out during the project. Once the flag was hoisted, it represented a challenge to the British assault squadron that was almost irresistible.

> *War was a new game to the Americans . . . but I can assure you, they have improved by experience and are beginning to be a formidable enemy.*
>
> — SERGEANT JAMES COMMINS OF THE BRITISH ARMY, AFTER FIGHTING THE AMERICANS IN NEW YORK.

At 6:30 A.M. on the humid, cloudy morning of September 13, 1814, the British bombship *Volcano* swung into position and opened fire on Fort McHenry. It was soon joined by 15 additional ships firing a wave of cannonballs, mortar bombs, and rockets at the American citadel.

Five hours later, there was still not the slightest hint that the defenders were weakening and Admiral Cochrane ordered the flotilla to move much closer to the fort. Almost immediately the *Volcano* took five serious hits and Armistead's gunners damaged several other ships so badly that the Royal Navy vessels quickly moved back to a long-range firing station. The confrontation then settled down to a long-range duel that lasted throughout the afternoon and night. One of the spectators on Cochrane's flagship *Tonnant* was a young attorney, Francis Scott Key, who had come aboard before the battle to seek the

Andrew Jackson spent much of the War of 1812 fighting pro-British Indians in Florida, Mississippi, and Alabama. After winning the final battle of the war at New Orleans he held a variety of appointments and offices before being elected to two terms as president of the United States in 1828 and 1832.

release of a family friend who had been captured during a British raid. Admiral Cochrane agreed to the release but only after the bombardment ended. At dawn the next morning Key could clearly see the enormous American flag waving defiantly in the sea breeze and he pulled out an envelope and scribbled a poem called "The Defense of Fort McHenry" which, when set to music a short time later, became "The Star Spangled Banner." The successful defense of the fort convinced Colonel Brooke to call off a planned army assault on the American entrenchments, and ships and soldiers pulled back into the Atlantic Ocean to await reinforcements and new orders. The American victory at Baltimore was soon complemented by a smashing land-sea victory at Plattsburgh, New York, in which a British naval squadron was virtually annihilated and a far superior army of Napoleonic War veterans was thrashed by a small force of American regulars. A veteran of Wellington's army, Sergeant James Commins, was astonished at the fighting ability of Americans compared to what he had been told to expect. "War was a new game to the Americans as they had not seen a hostile engagement in the country for forty years, but I can assure you, they have improved by experience and are beginning to be a formidable enemy."

The British army would confront this "formidable enemy" one final time in a battle that, rather ironically, was fought after a treaty of peace was concluded.

American and British negotiators had agreed upon the terms of peace between their governments on Christmas Eve of 1814 in the picturesque city of Ghent, Belgium. However, word of the treaty would not cross the Atlantic for several weeks, and in the meantime, a heavily reinforced British assault force was deploying for an attack on one of the richest prizes on the American continent, the city of New Orleans. The Duke of

Wellington's brother-in-law, Sir Edward Pakenham, was given command of a number of the Iron Duke's best regiments and sailed toward the Crescent City which was defended by the colorful, controversial Major General Andrew Jackson. The Tennessean had cobbled together a motley army of about 3,500 men, including Creole militia, free blacks, coastal pirates, and buckskinned frontiersmen, to repel the British invasion, and had quickly set his men to work building huge cotton-bale fortifications around the approaches to the city.

On the unusually frigid morning of January 8, 1815, as temperatures hovered around 20 degrees, and dense frost and fog permeated the air, 3,500 defenders stood behind their entrenchments and heard the eerie wail of bagpipes approaching in the mist. Sir Edward Pakenham, resplendent on a white horse, was leading over 6,000 of his men in a climactic assault toward the city. A British lieutenant echoed the confidence of his men as he insisted, "we expected to annihilate Jackson's force in an instant, but to our great mortification, we found that his army had entrenched itself in a strong position." "Old Hickory" had not only erected a formidable set of entrenchments, he had also cleverly concealed a number of lethal, canister-firing artillery batteries supported by hundreds of backwoodsmen, armed with one or more deadly long rifles that far outranged the redcoats' muskets.

As the bagpipers moved forward with the infantry, British rocket batteries fired salvoes of Congreve rockets at the cotton bales, but most of the missiles glanced off harmlessly after a spectacular visual display. Then Jackson shouted the order to open fire and entire rows of redcoats fell to the frozen ground. As Jackson shouted, "Give it to them boys, let's finish this business today," Sir Edward slid from his horse with a mortal wound and the panicky Regulars were unsure whether to continue to advance or retreat. One officer insisted, "Our brave fellows, with few exceptions, stood their ground neither advancing nor retreating, amidst a scene of carnage such as rarely been witnessed." Within the space of an hour, at an incredibly tiny cost of a half-dozen casualties, Jackson's motley army killed or wounded over 2,000 British soldiers and sent the conquerors of Napoleon reeling back toward the fleet in shock. As British

> *Give it to them boys, let's finish this business today.*
>
> — GENERAL ANDREW JACKSON ENCOURAGING HIS MEN IN DEFENSE OF NEW ORLEANS.

> *The glorious achievements of the last year have sealed the destiny of our country, perhaps for centuries to come, and placed our nation on high and honorable ground.*
>
> — AN AMERICAN CONGRESSMAN AS THE LAST BRITISH SOLDIERS LEFT AMERICAN SOIL.

Sergeant David Brown lamented, "Many a gallant man and officer wiped the tears from their eyes and looked back and on their comrades lying in the field." An American defender witnessed the same sight and admitted with some horror, "when the smoke cleared away and we could obtain a fair view of the field, it looked at first glance like a sea of blood."

As the last British invaders of American soil staggered back to their ships, an exuberant congressman noted, "The glorious achievements of the last year have sealed the destiny of our country, perhaps for centuries to come, and placed our nation on high and honorable ground." An America that was now beginning to stretch from "sea to shining sea" was expanding in several directions at once, and the expansion would soon provoke a conflict with an equally proud republic of the New World.

★ ★ ★

The end of the War of 1812 stimulated a western migration of Americans that prompted people to settle in not only newly purchased United States territories but also in the Republic of Mexico's northern province of Texas. After Mexico gained its independence from Spain, the new government decided to encourage settlement of its largely empty northern regions by enticing foreigners, mostly Americans, with a title to over 4,000 acres of land for a token payment of $30 and a promise to improve the homestead and abide by the laws of Mexico. By 1835 over 30,000 Americans had settled in Texas and the new president of Mexico, Antonio Lopez de Santa Anna, decided it was time to bring the Texans much more closely under supervision from Mexico City. When the president's brother-in-law led a column of Mexican troops into Texas to disarm the mostly Anglo inhabitants, he was defeated in a battle in the town of San Antonio and sent back to Mexico City as a paroled prisoner of war.

Eight hundred miles to the south, Santa Anna exploded in fury at this humiliation to the Mexican Republic, and quickly organized an army of over 6,000 men to march north and crush the "gringo" rebels. The first major barrier in Texas to the oncoming Mexican army was the mission fortress of San Antonio popularly called the Alamo. General Sam Houston, commander in chief of the Texan army, was convinced that the Alamo was untenable and he ordered Colonel James Bowie to take 30 men and blow up the fort. Houston insisted, "Our forces must not be shut up in forts where they can neither be supplied with men nor provisions." However, when Bowie arrived in San Antonio, he allowed himself to be persuaded by the local militiamen that the Alamo would become a significant impediment to Santa Anna and could be defended with proper reinforcement. Bowie was joined in turn by Colonel William Barret Travis, who commanded a small force of regular cavalry, and Colonel David Crockett, who had come south from Tennessee with a dozen volunteers. While Crockett largely deferred authority to the other two leaders, Bowie and Travis reluctantly came to an agreement that they would share command of San Antonio's garrison of about 150 men, retreat into the Alamo when the Mexican army arrived, and pressure Houston and a number of regional commanders to rush reinforcements to the mission.

James Bowie was intended to be joint commander of the Alamo but illness kept him confined to bed for the latter part of the siege. From his sick bed he may possibly have stabbed or shot several Mexican attackers before being killed.

On Washington's Birthday of 1836, the advanced units of the Mexican army appeared on a sunbaked plain outside of San Antonio, the local church bell began ringing furiously, and the motley force of Texan volunteers hurried into the mission. Bowie's health was now deteriorating rapidly and William Travis was emerging as the leader of the small garrison. Soon after the Mexican column surrounded the Alamo, Travis sent out a thrilling dispatch intended for "the people of Texas and all Americans in the world." The 27-year-old South Carolina lawyer implored the arrival of reinforcements as he noted, "I am besieged by a thousand or more of the Mexicans under Santa Anna; the enemy has demanded a surrender at discretion otherwise the garrisons are to be put to the sword if the fort is taken. I have answered the demand with a cannon shot and our flag still waves proudly from the parapet, I shall never surrender or retreat."

★ ★

Davy Crockett

Among the greatest of the frontiersmen, Davy Crockett's story has become a legend in American folklore. As a soldier, though, Crockett had an uneven career. He quit the army in disgust over atrocities inflicted on the Indians and later found time to regularly disappear into the woods for extended periods to pen fanciful tales about his adventures.

Crockett volunteered to serve in the Creek War of 1813 and 1814 and became acquainted with Andrew Jackson. But he left the service, providing a substitute to finish out his enlistment, and turned against Jackson over the army's treatment of Indians.

His wife died in 1815, and Crockett soon married a young widow, acquiring two additional children in the process. Successful neither as a farmer nor as a businessman, Crockett made something of a mark in local politics and was elected to a magistracy. Crockett was also elected a colonel in the militia and served several years in the state legislature.

Meanwhile, he took up writing about his adventures in the woods. His writings made him popular, and he was elected to serve four terms in Congress, although he became a bitter opponent of Jackson, with whom he disagreed on a variety of issues including Indian removal.

In 1835, Crockett made a campaign tour of the major cities of the East, where he was well-known because of his writings and because of what others had written about him. Defeated later that year by a Jacksonian candidate, Crockett told his constituents, "I'm going to Texas and you can go to hell."

Heading west, he brought a dozen followers and his fiddle to Texas and ended up in the Alamo, where he was one of several prisoners murdered in 1836 after the Mexicans had secured the mission. One of the legendary heroes of American history, the truth about him is almost as impressive as the myth.

Davy Crockett was a former Indian fighter and Congressman. In 1836 he led a small force of volunteers at the Alamo. This portrait dates from the 1820s.

★ ★

During the next 13 days, Santa Anna's troops gradually extended the siege lines and pounded the walls with field pieces as Texan sharpshooters attempted to keep the enemy gunners at a respectful distance. One Mexican captain noted, with considerable frustration, that "a tall man with flowing hair, was seen firing from the same place on the parapet during the entire siege. He wore a buckskin suit and a cap. He would kneel or lie down behind the low parapet, load his long gun to fire, and we all learned to keep at a good distance when he was seen to make ready to shoot. He rarely missed his mark and when he fired he always rose to his feet and calmly reloaded his gun seemingly indifferent to the shots fired at him by our men." This Mexican officer may very well have been watching the legendary Davy Crockett in action, although the former congressman was merely one of many excellent sharpshooters in the garrison.

Like many Texans of the time, William Barret Travis was a frontier adventurer who had immigrated from Alabama. Sketched in December 1835, this is the only known portrait of the Alamo's commander.

On the evening of March 5, 1836, an immense cold front swooped down from the northern plains and forced the Texans to huddle in their blankets next to fires as Santa Anna organized his grand assault. Most of the hoped-for American reinforcements had never arrived, and on the eve of the cli-

> *I am besieged by a thousand or more of the Mexicans under Santa Anna; the enemy has demanded a surrender at discretion otherwise the garrisons are to be put to the sword if the fort is taken. I have answered the demand with a cannon shot and our flag still waves proudly from the parapet, I shall never surrender or retreat.*
>
> — COLONEL WILLIAM TRAVIS IN A LETTER FROM THE ALAMO.

The final assault on the Alamo on March 6, 1836. Santa Anna's Second Column has broken through the south face of the defenses defended by only a palisade and are advancing on the last defenders in the chapel.

mactic battle only 182 men were spread over the adobe walls of the Alamo. At midnight, Santa Anna had a late dinner in his headquarters tent and then gave final orders for 1,800 men from his 6,000-man army to divide into four assault columns, collect a number of newly constructed ladders, and prepare for a pre-dawn assault.

At just past 5 A.M. in the frigid early morning darkness, the assault troops gave a huge cheer as they raced toward the Alamo's walls. The combination of the cheering soldiers and the Mexican trumpets playing the Moorish strains of the *Duguello*, which meant "to cut the throat," quickly awakened the sleeping defenders who rushed to the parapets and poured a devastating volley of fire into the Mexican ranks. Batteries of heavy guns tracked each of the assault columns and unleashed volleys of grapeshot that annihilated entire squads with each round. A number of defenders had stacked three or four loaded rifles next to their position and successively emptied each weapon into the oncoming troops. As one Mexican column commander admitted, "The initial rebel fire was very rapid and deadly; our columns left along their path a wide trail of blood, of wounded and dead."

As the earliest gray of dawn pierced the night, Santa Anna stood near one of his artillery batteries with his aides and, observing the decimation of his assault force, ordered the deployment of additional units. However, while the Texans were taking an enormous toll of the attackers, two events changed the course of the battle. First, two of the largest assault columns, staggering against the blizzard of enemy grapeshot, gradually began to come together at the weakest link in the Alamo's defenses. One section of the north wall had been badly damaged by Mexican artillery, and had been hurriedly repaired without the construction of new firing platforms. The Mexican troops were now gathering in front of a segment of wall that had practically no defenders. Soon, over 600 Mexicans were climbing over the eight-foot walls while William Travis and perhaps 25 defenders hurriedly deployed to confront them. Travis personally charged a squad of assault troops, blasting one or two with his shotgun and then dueling others with his sword. A moment later a Mexican rifleman shot the South Carolinian in the head and the small group of Texans were overwhelmed in a sea of bayonets.

The second turning point occurred at the opposite end of the fort, the Alamo's south wall. This area was covered by the mission's huge 18-pound cannon which had knocked down entire rows of assault troops. However, in the midst of this carnage, Colonel Jose Morales and about 100 of his men crawled over the gun emplacement and killed or dispersed the Texan gunners. A moment later, the imposing 18-pounder was swung around to begin blasting holes in the enclosed buildings that formed a refuge for Texans retreating from the now largely enemy held walls. A gruesome process began in which the captured cannon would smash a portion of the wall of a room, Mexican infantry would charge

---

★ ★ ★

The American army had Mexicans serving as scouts and spies, often under bizarre circumstances, as in this account by Adjutant General Ethan Allen Hitchcock:

Puebla, 23d June, [1847]. The robber Dominquez is a very curious and interesting man. When General Worth first arrived here, some person pointed out this man as a great robber and desired that he might be seized.
He was living quietly with his family here, the people fearing him or the laws being powerless in regard to him. General Worth arrested him, but, after a few days, sent to him saying that he was arrested on complaint of his own people, and, giving him to understand that he had no friends among the Mexicans, offered to take him into our service. The plan took, and when General Scott arrived, he at once sent Dominquez to me.
I tried him and found him faithful. When I settled with him, paying him about $110, including his outfit, I suggested his bringing into our service the whole band of professional robbers that line the road from Mexico to Vera Cruz. He assented, but frankly spoke of the difficulty of giving security for their good faith and honesty. I told him to think the matter over and we would talk again.
The next day, Major Smith's interpreter (Mr. Spooner) recognized our Dominquez as the fellow who had robbed him on the highway! Dominquez took $5 from him and gave him a pass of protection from other robbers
Last evening we saw Dominquez again and engaged five of his men at $2 a day, with himself at $3 a day. I told Dominquez to find out how many men he can control on the road. He thinks some 300. I have ordered the five men in different directions for information.

★ ★ ★

Sam Houston secured Texas independence by his victory at San Jacinto on April 21, 1836. He was later president of the Texas Republic and governor of the state of Texas, but lived the last few years of his life in seclusion after opposing the secession of Texas from the Union in 1861.

Victory is certain, trust in God and fear not! Remember the Alamo!

— GENERAL SAM HOUSTON TO HIS MEN ABOUT TO CHARGE SANTA ANNA'S ARMY.

in with bayonets, and after a brief melee, the defenders would be annihilated.

The Texans had no bayonets of their own, and were forced to use rifle butts, knives, tomahawks, and fists against the Mexican steel. A Mexican officer noted the outcome: "a horrible carnage took place, and some were trampled to death. The tumult was great, the disorder frightful; it seemed as if the furies had descended upon us."

After almost an hour of this bloody dueling, most of the defenders had been killed and the Mexican troops concentrated on the original mission chapel and its auxiliary buildings. At this point Jim Bowie met his end, while a number of women and children were spared at the last moment. At least six Alamo defenders were captured alive and it seems probable that one of these was Davy Crockett. However, when one of Santa Anna's generals requested that these prisoners be spared, the caudillo ordered his personal guard to hack the men to pieces with their swords and bayonets, a final gruesome bloodstained image of the battle of the Alamo. While every active defender of the Alamo was killed, these men were joined in death by between 400 and 600 of their opponents with dozens of other Mexican soldiers carried out of the fort severely wounded. Santa Anna could now continue his northward march, but at a cost of a large segment of his army.

Santa Anna's army now played a game of cat and mouse with Sam Houston's much smaller Texan army which prompted the caudillo to divide his force into a number of columns incapable of supporting one another, a situation that the Texan general quickly turned to his advantage. Houston placed his small army of 800 men along the San Jacinto River directly opposite the Mexican column personally led by Santa Anna. On the hot, sultry afternoon of April 21, 1836, while the Mexican president and his 1,200 men relaxed while waiting for the arrival of reinforcements, the Texan army surged into motion. Houston exhorted his men, "Victory is certain, trust in God and fear not! Remember the Alamo!" and the grim-faced settlers and backwoodsmen advanced across a wide plain towing two small cannons with them.

The Mexican general was convinced that no confrontation would occur until the next morning and Santa Anna himself was asleep in his tent. Suddenly the avenging Texans swarmed across hastily constructed barriers made of luggage and saddles and tore into the largely astonished Mexicans. The two artillery pieces sprayed lethal charges of horseshoe fragments and nails into poorly deployed masses of Mexican soldiers and the already shaky line began to unravel. In a battle that lasted only 18 minutes, the Texans simply slaughtered the panic-stricken enemy troops as Santa Anna ran for his life wearing bedroom slippers. Over 600 Mexican soldiers were killed before the painfully wounded Houston could stop the carnage, while the attackers had lost only nine men. The next morning, a shabbily dressed Mexican "private" was identified as Santa Anna when his fellow prisoners began shouting his name, and Houston offered the caudillo his life in return for the Mexican evacuation of Texas. While Santa Anna would go back on his promise within days after he returned to Mexico City, the next serious challenge to Texan borders would not occur until the Lone Star Republic had become the Lone Star State.

On July 4, 1845, the Congress of the Republic of Texas ratified a resolution of annexation to the United States and thus enjoyed the protection of the American Union. Almost immediately, an army of 3,900 American troops under General Zachary Taylor marched into Texas from adjoining Louisiana and soon after encamped on the Rio Grande River in an area that was still claimed by Mexico. On April 25, 1846, the first serious clash of arms occurred as General Anastasia Torrejon's column of 1,600 cavalrymen swept north of the river

Zachary Taylor had been an army officer since 1808, despite never having gone to West Point. His post as commander during the Mexican War was partially based on political considerations in Washington, but he proved his ability by victories at Palo Alto (May 8, 1846), Buena Vista (February 21-22, 1847) and other battles of the war. He was elected president in 1848 but died a little over a year after taking office.

Zachary Taylor won the battle of Palo Alto after heeding the advice of younger officers about the placing of artillery. Early prints sometimes showed American soldiers in antiquated uniforms, but in fact it was the Mexicans who wore uniforms inspired by the Napoleonic Wars.

and ambushed a patrol of 63 American dragoons at Rancho Carricitos. Eleven Americans were killed, and while the captured survivors were treated with consideration, a full-scale war was underway.

General Taylor now faced an immediate dilemma. His main fortification on the Rio Grande, Fort Texas, was well-garrisoned and strongly built but had almost no reserve food supplies. On the other hand, his main supply base, Point Isabel, 18 miles away on the Gulf of Mexico, had enormous stockpiles of food but few defenders. Therefore, Taylor left Major Jacob Brown with an infantry regiment and his heaviest cannons to hold Fort Texas, while 3,000 men and 300 wagons hurried toward the supply depot. The commander of Mexican forces in the region, General Mariano Arista correctly guessed Taylor's plans and crossed the Rio Grande with 4,000 men to intercept the Americans on their march.

Arista, a tall, aristocratic redhead who had attended school in the United States and lived in Cincinnati, was an able, energetic general who moved rapidly to interpose his army between Taylor and his supply base. However, when the Mexican general realized he couldn't quite catch the Americans on their outward journey, he ordered part of his army to lay siege to Fort Texas while his main force deployed along the main road between Point Isabel and the American fort.

On the early afternoon of May 1, 1846, Taylor's soldiers and wagons had begun their march to Point Isabel. After several hours of marching in the shimmering heat, the men camped for the night, a dreadful experience for all concerned. One officer noted, "The night was awful, the mosquitoes seemed as thick as the blades of grass on the prairie and swarmed and buzzed in clouds while parties of half famished wolves prowled and howled around us." The next day, as the men began loading the supply wagons at Point Isabel, the booming of cannons back at Fort Texas could be heard clearly. A young West Point graduate, Lieutenant Ulysses S. Grant, noted, "As we lay in our tents that evening upon the seashore, the artillery at the fort on the Rio Grande could be distinctly heard. The war had begun."

Taylor filled every wagon with supplies, deployed 500 men to guard the base, and began the return march to Fort Texas. Lieutenant James Longstreet, the future Confederate general, noted that the march was not an easy one: "The route of march was through a dense chaparral on both sides of the road; the infantry found their way as best they could while the dragoons and Texas Rangers moved both along the road and far off from our flanks whenever they could find a passage." As the column approached to within nine miles of Fort Texas, the Americans came upon Arista's army deployed in a double line across the width of a plain called Palo Alto or Tall Timbers, which straddled the main road. Arista had placed his army in a position that was anchored by a swamp on one side and a

> *I looked down that long line of armed men, advancing toward a larger force, and I thought what a fearful responsibility . . . commanding such a host and so far from friends.*
>
> — LIEUTENANT ULYSSES GRANT, ABOUT GENERAL ZACHARY TAYLOR'S RESPONSIBILITIES AS COMMANDER.

Lieutenant Ulysses S. Grant manned a cannon against Chapultepec Castle, a key point in the defenses of Mexico City. Most American soldiers in the campaign wore a practical uniform of shell jacket and forage cap.

★ ★

Frank S. Edwards

A native of England, Frank S. Edwards came to the United States and enlisted in the army when the Mexican-American War broke out. He was part of one of the most impressive wartime marches in history—one that saw his artillery company march 101 of 318 days after leaving Fort Leavenworth, traversing 2,230 miles through enemy territory to Mexico, walking more than 22 miles a day.

Little is known about Edwards, born in 1827, except for the personal information he included in *A Campaign in New Mexico with Colonel Doniphan*, a short and surprisingly detailed account of his war experiences, which he wrote after being discharged.

Edwards, who was a moderately well-educated young man, came to the United States sometime prior to 1845 and settled in New York. By chance he was in St. Louis when the Mexican-American War broke out in May 1846, and he enlisted in a volunteer battery, A Company, Missouri Light Artillery, writing that he did so because he thought the army might help him "obtain the restoration of my health, which had been for some time, very much impaired."

Edwards began marching out of Fort Leavenworth on June 30, 1846, as part of a column under Major General Stephen W. Kearny. Marching across arid plains and great rivers, the troops on August 18 reached Santa Fe, New Mexico, which fell without a fight, the Mexican army having withdrawn.

After several weeks at Santa Fe, Kearny split his force, taking some of the troops with him west across New Mexico and Arizona towards Southern California. He left the balance, including Edwards's company, at Santa Fe under Colonel Alexander W. Doniphan. Having organized New Mexico under U.S. administration, on December 6, Doniphan led the column out from Santa Fe south, with the intention of meeting up with Major General Zachary Taylor's army in northern Mexico.

What followed was an arduous march across deserts and mountains, with the temperatures often well below freezing at night and well over 100 degrees by day. Unlike the advance from Fort Leavenworth to Santa Fe, the troops several times found themselves in action against Mexican troops or Indians, each time coming away victorious.

The march was made in several stages, with lengthy halts at El Paso and Chihuahua. By mid-May, the column had reached Parras, in Coahuila, where contact was made with Taylor's army. Later that month, the column reached Monterey. After a few days in Mexico, the troops marched across Texas to the coast and boarded a ship bound for New Orleans. From there, they were returned to St. Louis, where the troops were discharged on June 24, after marching for almost exactly one year.

★ ★

War of 1812 veteran and frontier explorer Stephen Kearny played a major role in defeating Mexican forces in California. Weakened by yellow fever, he died just after the war's end in October, 1848.

wooded knoll on the other, a situation which forced Taylor to launch a frontal assault against a larger army.

Taylor had enormous confidence in his men and quickly devised a plan where he would use his crack mobile artillery batteries to blast a hole in Arista's lines which would then be followed up by a coordinated infantry-cavalry assault. Ulysses Grant was involved in the advance and he noted, "I looked down that long line of armed men, advancing toward a larger force, and I thought what a fearful responsibility General Taylor must feel—commanding such a host and so far from friends." However, luckily for the Americans, the Mexican artillery fired from such a great distance that the men could simply sidestep the cannonballs as they bounced through the tall grass, while the enemy Brown Bess muskets were nearly useless at long range. As Grant insisted, "at the distance of a

We are very uncomfortable for more reasons than one. The last Norther we were washed out of our tents by the sea. However tis an ill wind that blows no good. A great number of turtle[s] were blown ashore, so numbed with cold that they were easily taken, & calipee & calipash some what consoled us for our disaster. If this wind continues long we can again sing, " We're afloat, we're afloat on the fierce rolling tide." Old Sumner has had one good effect on us—he has taught some of us to pray who never prayed before for we all put up daily petitions to get rid of him.

The water here unless well qualified with brandy has a very peculiar effect on one,—it opens the bowels like a melting [fat?]. Gen. Scott came to see us the other day. He complimented Major Sumner very warmly on our improvement & especially on the extraordinary vigilance of our scouts-who, as he said, were peering at him from behind every bush as he approached the camp. To those aware of the disease prevalent here, the mistake of the general is extremely ludicrous. When we go to drill, the men have to leave the ranks by dozens, & as the plain is bare as a table, make an exposé of the whole affair. The effect is unique as they squat in rows about a hundred yards from the battalion & when we deploy as skirmishers, we run right over them.

I have been on my knees almost all day, don't think I am afflicted with an untimely attack of piety,-but the fact is, chairs & tables are luxuries unknown in camps, I have to kneel by the side of a box to write.

— THOMAS EWELL IN WINFIELD SCOTT'S COLUMN

few hundred yards, a man might fire at you all day without your finding out." Major Samuel Ringgold unleashed his "flying artillery" batteries and ripped huge holes in Mexican defenses while Arista's cavalry counterattack was smashed by American infantry forming a deadly square of riflemen. The Mexican general ordered a retreat after losing over 400 men to Taylor's 50 casualties and a new defensive line was formed along a mostly dry riverbed called Resaca de la Palma.

The Mexican army deployed during the night of May 8 along a 200-foot-wide ditch with walls three or four feet deep and flanked by dense formations of chaparral. The next morning, May 9, 1846, Taylor ordered Colonel Charles May to take a squadron of cavalry and capture a Mexican artillery battery that covered the American line of advance. May's horse soldiers initially drove off the enemy gunners, but the dragoons were in turn surrounded by an overwhelming force of Mexican infantry. At this point, Taylor ordered a regiment of infantry forward to rescue the horsemen and James Longstreet accompanied the advance. As the column waded through a series of shallow lagoons, men stopped long enough to take a drink. The future general noted that "this halt gave us a moment for other thoughts; mine went back to her whom I had left behind. I drew her daguerreotype from my breast pocket, had a glint of her charming smile and with quickened spirit mounted the bank."

While the men in Longstreet's column occupied the Mexicans from the front, a small force of American troops located a rear approach to the enemy line and caught Arista's troops in a devastating pincers. The general narrowly avoided capture while hundreds of his men surrendered and dozens of other soldiers drowned attempting to swim the Rio Grande back to their base at Matamoros. At a cost of 35 dead and 75 wounded, the American army had inflicted 2,000 casualties on the Mexican army and opened the gate to an invasion of northern Mexico.

After the battles of Palo Alto and Resaca de la Palma, Taylor's army rested, refitted, and processed reinforcements before setting out to capture the capital of the state of Nueva Leon, the city of Monterrey. During a two-day battle on September 20 and 21, 1846, against Mexican defenses with colorful names such as El Diablo, The Black Fort, and The Citadel, the Americans won a vicious house to house contest and forced the evacuation of the city by the Mexican army. However, when the capture of northern Mexico failed to produce Mexican agreement to peace terms, President James Polk decided to strip Taylor's army of its regulars and attach this force to Winfield Scott's invasion army that would attempt to capture Mexico City itself. Unfortunately for Taylor, just as his best troops marched away, newly reinstated Mexican president, Antonio Lopez de Santa Anna, assembled an army of 20,000 men and marched north to annihilate the Yankee army around Monterrey.

On February 20, 1847, a scouting party of American cavalry spotted the enormous Mexican army marching into the town of Encarnacion, a few miles south of the Buena Vista ranch near the city of Saltillo. Taylor quickly deployed his small force of 4,700 newly recruited volunteers around the ranch house, its outbuildings, and a nearby pass that was the only direct approach to the estate. On February 23, while part of Taylor's army engaged in a furious fire fight with a Mexican column moving through the pass, a portion of Santa Anna's army pushed over an almost impenetrable rocky terrain on the flank and charged down on the ranch buildings. American riflemen fired from every roof, window, and door of the ranch house

Better known for his Civil War career, Samuel F. Du-Pont was very active in the Mexican War as commander of the sloop Cyane, *principally along the coast of California.*

The assault on Chapultepec Castle in Mexico City was the culminating moment of the War with Mexico. The final attack was led by two young U.S. Army officers, George Pickett and James Longstreet.

while a regiment of Mexican lancers closed in on the buildings. However, before the ranch house was overwhelmed, Colonel Jefferson Davis's redshirted Mississippi Rifles rushed into the adjoining fields, formed an inverted V with the open end toward the enemy, and virtually annihilated the Mexican charge. By the end of the day, at a cost of 700 men killed or wounded, Taylor's army had repulsed Santa Anna and inflicted 4,000 casualties on the republic's most imposing army. Northern Mexico was now firmly held by the American army, but the scene of action quickly shifted southward.

On February 21, 1847, as Santa Anna's army began deploying near Buena Vista, General Winfield Scott arrived at his staging area of Lobos Island about 50 miles south of the Mexican port of Tampico. By March 2, the last of 80 assorted American paddle wheelers and sailing vessels had arrived to transport Scott's relatively modest force of 12,000 men to Vera Cruz, 200 miles to the south. Before attempting a full-scale landing, Scott steamed into the city harbor for a personal reconnaissance accompanied by a number of aides including George Meade, Robert E. Lee, Joseph Johnston, and Pierre Beauregard. Suddenly a well-concealed Mexican battery opened fire and sent a salvo of shells plummeting around the small American vessel. The guns narrowly missed demolishing the craft, which might have dramatically changed the course of both this war and the Civil War as well. The boat quickly chugged out of harm's way, and plans were finalized for a major amphibious landing.

At 1:00 on the beautiful spring afternoon of March 9, 1847, 65 landing craft headed for the Mexican shoreline shepherded by a squadron of gunboats and supported by massive naval gunfire. A few minutes later, 4,500 men jumped into the surf and waded ashore while being serenaded by naval bands aboard ship playing "The Star Spangled Banner." The men waded through waist-deep water, sprinted up the nearby sand dunes, and raised the flag as a covering force of Mexican lancers warily withdrew toward their main defense line. By midnight, 10,000 American soldiers were ashore and the first step to Mexico City had begun.

The American army was able to push through the defenses of Vera Cruz with the aid of extensive naval support but as Scott moved inland, Santa Anna returned from his northern disaster and raised a new army to defend the national capital. A bloody preliminary battle outside Mexico City at the town of Cerro Gordo allowed Scott to push his small army toward its major objective. But though over 31,000 Mexican soldiers guarded the metropolis, excellent scouting work by Captain Robert E. Lee allowed the American army to outflank the main enemy defenses and emerge from a gigantic petrified lava bed onto the main causeway into Mexico City.

On the morning of September 13, 1847, General Scott met with his division commanders to discuss the most effective means to capture the capital city. The most imposing segment of the Mexican defense network was the enormous, ancient Chapultepec Castle which glowered over the nearby plain and seemed invulnerable to attack. Most of Scott's officers were convinced that the castle could not be stormed and some other approach must be found. However, General Franklin Pierce and Lieutenant Pierre Beauregard insisted that Santa Anna would feel the same way and deploy most of his army elsewhere. The future American president and the future Confederate general convinced Scott to attempt the risky assault and the operation went into effect.

Active operations in the Mexican War ended when Winfield Scott entered Mexico City on September 13, 1847. Scott depended less on instinct and more on military theory than Zachary Taylor. The elderly Scott was still on active duty at the beginning of the Civil War and his tactics were imitated by both sides.

Chapultepec Castle stood on a 200-foot hill surrounded by a large municipal park which opened onto a causeway across a large cypress swamp. As Pierre Beauregard suspected, Santa Anna had only deployed 850 men in the castle and adjacent grounds, and after a marine artillery bombardment, an American assault column waded through the cypress swamp, sprinted through the park, and began to scale the castle walls. The commander of the castle garrison, Colonel Nicholas Bravo, ordered his men to retreat into the inner citadel which housed the National Military College. Here 80 cadets aged 13 to 19 fought furiously against a force of Americans under Captain Joseph Johnston. The defenders, eventually called "Los Ninos Heroicas," fought with swords, knives, and clubbed muskets as the battle swayed back and forth under the national flag waving over the grounds. One cadet dueled a half-dozen Americans sprinting for the flag until Lieutenant George Pickett grabbed the colors and replaced them with the Stars and Stripes. Outside the walls, hundreds of American soldiers cheered themselves hoarse as the "Halls of Montezuma" were captured. At noon on September 13, 1847, General Winfield Scott rode triumphantly through the City Square and supervised the raising of the American flag over the Grand Plaza. The United States had added vast new territories to the American Union, but, ironically, within 15 years, the Northerners and Southerners who had fought together in this emotional battle would be taking opposing sides in a far more monumental conflict.

The 7th New York Regiment marches through the city before embarking for Washington. After Fort Sumter, hastily assembled volunteers from a few Northern cities were the only defenders of the nation's capital.

CHAPTER III

The Blue and the Gray

*I*n the pre-dawn hours of Thursday, April 11, 1861, alarm guns were fired at Citadel Square in Charleston, South Carolina, and militia companies began to form up and move to their assigned positions. One hundred and two days after the state of South Carolina had seceded from the American Union the time for diplomacy had ground to an abrupt halt and the bloodiest war in the nation's history was about to begin. Brigadier General Pierre Beauregard had just received orders from the Confederate government in Montgomery, Alabama, to demand the surrender of Fort Sumter and its Federal garrison of slightly more than 70 men, commanded by Beauregard's former West Point teacher, Major Robert Anderson.

Shortly after lunch on this climactic day, three Confederate staff officers, Colonel James Chestnut, Lieutenant Colonel James Chisholm, and Captain Stephen Lee, rowed out the three miles to the Federal fort and presented the Kentucky-born commander of the structure with a courteous but firm demand for the surrender of the post. Beauregard, who greatly admired his mentor and friend, offered generous terms, including permission to evacuate the fort with all arms and property, and provision for a final 100-gun salute to "the flag you have upheld so long with so much fortitude under the most trying circumstances." After a final fruitless round of negotiations, the three emissaries returned to Sumter at 3:30 on

Major Robert Anderson commanded the Federal garrison at Fort Sumter in 1861. Born in Kentucky and a West Point graduate, he knew many of his Confederate opponents.

Friday morning and informed Anderson, "By the authority of Brigadier General Beauregard, we have the honor to notify you that he will open fire of his batteries on Fort Sumter in one hour from this time." Anderson accompanied the officers to the fort's small wharf and whispered, "If we never meet in this world again, God grant that we may meet in the next." Exactly one hour later, at 4:30 A.M. on April 12, 1861, a shell from a Confederate mortar battery arced high over the water, its fuse glowing a dull red, and began a rapid descent over Fort Sumter. A Confederate artilleryman thought that the shell "looked like the wings of a firefly," while a Federal defender on the receiving end noted that "the shell descended with ever increasing velocity until it landed in the fort all burnt." He noted, with a cannoneer's keen eye, "it was a capital shot."

In Charleston itself hundreds of citizens scampered onto rooftops or rushed to beachfront parks, carrying with them many different emotions ranging from exultation to despair. One eyewitness noted enthusiastically: "At the gray of the morning the roar of cannon broke upon the ear. The houses were in a few minutes emptied of their excited occupants and the living stream poured all through the streets leading to the wharves and battery. On reaching our beautiful promenade, we found it lined with ranks of eager spectators. On no occasion have we ever seen so large a number of ladies as on this eventful morning. There they stared, with palpitating hearts and pallid faces, watching the white smoke as it rose of wreaths, and breathing out fervent prayers for their gallant kinfolk at the guns."

Three hours later, the tiny Federal garrison, which was desperately short of ammunition, ate a meager breakfast of salt pork and water and prepared to return fire. Major Anderson, whose father had defended Charleston against the British in the War of Independence, decided to conserve his

Red hot shot and bursting shells soon set the wooden barracks on fire and nearly the whole interior of the fort blazed like a furnace.

— DESCRIPTION OF THE BOMBING OF FORT SUMTER.

ammunition supply by firing only six guns to counter the nearly 50 cannons firing from Rebel batteries. Anderson's senior battery commander, Captain Abner Doubleday, personally sighted the first gun and noted proudly "fired the first shot against the rebellion." For the next 33 hours a one-sided duel developed between Confederate and Federal artillerists as Rebel shells broke off huge chunks of Sumter's walls and started blazing fires in the fort's barracks and offices. Frustrated Union gunners watched their shells bounce off Confederate batteries reinforced with railroad iron and cotton bales so that the impact of Federal shells "was much like that of peas striking a wall." On the other hand, Rebel guns were gradually demolishing the Federal stronghold. One contemporary observer noted, "It is difficult for one to imagine the power of the missiles which modern science has constructed. Cannons weighing thousands of pounds were thrown from their carriages by the explosion of shells. Red hot shot and bursting shells soon set the wooden barracks on fire and nearly the whole interior of the fort blazed like a furnace."

By the early afternoon of Saturday, April 13, while the Stars and Stripes still waved in the humid Carolina air, it was becoming increasingly obvious to both the defenders of Sumter and their adversaries that the fort was becoming untenable. Red-hot shot was sending blinding smoke cascading through the casemates, and gunners were staggering to their weapons with wet rags covering their faces. The post's chief surgeon, Samuel Crawford, noted the rapid deterioration of conditions as "the roaring and crackling of the flames, the dense masses of whirling smoke, the bursting of the enemy's shells and our own, which were exploding in the burning rooms, the crackling of the shot and the sound of the masonry falling in every direction made the fort pandemonium."

General Beauregard could see the havoc that the bombardment was inflicting on his former instructor's command, and he decided to send a party of aides out to the fort to see if

---

★ ★ ★

The boat containing the two aides and also Roger A. Pryor, of Virginia, and A. R. Chisolm, of South Carolina, who were also members of General Beauregard's staff, went immediately to Fort Johnson on James Island, and the order to fire the signal gun was given to Captain George S. James, commanding the battery at that point. It was then about 4 A.M. Captain James at once aroused his command and arranged to carry out the order. He was a great admirer of George A. Pryor, and said to him, "You are the only man to whom I would give up the honor of firing the first gun of the war"; and he offered to allow him to fire it. Pryor, on receiving the offer, was very much agitated. With a husky voice he said, "I could not fire the first gun of the war." His manner was almost similar to that of Major Anderson as we left him a few moments before on the wharf at Fort Sumter. Captain James would allow no one else but himself to fire the gun.

—STEPHEN D. LEE, ON THE FIRING OF THE FIRST SHOT AT FORT SUMTER

★ ★ ★

Abraham Lincoln was elected president in 1860. Although a lawyer from rural Illinois with no military experience, he learned from early mistakes and effectively directed the mass mobilization of an industrialized society.

Anderson required any help in fighting the obviously spreading fires. When the Federal commander was essentially offered the same generous terms as two days earlier, he quickly accepted them and at 1:30 P.M. Sumter's guns fell silent and the American flag was replaced by a white emblem of surrender. The next morning, as Charleston ferry owners did a brisk business carrying tourists around the outside of the fort at 50 cents a person, the Federal garrison began a 100-gun salute in preparation for evacuation. Up to this point in the battle not one soldier on either side was either killed or even seriously wounded, but as the 50th salute gun was fired, a burning fragment of powder was caught by the wind and dropped into a pile of ammunition next to a cannon; exploding fragments went flying in all directions and Private Daniel Hough was killed instantly. A short time later, Hough's body was carried by an honor guard of South Carolina militia to a funeral service conducted by a Confederate chaplain and the first of 640,000 Americans to die in the Civil War was lowered into the ground. The war that many Americans had called an "irresistible con-

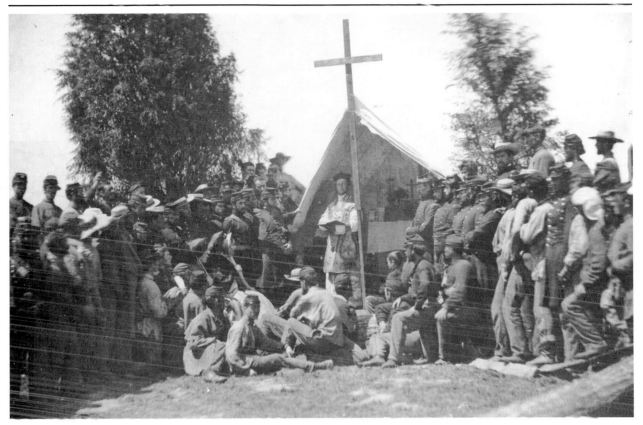

flict" had finally begun and amateur armies of Yankees and Rebels began massing in villages, towns, and cities across the continent as the last hope of peaceful reconciliation flickered and died.

The news of Anderson's surrender generated a wide spectrum of emotions depending on geographical location. Governor Francis Pickens of South Carolina emphasized that the capture of Fort Sumter would serve as a firebreak against an invading horde of Yankees. "They have vauntingly arrayed their twenty millions of men against us . . . but we have rallied; we have met them and we have conquered." On the other hand, Northern publisher Charles Abbott saw the confrontation quite differently: "Fort Sumter was the Bunker Hill of the Civil War. In both cases, a proud aristocracy were determined to subject this country to its sway. In both cases, the defeat was a glorious victory. This little band of heroes withstood the attack of an army, provided with the heaviest batteries which Europe and America could afford. And then, when they had not another cartridge to fire or not another biscuit to divide,

A Catholic chaplain conducts mass for the predominantly Irish 69th New York Militia. Religious services were well-attended on both sides.

Irvin McDowell lost the first major battle of the Civil War at First Bull Run. He came closer to victory than many realize, but his battle plan was too complicated for his untrained troops.

they evacuated the ruins, the Stars and Stripes still waving over them."

On Sunday, April 14, as Major Anderson was preparing to evacuate Fort Sumter, Abraham Lincoln called an emergency meeting of his cabinet and military advisors, and the next morning issued a call for 75,000 volunteers to put down what was now labeled as an insurrection. Almost immediately the governors of Virginia, Tennessee, Arkansas, and North Carolina refused Lincoln's request and set in motion the secession of those states from the Union. This second wave of secession encouraged the Confederate government in Montgomery, Alabama, to accept Virginia's offer to house the new republic's officials in Richmond, thus placing the capitals of two belligerent nations only 100 miles apart.

For the next three months, huge numbers of boys and young men from the now seperate regions of the country rushed into recruiting offices and joined the dozens of state regiments that would eventually form the Union and Confederate armies. While Confederate President Jefferson Davis was tempted to launch an attack towards the Union capital during the first weeks of the war, there was considerably more pressure on

Washington was defended throughout the war by heavy artillery units such as Company A of the First Connecticut. Their duties were largely ceremonial, as reflected by the well-cared-for weapons and the regulation coats; the officers and NCOs at left have trouser stripes in the red artillery arm-of-service color. The heavy artillerymen were thrown into the war's final battles as infantry, with tragic results.

Abraham Lincoln to order a general offensive as Northern newspaper headlines screamed "On to Richmond," and proclaimed that the first session of the Confederate Congress due to meet in Richmond in late July should never be permitted to convene. By mid-July almost 40,000 green Yankee troops were encamped around Washington and their new commander, 43-year-old Irvin McDowell, was under enormous pressure to use this huge army to capture the Rebel capital.

McDowell's main nemesis was the Confederate hero of Fort Sumter, General Pierre Beauregard, who commanded an army only slightly more than half as large as the Yankee force. However, Beauregard's lack of numbers was at least partially mitigated by an effective intelligence network in the Northern capital, led by a vivacious and popular young widow named Rose O'Neal Greenhouse. Mrs. Greenhouse, an ardent Southern sympathizer, owned an impressive home across the street from the White House and regularly entertained cabinet members and senior officers of the Union army. At least some of these dignitaries were less than silent about their knowledge of the national army's campaign plans and the young widow was able to secure a sensational intelligence bonanza. On July 10, one of Mrs. Greenhouse's proteges, young socialite Bettie McDowell, drove away from Washington disguised as a farmer's wife who had driven to the city to deliver vegetables. Her cover story worked through a series of roadblocks until she passed into northern Virginia, when she dashed away from a suspicious Union provost guard with bullets flying over her head. Miss McDowell supplied Beauregard with the exact starting date of the Union offensive and a yard square map drawn by Mrs. Greenhouse which contained a detailed image of the Yankee advance route. This vital information allowed the Confederate general to risk calling in reinforcements from all over Virginia knowing that the Yankees could not attack in every direction at once.

Six days later, with Beauregard's full knowledge that they were coming, Irvin McDowell's army rumbled southwest from Washington, accompanied by sightseers who had come to watch the battle and cheer the Union to victory. The march soon slowed to a crawl as inexperienced troops fell out of line

. . . the defeat was a glorious victory.

— A NORTHERN NEWSPAPER'S DEPICTION OF THE LOSS AT FORT SUMTER.

General Daniel McCook Jr., son of an Ohio family that lost many members in the Union cause.

General Robert L. McCook. Like many other members of his family, he served and died in the war's Western theater.

☆ ☆

A Family's Brave Sacrifice

Throughout the history of the United States it has not been unusual for a family to have several sons in the service at the same time, but few have matched the "Fighting McCooks of Ohio," as they were known. The McCook patriarchs, brothers Daniel and John, together saw 15 of their sons in Union blue and wore it themselves, despite their rather advanced age.

McCooks served in all ranks, from private to major general. Some served as physicians, chaplains, recruiters, or staff officers. But most of them were combat troops. To distinguish among the numerous McCooks in the service, people would add "of the tribe of Dan" or "of the tribe of John" when mentioning their names. One of the numerous clan, Alexander, was a West Point graduate, and two, Edwin and Roderick, graduated from Annapolis. Four of the boys, Robert, Alexander, Daniel Jr., and Edward, became generals in the volunteer army, while three others held honorary commissions as generals in the volunteers.

Several McCooks were at First Bull Run, where young Charles, a private in the 2nd Ohio, was killed while his father, Daniel, who was serving as a volunteer nurse, looked on. While some members of the family served in West Virginia and Virginia and on duty with the fleet, most of the clan fought in the Western theater. There were McCooks present at Forts Henry and Donelson, Shiloh, Wilson's Creek, Corinth, the Vicksburg campaign, Perryville, Murfreesboro, Tullahoma, Chickamauga, Chattanooga, as well as during the Atlanta campaign, in Alabama, the Carolina campaign, and on the March to the Sea.

The family paid a heavy price for its devotion to the Union. Charles died at Bull Run; patriarch Daniel died of wounds incurred during a Confederate cavalry raid; Robert was murdered by Confederate irregulars while recovering from wounds; and Daniel Jr., who before the war had been one of William Tecumseh Sherman's law partners, was killed leading an attack at Kenesaw Mountain.

In addition to the four who died in the war, John, father of five of the Fighting McCooks, who had served as a military surgeon, died of natural causes shortly after the war ended. Naval officer Roderick was permanently disabled in the fighting at Fort Fisher in late 1864 and early 1865, and other members of the family accumulated an imposing number of wounds.

Amazingly, some families had even more stirring records than the brave McCooks. Curtis King, an Iowa farmer who served in a homeguard unit in his 80s, had several sons, 20 grandsons, and four or five great-grandsons who fought for the Union, a number of whom were killed in action. Ora Palmer of North Carolina lost all four of her sons at Gettysburg, and Polly Ray, also of North Carolina, lost her seven sons in the war.

★ ★

to take naps or loot nearby towns. Soon hundreds of soldiers were inching southward encumbered with mattresses, mirrors, clocks, and other less than essential equipment. Finally, on the night of July 20, 1861, as elements of Joseph Johnston's Confederate army steamed into Manassas Junction from their camps in the Shenandoah Valley, the Union army bedded down in the hamlet of Centreville and prepared to launch an attack against Beauregard along Bull Run Creek.

Sunday, July 21, dawned sunny and hot, and as the mercury soared into the 90s McDowell's complex plan surged into operation. The Union commander's plan was to keep Beauregard occupied along his defenses on Bull Run while a large flanking force of over 14,000 men crossed the creek at Sudley's Springs Ford, several miles west of the Confederates and smashed into the Rebels's unprotected flank. The plan was a decent one, but McDowell's green recruits were simply incapable of the pinpoint coordination needed for the complex plan to succeed, and piece by piece the Union offensive began to unravel.

The Union demonstration attack in Beauregard's front, which was supposed to divert the Rebels's attention from the threat

> *With cheers and at double quick we dashed forward, throwing away knapsacks and coats and everything which could retard our charge.*
>
> — A MEMBER OF THE 69TH NEW YORK REGIMENT.

8th New York Militia in the field, 1861. As with a number of Northern volunteer units in the early months of the war, they were confusingly dressed in grey. Some Southern units were also wearing blue at the time.

to their flank, was so lackluster and disorganized that virtually no one was fooled in the Confederate lines. Most importantly, the grizzled Southern general, Nathan Evans, who was responsible for holding a key bridge across Bull Run, quickly recognized the Union frontal "attack" as a sham and ordered most of his brigade of South Carolinians and Louisianians to march double time through a series of fields and streams toward the Federal flanking column. The Rebels arrived, panting and winded, at a farmhouse near the main road the Yankees would have to cross in order to flank the Confederate army. When Ambrose Burnside's brigade of New York, New Hampshire, and Rhode Island men marched confidently down the turnpike they were met by a hail of bullets that stalled the Union advance and allowed desperately needed Southern reinforcements to arrive.

Pierre G. T. Beauregard commanded Confederate troops capably at the beginning and end of the Civil War, but personality conflicts kept him in isolated posts for much of the time.

McDowell still had more men on the battlefield than Beauregard, and sheer weight of numbers gradually pushed the Confederates back to the dominant position on the field, Henry House Hill. This high ground featured a large farmhouse owned by the octogenarian widow of one of the officers of the legendary ship U.S.S. *Constitution*, and when the crack of gunfire approached her home, widow Henry categorically refused to leave her bedroom. Her home now became the focal point for the first significant battle of the Civil War. Young men from New York and Virginia whose fathers and older brothers had fought together against the British and the Mexicans now lined up on opposite ends of a treeless field and fired volley after volley at one another. Colonel Michael Corcoran lined up the 1,600 Irishmen of his 69th New York Regiment and shouted, "Come on boys! You have got your chance at last," and led his men against a Confederate artillery battery. As one member of the regiment noted, "with cheers and at double quick we dashed forward, throwing away knapsacks and coats and everything which could retard our charge," and entered a contest in which the regiment took and lost a commanding position eight

Come on boys! You have got your chance at last...

— COLONEL MICHAEL CORCORAN URGING THE MEN OF THE IRISH 69TH NEW YORK REGIMENT INTO THE BATTLE OF FIRST BULL RUN.

There is Jackson standing like a stone wall! Rally behind the Virginians!

— THE RALLY CALL THAT EARNED STONEWALL JACKSON HIS NICKNAME.

Thomas J. Jackson earned his nickname "Stonewall" at First Bull Run. The eccentric general was Robert E. Lee's greatest commander, and was irreplaceable after his death at Chancellorsville.

times in succession. Finally, as they threw themselves panting and fainting on the ground, they were replaced by a regiment of Connecticut men who "came rushing through the smoke of the conflict, swept up the hill like a whirlwind, unfurled the Stars and Stripes over the captured guns and gave three cheers which blended exultingly with the roar of the battle."

However, as the Yankees were about to chase the Rebels from a key position, a dour, shabbily dressed former professor from Virginia Military Institute gave new hope to the Confederates. General Thomas Jackson calmly refused the unraveling Southern line of battle while an admiring colleague shouted to his men, "There is Jackson standing like a stone wall! Rally behind the Virginians!" By late afternoon of this agonizingly hot day, the tide of battle slowly began to shift in favor of the Confederates. At this point the Henry House itself was a shambles, and Mrs. Henry had been killed when a shell blew apart most of her bedroom, but the Rebel line around the house stiffened as Joseph Johnston's men jumped from troop trains chugging into nearby Manassas Junction and charged excitedly onto the battlefield. One by one, exhausted, inexperienced Union regiments began to withdraw from the firing line until the equally fatigued Southerners began to sense that they might win the battle. As the bluecoats pulled back toward Bull Run Creek, a few well-placed Confederate cannon shots began to land among the men and orderly retreat quickly degenerated into chaotic flight. A Northern spectator, caught up in the panic, recounted the scene as an image of hell: "The rush was like that of a mountain torrent detached from its bed. Broken regiments, bleeding men, wounded horses frenzied in agony, wagons, caissons were all flying so wildly that no individual energy or courage could by any possibility stop the flood. The cool and the brave were swept along. Many riderless horses, in their death agony, plunged through the mass, striking down or trampling the fugitives."

In one sultry Sunday afternoon, the largest,

best-equipped army in the history of the United States had been sent fleeing northward in panic after losing almost 4,000 men and nine regimental battle flags. Only the chaotic condition of the victorious Rebel army prevented the Southerners from marching into Washington and planting the Confederate flag on the Capitol and White House. However, despite the enormity of the defeat and a few newspaper editorials calling for recognition of Southern independence, most Northerners from

> *If I had ten sons, instead of five, I would give them all sooner than have our country sent into fragments.*
>
> — A NORTHERN MOTHER ON SENDING HER FIVE SONS OFF TO WAR.

Abraham Lincoln to common citizens began to see the defeat as a necessary object lesson from which much could be learned. A Southern woman living temporarily in Massachusetts warned her Virginia relatives, "I would not advise you of the South to trust too much in the idea that the Northerners will not fight, for I believe they will and their numbers are overwhelming." A New York woman wrote her officer husband a poignant letter informing him that all five of his sons had enlisted in the Union army: "I could not withhold them and in the name of their God, and their mother's God and their country's God, I bid them to go. If I had ten sons, instead of five, I would give them all sooner than have our country sent into fragments." The initial confidence among Northerners and Southerners that one great battle would determine the fate of Union and Confederacy now gradually gave way to the realization that a long war was probable and 1861 was little more than a year of preparation.

While Union and Confederate military leaders spent most of the fall and winter following First Bull Run in preparation for a new Virginia campaign in the spring of 1862, a little-known Federal general in the West was making rapid inroads on the Rebels's hold on the crucial state of Tennessee. General Ulysses S. Grant, a man who had virtually been forced to resign his commission due to drunkenness, had only escaped a dreary fate of working indefinitely in a saddle and harness store by the desperate need for trained officers to take over the new volunteer regiments. In February of 1862, Grant led

Black units, known as the "U.S. Colored Troops," began to be recruited after the issuance of the Emancipation Proclamation. This soldier wears a pre-war coat cut short to resemble the four-button fatigue jacket worn in the field by most Union troops.

ELLSWORTH

A Battle Hymn for Ellsworth's Zouaves

Who is this ye say is slain?
Whose voice answers not again?
Ellsworth, shall we call in vain
    On thy name to-day?
No! from every vale and hill
One response all hearts shall thrill:
"Ellsworth's fame is with us still,
    Ne'er to pass away!"

Bring that rebel banner low,
Hoisted by a treacherous foe:
'Twas for that they dealt the blow,
    Laid him in the dust.
Raise aloft, that all may see,
His loved flag of liberty.
Forward, then, to victory,
    Or perish if we must!

Hark to what Columbia saith:
"Mourn not for his early death;
With each patriot's dying breath
    Strength renewed is given
To the cause of truth and right,
To the land for which they fight.
After darkness cometh light,
    Such the law of heaven."

So we name him not in vain,
Though he comes not back again!
For his country he was slain;
    Ellsworth's blood shall rise
To our gracious Saviour-King–
'Tis a holy gift we bring;
Such a sacred offering
    God will not despise.

———— ★ ★ ★ ————

Ephraim E. Ellsworth had worked in Abraham Lincoln's law firm and helped popularize Zouave-style volunteer units in a series of pre-war parades and demonstrations. He was killed in the first days of the war as the Union army advanced through Alexandria.

a relatively small army against the vital Confederate bastions of Fort Henry and Fort Donelson and ended up capturing over 12,000 Rebel soldiers and forcing the Southern evacuation of Nashville. By April of 1862 Grant's army had marched almost to northern Mississippi and Jefferson Davis was desperate to prevent the unraveling of the entire Western theater of war.

President Davis turned over command of Western operations to the general he considered the most talented officer in either army, Albert Sidney Johnston, who was in turn assisted by the hero of Fort Sumter and Bull Run, Pierre Beauregard. These two commanders cobbled together an attack force that matched Grant's 40,000-man army, and planned a massive surprise assault on the Yankees who were rather leisurely encamped along the Tennessee River at the small port of Pittsburg Landing. Grant had little idea that the

Confederates were about to attack him, and on the morning of April 6 was comfortably quartered in a gracious plantation house several miles upriver. Suddenly, just as dawn broke, Johnston's hard-driving Rebels slammed into the Yankee camp just as the Federals were preparing breakfast. Graycoats overran the rows of tents and one Confederate general noted approvingly, "The enemy was found utterly unprepared, many being captured in their tents, and others, though on the outside, were in costumes better fitted to the bedroom than the battlefield." When Grant heard the distant sound of gunfire, he commandeered a steamboat and hurried to the scene of the action. First, he conferred with the commander of one of his reserve divisions, General Lew Wallace, and ordered him to start a forced march to cover the Union flank. The future author of the best-selling novel *Ben Hur* promptly put his regiments in motion while Grant steamed down to Pittsburg

Albert S. Johnston organized an effective Confederate surprise attack on Union units at Shiloh. Confederate forces faltered after Johnston was killed, and eventually had to withdraw.

Officers of the 2nd New York Artillery in the field. Liquid refreshment is clearly visible on the table in the tent, although troops on both sides generally avoided any public display of playing cards, alcohol, etc.

William T. Sherman served under Grant at Shiloh, and first showed his capabilities in that hard-fought engagement. By war's end he was commanding the Union's second largest army.

Landing and began to throw together a final line of defense along the high banks overlooking the river.

For most of this gorgeous spring morning and afternoon, the advancing Confederates overran successive Union defense lines and began capturing entire Yankee regiments. However, just as Johnston was directing a possibly overwhelming attack on a key Union position called "The Hornet's Nest," the Texan slid from his horse with a bullet wound behind the knee. The wound should not have been fatal, but while blood filled the general's boot, none of his accompanying staff officers thought to apply a lifesaving tourniquet. Sadly the army's chief physician had just been dispatched by the chivalrous general to attend to a number of severely wounded Federal soldiers who had received no medical attention from their own surgeons. Within a few minutes Johnston had bled to death, and the energy behind the Confederate advance dissipated quickly. Several Confederate regiments were able to penetrate to the riverbank, but Grant had set up a formidable line of over 50 cannons backed up by the naval gunfire of several gunboats steaming up and down the Tennessee River.

The next morning as Pierre Beauregard assumed full command of the Confederate army, long lines of Federal reinforcements began deploying alongside the survivors of the first day's fighting and Grant, accompanied by redheaded, voluble William T. Sherman, ordered a massive Union counterattack. Beauregard was an energetic field commander and as one Confederate officer noted, he "was everywhere in person, inciting the troops to the most desperate valor." Units such as the Crescent Regiment of New Orleans and the Washington Artillery fought desperately to hold the Rebel lines, but blue-coated reinforcements were pouring across the

> ## *The storm of lead was so great that it is a marvel that anyone could have escaped unshot.*
>
> — Eyewitness description of the fire power of the Federal army.

94

Tennessee River in ferryboats and Beauregard had no more reserves. A huge line of Federals stepped into firing formation and the result was catastrophic to the Southerners as "nearly every bullet performed its mission. The foe staggered, recoiled and fled leaving the field covered with the slain. Tents were riddled with bullet holes. The storm of lead was so great that it is a marvel that anyone could have escaped unshot. One tree, not 18 inches in diameter was struck with 90 balls." Beauregard's desperate men gradually withdrew to a ridge that featured a small meetinghouse, Shiloh Church, and deployed for a final climactic assault. For several hours a fierce fight continued along this line but the woods around the church were rapidly filling with even more bluecoats. Suddenly "cheer after cheer rang through the woods as the Union troops received increasing assurance that the day was theirs." At about 4:00, the main Confederate line simply disintegrated and the retreating Rebels rushed through the Union camps they had occupied overnight, pressed on to their own encampment about two miles further from the river, and caught their breath just long enough to begin a retreat back to their main entrenchments at Corinth, Mississippi. Grant's exhausted army made no attempt to pursue the retreating Rebels as they instead tended to the victims of the battle which included thousands of Union and Confederate casualties. One officer noted of the area around Shiloh Church, "where the charges were made the bodies lay in rows forming parapets of flesh which might serve as breastworks. Mangled horses, mutilated men, broken gun carriages and all the nameless debris of a battlefield were spread around in appalling confusion."

Grant's army had lost an appalling total of 13,000 men killed, wounded, or captured while the Confederate attackers had suffered a near-

Although not a trained military professional, Lew Wallace served ably at Shiloh and later campaigns of the Civil War. As post-war governor of the New Mexico territory, he wrote the novel Ben-Hur *by night while conducting the search for Billy the Kid by day.*

Cheer after cheer rang through the woods as the Union troops received increasing assurance that the day was theirs.

— ACCOUNT OF THE UNION VICTORY AT SHILOH.

George B. McClellan got Union forces close to Richmond by his bold landing on the Peninsula and won the battle of Antietam, but his reluctance to follow up his successes aggressively led to his eventual dismissal by Lincoln.

I cannot spare this man! He fights!

— ABRAHAM LINCOLN ABOUT ULYSSES GRANT.

ly as severe 10,700 casualties. Despite these losses, the Federals were clearly on the offensive in the Western theater of the war and when a Union politician questioned Grant's alleged drinking and high casualties, Abraham Lincoln responded tersely, "I cannot spare this man! He fights!"

Unfortunately for the president's piece of mind, his main Eastern commander was very much the opposite of Grant. Brilliant, rich, 35-year-old George Brinton McClellan, one of the highest profile officers in the pre-war army, had been called from a moderately successful campaign in western Virginia to take over the army around the capital in the wake of the Bull Run disaster. McClellan, who was often referred to as the "Young Napoleon," spent almost a year reorganizing and training the huge Union army at his disposal and finally, in April of 1862, over 100,000 bluecoats boarded a flotilla of naval transports and set sail for Union held Fortress Monroe on the tip of the Virginia peninsula. The movement was so impressive that one observer called the operation "the leap of a giant" as men, horses, cannons, and even two newly developed observation balloons were landed in Virginia for an offensive toward Richmond.

McClellan's huge army advanced with agonizing slowness against famous colonial towns such as Williamsburg and Yorktown, but by late May the enormous force was close enough to the Confederate capital to hear the Richmond clocks strike the hour. The equally cautious commander of the Confederate defenders, General Joseph Johnston, finally organized a massive counterattack as McClellan was preparing to besiege the city, and in the confused battle of Fair Oaks slowed down the Federal momentum while being severely wounded in the process. President Jefferson Davis, who had ridden out from the Confederate White House to observe the battle, was stunned at the loss of his senior commander, but quickly made a decision that would change the course of the war. Davis turned to his chief military advisor, Robert E. Lee, and offered him command of the Confederate field army. Up to this point in the war, Lee had been derided as "The King of Spades" and "Granny Lee" for his cautious direction of several minor campaigns. Now the "real" Lee emerged in this moment of crisis; as one aide noted to another Confederate officer, "audacity will be his name."

Lee's first significant move was to order one of the heroes of First Bull Run, Stonewall Jackson, to take a relatively small army of 17,000 men and challenge Union operations in the Shenandoah Valley. In one of the most celebrated military feats in American history, Jackson's army of fast moving "foot cavalry" first mystified and then defeated a collection of Federal armies numbering over 70,000 men, and created such a panic in Washington that Lincoln recalled most of the reinforcements which McClellan intended to use for a final assault on Richmond. Lee then recalled Jackson from the Valley, and beginning on June 26, 1862, launched a series of attacks that pushed McClellan's army from the suburbs of Richmond all the way down to the James River, out of direct range of the capital.

Lincoln was so appalled at McClellan's lack of aggressiveness during the Seven Days campaign that he called Western theater commander Henry Wager Halleck to Washington as new commander of all American forces, and installed another westerner, General John Pope, as commander of a newly organized Army of Virginia. Lincoln and Halleck hoped to trap Lee in a pincers between McClellan's Army of the Potomac and Pope's new army but the audacious Virginian promptly left a small covering force to deal with McClellan and marched north with his chief lieutenants, Stonewall Jackson and James Longstreet, to "suppress" Pope. While Lincoln ordered much of McClellan's army northward to support Pope, Lee goaded Pope into a bloody series of assaults on Jackson's corps near

---

★ ★ ★

I tried to keep clean while in the army, and made it a rule to take a bath once a week and oftener when convenient; this included winter as well as summer. It looked very formidable to take a bath on some of those cold and stormy days which we had in the army, but it was more in looks than in reality. Here is a winter's day experience in this camp. One day about noon the sun shining brightly and little wind stirring, I thought I would take my bath. I walked over to Madison Run, a large stream about half a mile from camp. I found the stream frozen over solid. I got a large rock, walked to the middle of the stream, raised the rock over my head, and hurled it with all my force on the ice, but it made no impression. I repeated this eight or nine times without breaking the ice. I then returned to camp, got an axe, went back to the run, cut a large hole in the ice, which was about seven inches thick, cleared the hole of all floating ice, undressed, took a good bath, dressed, and when I returned to camp was in fine condition.

—JOHN WORSHAM,
ONE OF JACKSON'S FOOT CAVALRY

★ ★ ★

John Pope took command of the Army of the Potomac in early 1863 after a string of victories in the West. His personality irritated Eastern officers and none regretted his dismissal after his defeat at Second Bull Run.

the old Bull Run battlefield and then, just as the Federal army was fully committed, sprung Longstreet's well-concealed men on the unprotected Federal flank. The battle of Second Bull Run was an even worse Union disaster than the first encounter, and by early September of 1862 a dazed and shattered bluecoat army was back in the Washington defenses wondering what had hit them.

In the wake of this disaster, Pope was promptly sent west to fight Indians and McClellan was given orders to defend the capital and counter a Confederate invasion of the North. In early September, Lee's victorious army crossed the Potomac River into Maryland with the intention of adding that state to the Confederacy while threatening the Federal capital. Unfortunately for the Confederate cause, Lee was now becoming somewhat overconfident and he rashly divided his relatively small army into five separate forces with large distances between each unit. Soon after the general had divided his army, one of his staff officers used a copy of the army's latest set of orders to wrap several of his cigars and then dropped the document as he was about to leave camp. The next day a Federal army occupied the same campsite and a sharp-eyed corporal retrieved the cigars and the invaluable orders. McClellan now had the entire battle orders of the enemy army and, if he moved quickly, could throw an army of almost 80,000 on each of five separate Rebel forces that were only a fraction as large. However, the "Young Napoleon" was afflicted with a malady that Lincoln sarcastically called "the slows" and he took so long to get organized that Lee was given time to hurriedly begin concentrating his scattered divisions along the Antietam Creek near the little town of Sharpsburg, Maryland.

On the morning of September 17, four days after the lost orders were discovered, McClellan finally closed with Lee's army and began a series of disjointed attacks against a Rebel army that was still not fully unified and was outnumbered about three to one. Lee had rather unwisely chosen to make his stand with his back to the Potomac River which had only one fordable crossing spot in the area; thus if the bluecoats broke through the Rebel lines there was nowhere to retreat and McClellan could effectively end the war in a single day. However, the brilliant but cautious Pennsylvanian never properly organized his assault forces and his opponent was able to shift his forces from one threatened point to another for most of the early autumn day.

As the sun rose on September 17, the first Union assault forces approached the four-mile-long Rebel defense line through seas of waving corn, smoothly plowed fields, and scattered orchards. General Joseph Hooker's men moved cautiously through alternating cornfields and woods and smashed into the Confederate left flank. Hundreds of Federal cannons

Robert E. Lee commanded the Army of Northern Virginia, the principal army of the Confederacy. The greatest testimony to his ability and character is the esteem in which he was held by his opponents.

★ ★

THE WRITING OF
"THE BATTLE HYMN OF THE REPUBLIC"

"We were invited one day to attend a review of troops at some distance from the town. While we were engaged in watching the maneuvers, a sudden movement of the enemy necessitated immediate action. The review was discontinued, and we saw a detachment of soldiers gallop to the assistance of a small body of our men who were in imminent danger of being surrounded and cut off from retreat. The regiments remaining on the field were ordered to march to their cantonments. We returned to the city very slowly, of necessity, for the troops nearly filled the road. My dear minister was in the carriage with me, as were several other friends. To beguile the rather tedious drive, we sang from time to time snatches of the army songs so popular at that time, concluding, I think, with: John Brown's body lies a-moldering in the ground; His soul is marching on.

"The soldiers seemed to like this and answered back, 'Good for you!' Mr. Clark said, 'Mrs. Howe, why do you not write some good words for that stirring tune?' I replied that I had often wished to do this but had not as yet found in my mind any leading toward it.

"I went to bed that night as usual and slept, according to my wont, quite soundly. I awoke in the gray of the morning twilight, and as I lay waiting for the dawn, the long lines of the desired poem began to twine themselves in my mind. Having thought out all the stanzas, I said to myself, 'I must get up and write these verses down, lest I fall asleep again and forget them.' So with a sudden effort I sprang out of bed and found in the dimness an old stump of a pen which I remembered to have used the day before. I scrawled the verses almost without looking at the paper. I had learned to do this when, on previous occasions, attacks of versification had visited me in the night and I feared to have recourse to a light lest I should wake the baby, who slept near me. I was always obliged to decipher my scrawl before another night should intervene, as it was only legible while the matter was fresh in my mind. At this time, having completed my writing, I returned to bed and fell asleep, saying to myself, 'I like this better than most things that I have written.'"

—JULIA WARD HOWE

★ ★

supported this advance, and, after an hour of desperate fighting, the Rebel line began to waver, and the Southerners began to retreat into a series of wooded lots while the pursuing Yankees let out huge cheers. As the bluecoats pursued their enemies into the woods, General John Bell Hood's Texans rushed onto the scene and simply annihilated the most advanced units of Federals. Each general now began sending massive reinforcements into the struggle for control of the woods and the adjacent cornfields, and regimental and division commanders on both sides began dropping as fast as their men. The 15th Massachusetts entered the battle with 617 men, an hour later only 143 were still standing. Within 30 minutes the 34th New York Regiment had been reduced from 500 to 34 soldiers. Hood's crack assault unit, the 1st Texas Regiment lost 410 of its 450 men in a little more than 15 minutes as bodies covered the red-tinged cornfields.

John B. Hood was an aggressive Confederate commander at Antietam, Gettysburg, and the later campaign against Sherman. He continued to command despite being seriously wounded several times.

As the battle on the Confederate left flank and center devolved into a bloody stalemate, Federal hopes for a decisive breakthrough were focused on General Ambrose Burnside's attempts to cross Antietam Creek below Sharpsburg and roll up the Southern right flank. At one point during the battle, Burnside's attack force outnumbered the Confederate defenders more than 10 to 1, and his scouts reported that there were several places where the Antietam could be crossed by wading; but the Rhode Island general became obsessed with capturing a long, stone bridge across the creek and the graycoats were able to prevent the capture of the span for most of the afternoon. Finally, when the Yankees overwhelmed the thin line of Rebels, they smashed into Ambrose Powell Hill's crack division which had just arrived after a grueling march from Harper's Ferry. As one soldier noted, "Hill's timely arrival was our salvation; forming on the right, his columns were seen marching over the fields to reinforce their comrades, who had

Ambrose E. Burnside enjoyed enduring popularity among his own IX Corps troops, but his command decisions at Antietam were ill-advised, and he later led the Army of the Potomac to disaster at Fredericksburg.

fought heroically, despite their reverses. Our fresh brigades advanced in long, dark lines upon the Federal troops and our batteries on a semicircular ridge above them lay low many a brave soldier by a sharp crossfire." A Union soldier saw the arrival of the reinforcements from a different perspective: "The rebel columns increased their pace, the guns on the hill above sent an angry tempest of shell down among Burnside's men. In another moment, a rebel battle line appears on the brow of the ridge, moves swiftly down in the most perfect order and though met by incessant discharges of musketry, of which we plainly see the flashes, does not fire a gun. White spaces show where men are falling but they close up instantly and the line advances. Burnside is outnumbered, outflanked, compelled to yield the ground he took so bravely."

Lee had sent every available unit in his army to confront Burnside; he had absolutely no reserves left. However, when Burnside sent a messenger to McClellan urging him to dispatch some of the 20,000 Federals who had not yet entered the battle, the Young Napoleon hesitated. His subordinates emphasized that Lee might attack elsewhere on the field and McClellan ordered Burnside to merely hold a good defensive position; any further offensive from the Army of the Potomac was out of the question. As the sun set on a battlefield that one eyewitness called "a landscape turned red," the opportunity to annihilate a now desperately over-extended Southern army slipped through McClellan's fingers. Lee defiantly held his position throughout the next day, almost daring his opponent to attack, and then slipped across the Potomac overnight, ending the first invasion of the North. The Army of Northern Virginia had lost a stupendous 14,000 of the 39,000 men engaged while the Federals had lost an almost equally appalling 13,000 men. This battle produced the single bloodiest day of the Civil War and the armies'

> ## *Burnside is outnumbered, outflanked, compelled to yield the ground he took so bravely.*
>
> — A UNION SOLDIER'S ACCOUNT OF THE REBEL ATTACK ON BURNSIDE'S TROOPS AT ANTIETAM.

medical staffs were simply overwhelmed by the flood of casualties. One of the "angels" of this gruesome battlefield was a former Patent Office clerk who had organized efforts to collect bandages and food for casualties by advertising in Northern newspapers. At the battle of Antietam, Clara Barton provided surgeons with desperately needed anesthetics, tended to the wounded in the field, and was nearly a casualty herself when a bullet pierced her sleeve and killed the soldier she was attending. A few minutes later she used a pocket knife to remove a musket ball from a soldier's cheek when it became obvious that it would be hours before a surgeon could provide relief. However, despite Miss Barton's best efforts, thousands of wounded Rebel and Yankee soldiers would never leave the peaceful fields along Antietam Creek alive.

The Union had technically won a victory at Antietam, to the extent that the Southern invasion of Maryland was repulsed, and Abraham Lincoln used this "triumph" to announce the Emancipation Proclamation to the people of the North and the South. However, the weeks between the announcement and its official implementation of January 1, 1863, were particularly dismal ones for the Union cause. Lincoln finally tired of McClellan's excessive caution and replaced him with Ambrose Burnside, who promptly blundered into one of the most one-

Clara Barton had her first experience of nursing troops under fire at Antietam, a week short of her 41st birthday. Her wartime experiences led her to found the American Red Cross.

★ ★ ★ ★ ★ ★ ★ ★ ★ ★ ★ ★ ★ ★ ★ ★ ★ ★ ★ ★

An Ordinary Man Who Didn't Flinch

Charles Brunner was one of numerous ordinary people caught up in the nation's greatest conflict. He is known for rallying the troops during the most trying of times, and he fought in more than a dozen major battles, personally capturing three enemy battle flags. He appears to never have been wounded, although nearly 100 of his comrades were killed or injured.

A native of Northampton County, Pennsylvania, Brunner happened to be in Wisconsin in August 1862 and enlisted in B Company of the newly raised 23rd Wisconsin Volunteer Infantry, the only Pennsylvanian in the regiment.

Brunner first attracted attention at Port Gibson, during the opening battle of Grant's final Vicksburg campaign. After landing on the east bank of the Mississippi, Brunner, by this time a sergeant, led about 50 of his comrades in storming the Confederate defenses. As they attacked, the color sergeant was hit. Seizing the colors, Brunner led his men forward, planting the flag on the ramparts despite heavy enemy fire.

Two weeks later, at the battle of Champion's Hill, the regiment wavered as it attempted to assault Confederate trenches. Once more seizing the colors, Brunner cried out, "Boys, follow! Don't flinch from your duty!" and led the men forward again, to take and hold the enemy position. On the very next day, Brunner's regiment was again in action, at the battle of the Big Black River.

At the Big Black, a short but heated affair, Brunner's company was ordered to defend a Union cannon so that a troublesome Confederate battery could be brought under fire. The piece was sighted and soon hotly engaged. Very quickly most of the artillerymen and their infantry supports were put out of action. Brunner rallied the men in time to beat off a determined enemy attack in hand-to-hand combat, during which he was several times on the verge of capture.

There followed the siege of Vicksburg, which surrendered on July 4, 1863, and a short expedition against Jackson, Mississippi, to beat off a Confederate relief column. By this time, Brunner had received a commission as a second lieutenant. In August 1863, his one-year enlistment expired and Brunner resigned from the army. With that, he disappeared into the mists of history.

★ ★ ★ ★ ★ ★ ★ ★ ★ ★ ★ ★ ★ ★ ★ ★ ★ ★ ★ ★

sided defeats of the entire war when he sent 120,000 Federals marching in perfect formation against Lee's superbly deployed graycoats on the heights above Fredericksburg, Virginia. In the chill December air, over 12,000 Yankees fell onto the snowy, frozen ground as seven separate charges were pulverized by Confederate rifles and cannons. While Burnside's men were bleeding and dying in front of Marye's Heights, Rebel cavalrymen in the Western theater were devastating Ulysses Grant's supply lines and destroying his food depots; at one point they even captured Grant's wife and children who were chivalrously escorted back to the Union general by a Confederate cavalry leader. Finally, a third Federal army under General William Rosecrans confronted General Braxton Bragg's Army of Tennessee along Stones River near the town of Murfreesboro, Tennessee, and in one of the bloodiest New Year's Eves in American history, barely avoided annihilation. Only a desperate, backs-to-the-wall performance by the Federals on the second day of the battle prevented a stupendous defeat. Even though Bragg eventually retreated, the Union forces would be unable to launch offensive operations for over seven months. As the second year of the Civil War sputtered to an end on the last day of 1862, the Confederate cause seemed stronger than ever and not a few Northern politicians, editors, and even military officers suggested the time for peace negotiations was clearly at hand. Few people, North or South, could have foreseen that exactly one year later the Union armies would be on the offensive on all fronts and the Confederacy would be a dying, if still dangerous and valiant, entity.

The Confederate garrison at Vicksburg was eventually starved into submission, but Union troops won a number of victories at outlying redoubts.

CHAPTER IV

Union Restored

Presidents, generals, and citizens of both the North and South approached the onset of 1863 with the growing realization that the whole grand experiment in American republicanism was now adrift in a sea of blood that seemed to have no discernible end. A wide spectrum of Northern opinion ridiculed Lincoln's Emancipation Proclamation as illegal, unconstitutional, and producing an insurmountable barrier to any hope of peaceful reconciliation of the two divided sections of America. On the other hand, while Confederate armies had been fairly successful during the past year of campaigning, Southern soldiers and civilians decried the government of Jefferson Davis for ongoing shortages of food and clothing that were now plaguing almost everyone living in the secessionist republic. Both presidents were now coming under intensive pressure to produce a decisive victory that would end the struggle and restore prosperity to the American people.

Lincoln began the new year by relieving the failed Ambrose Burnside of command of the Army of the Potomac and replacing him with the general's harshest critic, General Joseph "Fighting Joe" Hooker. Hooker was a hard-drinking, hard-living officer who was despised by many of his fellow generals but extremely popular among his men. The controversial general soon developed a campaign plan that very nearly ended the Civil War in 1863. Unlike Burnside's unimaginative battering-ram tactics, Hooker sent his men on a brilliant, unexpected flank march over the Rappahannock and Rapidan Rivers and by

Joseph Hooker did not perform well while leading the Army of the Potomac in the field, but his reorganization of the army played a considerable role in its later victories.

May 1, 1863, was launching a seemingly irresistible assault force against the Rebels near Chancellorsville, Virginia. However, as Federal troops under Pennsylvanian George Gordon Meade trekked through an eerie forest of oversized trees and undersized bushes called the Wilderness, Hooker's nerve failed him and he ordered his nearly victorious army to dig in and await a Confederate attack. While Meade fumed that his superior had just thrown away the best opportunity ever to beat the Rebels, Robert E. Lee and Stonewall Jackson counted their blessings and prepared a daring countermove. While a tiny Confederate holding force under Lee made a noisy demonstration against Hooker's front lines, Jackson marched 26,000 men on a long, 12-mile flanking march that placed his men on the unprotected right flank of the Union army.

At 6 P.M. on the mild, pleasant evening of May 2, 1863, the blue-coated troops of General Oliver Howard's XI Corps sat by their supper fires at the terminus of the Federal line and played cards, smoked pipes, and congratulated themselves on their deployment in such a safe spot on the battlefield. Suddenly, squirrels, rabbits, and other animals charged out of the woods as if escaping from a forest fire and a moment later they were followed by thousands of screaming Rebels who were thought to be at least a dozen miles away. Jackson's grim infantrymen smashed through one hastily constructed defense line after another and by nightfall had pushed the Federals back nearly to Hooker's headquarters at the Chancellor mansion. Stonewall Jackson intended to launch a rare night assault, but the disorganized condition of his units forced him to spend the night hours scouting locations for a morning attack. As the Rebel general and his staff rode back toward their own lines, a company of nervous Confederate sentries opened fire in the belief that they were under attack by Union cavalry and Jackson went down with what would prove to be a mortal wound. Lee, stunned at the loss of Jackson, was able to organize a series of follow-up attacks that ultimately pushed Hooker back across the river, but the Virginia general promptly realized that his victory was indeed a hollow one. Not only was the Army of the Potomac still very much intact, but the Federals's Western counterparts were embarking on a campaign that would ultimately prove to be an irretrievable disaster for the Confederacy.

On April 9, 1863, while Joseph Hooker was planning his flanking operation against Lee, his Western counterpart, General Ulysses Grant, was setting into motion an equally daring campaign to capture the Confederacy's last major bastion on the Mississippi River, the town of Vicksburg. For the last several months a succession of operations against the citadel's river defenses had proved to be humiliating failures; so now the taciturn Grant decided that his best course was to swing in a wide-flanking movement around the city and approach the Rebels from the more vulnerable rear entrenchments. Thus, on the warm, moonless night of April 16, 1863, as Grant, his wife Julia, and their two young sons sat on deck chairs on the steamer *Magnolia* and observed the operation, Commodore David Porter's naval squadron steamed down river from the Union lines and passed under the Vicksburg batteries mounted on bluffs 200 feet above them. Confederate gunners sank the *Patrick Henry* and caused damage to most of the other ships,

Black laborers, recently freed from local plantations, dug canals under the direction of Union engineers to help out-flank Confederate positions at Vicksburg.

★ ★

UNION JIM

"Jim Williams, whose portrait we publish on this page, is of small, compact stature, twenty-six years of age, was born in the District of Columbia, from whence he was sold about six years ago to Benjamin Barber, of Carroll Parish, Louisiana. Williams, learning the arrival of General M'Arthur's division at Lake Providence, left his master about the 1st of February last, and joined the army in capacity of cook in the Ninety-fifth Illinois Regiment. On Tuesday, the 10th of February, learning that a scouting party had just gone out to make a reconnaissance in the neighborhood of his home, Williams determined to join them; and, borrowing a mule and musket, followed and overtook the party about five miles distant, and just before they fell into a rebel ambuscade of guerrillas, numbering about two hundred and fifty, who had left their horses in the rear, and, under cover of canebreaks and bushes, were reserving their attack until our advanced-guard of about forty infantry should be fairly within range. At this a volley was discharged by the rebels which prostrated one quarter of our men; the remainder charged bayonets and drove the rebels from their shelter. Now commenced a running fight. Jim Williams

dashed to the front and swept on about one hundred and fifty yards in advance. When under cover of a tree he commenced firing; this started up three guerrillas a short distance from him. The wily scout, observing them rise, leveled his musket and demanded their surrender, upon which two threw down their arms; the third, at the same instant, fired at Williams, the ball cutting off his belted knife. Williams returned the fire, sending a ball through the head of the rebel and killing him instantly. He then brought in his two prisoners with their guns, one of which he was allowed to keep as proof that negroes can fight. The little party of forty succeeded in dispersing the rebels and taking thirty-one prisoners before the remainder of the troops arrived.

On returning to camp a guerrilla scout was observed by the quick eye of Williams a quarter of a mile off. He darted after him like a hound for his prey. The rebel waited the onset, when Williams, coming within about fifty yards, delivered an off-hand shot which sent the foe reeling on his horse's neck, crying "O God! I'm shot."

Williams is very anxious to raise a company of negroes for scouting service, and said to the writer of this, on leaving him a few days since, "I am willing to work, but would rather fight." General M'Arthur, who appreciates true bravery without regard to color, holds him in the highest estimation, and freely gives him the post of honor in scouting the swamps of Louisiana."

—HARPER'S WEEKLY, MARCH 28, 1863

★ ★

but by midnight 10 formidable Union warships were safely below the city. A few days later they were covering a huge ferrying operation in which Grant marched an army of 30,000 men down the Louisiana side of the river and then crossed them over to the Mississippi side almost 50 miles below Vicksburg.

Grant's Confederate counterpart, Pennsylvania-born Lieutenant General John Pemberton, commanded a garrison of over 40,000 men, but frittered away this numerical advantage when he began dispersing troops all over Mississippi in an attempt to cut the Yankees' supply lines. This was an impossible task for the simple reason that Grant now had no supply lines to cut; in one of the most daring moves in military history, the Union general had

The surrender of Vicksburg on July 4, 1863, was the greatest in a string of victories in the Western theater that led to Ulysses S. Grant being given supreme command of the Union armies.

ordered his men to stock up on all the coffee, sugar, and hardtack they could stuff into their haversacks and then ordered his men to forage whatever else they required from the lush countryside. The Federals now had a totally mobile army that was virtually impervious to Confederate attempts to cut their lines of communication. Grant feinted against Vicksburg and then suddenly thrust his army at the vital railroad center of Jackson, Mississippi, 44 miles to the east. The Union general knew that any reinforcements for Pemberton would have to be transported through the railhead at the state capital. The bluecoat army brushed away a small defense force under General Joseph Johnston and destroyed the city's railroad facilities.

Pemberton was caught in an almost impossible dilemma; Johnston, his nominal superior, was urging the Pennsylvanian to link up with his own army to smash Grant near Jackson, while Jefferson Davis ordered him to defend Vicksburg at all cost and sit tight until reinforcements could be transported from the east. The Vicksburg commander made a fatal compromise. He left two divisions to guard the city and marched toward Jackson with about 20,000 men. In two successive bat-

Henry W. Halleck directed Union armies from Washington for much of the war. After being replaced by Grant, he remained in the capital in a staff position that left Grant free to campaign in the field.

tles about halfway between Jackson and Vicksburg, at Champion Hill and Big Black River, the outnumbered Confederates were mauled by Grant's army and the survivors were sent fleeing back into the defenses of the "Gibraltar of the West" minus almost half of their total strength. By late May, the Federals had virtually besieged Vicksburg and as their lines gradually constricted the Rebel garrison, it appeared that only a dramatic reinforcement from the east could save the city from capitulation.

While 32,000 soldiers and the 5,000 remaining civilians gradually watched their rations reduced to mule meat and then rat meat, and counted the arrival of new Union regiments almost every day, Jefferson Davis, Robert E. Lee, and other Confederate leaders were meeting in Richmond to attempt to solve this potentially disastrous crisis. General James Longstreet, Lee's senior corps commander, suggested the transfer of his three divisions, about one third of the Army of Northern Virginia, to the Western theater where, reinforced by units from General Braxton Bragg's Army of Tennessee, they would attempt to lift the siege of Vicksburg by attacking Grant from the rear. However, Lee insisted that the best way to relieve the pressure on Pemberton was through a second invasion of the North in which a possible thrust at Philadelphia or Baltimore might force Lincoln to recall much of Grant's army to protect the Eastern manufacturing centers. Since Lee was now clearly the most successful general the Confederacy had, his influence was enormous, and Davis, somewhat against his better judgment, approved the invasion of Maryland and Pennsylvania.

Lee's new offensive caught the Union army in a state of flux as General Hooker was currently involved in a series of disputes with Lincoln and senior General Henry Halleck. The immediate result of this feud was the resignation of Hooker and his replacement with General George Meade only a few days before the largest battle on the North American continent. When the Pennsylvanian took command of the Army of the Potomac, most of the Confederate army was already loose in his home state and the capital of Harrisburg was expected to fall at any moment. Meade, who was a cautious but competent commander, immediately ordered construction of an imposing defense line along Pipe Creek, just south of the Pennsylvania-Maryland border, with the expectation that this move would cover Washington should Lee wheel south toward the Federal capital. However, the anticipated "Battle of Pipe Creek" never occurred as two relatively small units of the opposing armies accidentally collided a short distance to the north in the quiet college town of Gettysburg, Pennsylvania.

On Tuesday, June 30, 1863, a small Union cavalry division under Kentuckian John Buford was scouting the region around Gettysburg in an attempt to discover the location of the main Confederate army. Buford's advance units came into contact with leading elements of Confederate General Henry Heth's division, which had been dispatched to confirm earlier reports that significant supplies of desperately needed shoes were available in the small crossroads town. While Buford wisely began fortifying the high ground outside the town and alerted Federal wing commander General John Reynolds that he might have discovered the Confederate army, the Rebel scouts mistakenly identified the Federal horsemen as local militia, a force that Heth thought could be easily brushed aside. Thus on Wednesday morning, July 1, as the sun rose on what was to be a torrid summer day, Heth's infantrymen, perhaps 7,000 strong, confidently approached the town with its distinctive Lutheran seminary building tower clearly in sight atop one of several ridges that bracketed the community. Buford's 2,500 cavalrymen dismounted and formed along McPherson's Ridge, under orders to hold long enough for Reynolds's I Corps infantry to arrive from a forced march several miles away.

In the midst of the wildest disorder in his ranks, and through a storm of bullets, a Union officer was seeking to rally his men to a final stand. He, too, went down, pierced by a minie ball. Riding forward with my rapidly advancing lines, I discovered that brave officer lying on his back, with the July sun pouring its rays into his pale face. He was surrounded by the Union dead, and his own life seemed to be rapidly ebbing out. Quickly dismounting and lifting his head, I gave him water from my canteen, asked his name and the character of his wounds. He was Major Francis C. Barlow, of New York, and of Howard's Corps. The ball had entered his body in front and passed out near the spinal cord, paralyzing him in the arms and legs. Neither of us had the remotest thought that he could possibly survive many hours. I summoned several soldiers who were looking after the wounded and directed them to place him upon a litter, and carry him to the shade in the rear. . . . He had but one request to make of me. That request was that if I should live to the end of the war and should ever meet his wife, I would tell her of our meeting on the field of Gettysburg and of his thoughts of her in his last moments. He wished me to assure her that he died doing his duty at the front, that he was willing to give his life for his country, and that his deepest regret was that he must die without looking upon her face again.

—John B. Gordon, General, CSA, at Gettysburg

★ ★ ★

Winfield S. Hancock, commander of the II Corps, took control of all Union troops in the Gettysburg area to stem the Confederate advance on the crucial first day of the battle.

Here an ill destiny awaited us. . .

— A SOLDIER'S ACCOUNT OF THE FIRST
DAY AT GETTYSBURG.

Heth's graycoats were in a rollicking mood as they expected to easily sweep away a few poorly organized militia units and then help themselves to the shoes and other luxuries that Gettysburg might offer. But suddenly Buford's men, many of them armed with new rapid-firing repeating rifles, opened a stunning volume of fire against the advancing Southerners, and the Confederate field commanders quickly sent requests for additional units to converge on Gettysburg in order to drive the stubborn Yankees back. Reynolds arrived before most of the Confederate reinforcements did, and for a while the Federals not only held their own, but launched several counterattacks that resulted in the capture of some entire Rebel regiments. Then the tide of battle shifted very quickly. Reynolds was killed leading an energetic Union attack and much of the offensive spirit of the Yankees melted away in the temporary command vacuum. By late afternoon, Lee had arrived to direct the Confederate operations and a series of brilliant flanking maneuvers pushed the Federals from McPherson's Ridge and then even threatened their fallback position of Seminary Ridge. One Michigan regiment was reduced to 96 men in 10 minutes as a new series of flanking attacks rolled up the bluecoats holding the ground around the seminary, and by late afternoon a stream of Yankees was hurriedly abandoning the ridge and running through the streets of the town looking for a clear path to the final ridge line around Gettysburg cemetery on the far side of town. One of the Federal officers caught in this chaotic movement noted, "Here an ill destiny awaited us, confused as we attempted to maneuver through cross streets and stung by the familiar battle yell of 'Stonewall' Jackson's men in our rear; we broke into inextricable confusion and fell an easy and wholesale prey to our pursuers, losing one thousand two hundred men in only twenty minutes. The remainder of us fled, in utter rout, to the hills to the south."

114

While Rebels and Yankees fought a desperate battle in the streets of Gettysburg, the senior Union general on the field, General Winfield Scott Hancock, arrived at the gates of the town cemetery and immediately decided that this should become the final line of defense. If Cemetery Ridge was overrun by the Rebels, Lee would gain a stunning one-sided victory as the surviving Federals would be caught in the open during a chaotic retreat. Therefore, Hancock ordered every newly arriving infantry unit and artillery battery to be posted along the ridge and personally deployed the decimated units retreating from the town as a crucial reserve in a wide arc from Culp's Hill down through the cemetery.

By Thursday morning George Meade had arrived, along with substantial elements of the Army of the Potomac, although it would be almost nightfall before every available unit was deployed for battle. Over on Seminary Ridge on the opposite side of Gettysburg, Lee and his lieutenants squinted through their binoculars and discussed the next logical move for the Army of Northern Virginia. James Longstreet pleaded with Lee to swing the Confederate army around Meade's left flank and then deploy the Rebel divisions on the next parcel of defendable ground between Gettysburg and Washington. Longstreet's reasoning was that Meade would be under enormous pressure from Lincoln to attack the Confederates before they could directly threaten the Federal capital and the result would most likely be at least as favorable as the battle of Fredericksburg. However, Lee was convinced that he had badly mauled the Union army on Wednesday afternoon, and that one massive, coordinated attack would send the Yankees scurrying in panic from their positions on the ridge where they could be annihilated in the open fields beyond the cemetery. The Confederate commander ended the discussion with the single statement, "The enemy is there and there I will

George G. Meade, commander of the Army of the Potomac, 1863-1865. Overshadowed by Grant as the war progressed, he is remembered as the victor of Gettysburg.

The enemy is there and there I will strike him, I will either whip him or he will whip me.

— GENERAL ROBERT E. LEE AS HE FACED THE DECISION THAT STARTED THE BATTLE OF GETTYSBURG.

The II Corps became one of the best units of the Army of the Potomac. Here corps commander Winfield S. Hancock is seated with his three principal subordinates: the First Division's Francis C. Barlow (who in fact survived the wounding witnessed by John B. Gordon at Gettysburg), the Third Division's David B. Birney, and the Second Division's John Gibbon.

strike him, I will either whip him there or he will whip me."

Lee's basic plan was to initiate a serial attack in echelon starting on the extreme left flank of the Union line at Culp's Hill and progressing down to the right flank which ended just short of two hills called the Round Tops. If all went well, Meade simply couldn't rush reinforcements to each threatened position in time, and the Union line would be penetrated and then rolled up. However, the Confederate attack plan depended on pinpoint coordination between all three corps and all nine divisions and this coordination simply never appeared at any point on this scorching second day of July. Confused and exasperated Confederate generals spent most of the day ordering marches and countermarches to properly deploy their men for attack and by late afternoon not one fully developed Rebel assault had been accomplished. Finally, shortly after 4 P.M., most of Longstreet's corps fanned out along the left end of the Union line and attempted the major attack of the day.

The Confederates nearly scored a significant breakthrough when Union corps commander Daniel Sickles pulled his force out of the main defense line along Cemetery Ridge and marched them forward to a peach orchard well in front of the rest of the Union army. Confederate troops smashed into this vulnerable Federal position from three sides and Sickles went down with a wound that would cost him his leg. However, other Union divisions along the ridge provided enough covering fire that most of Sickles's men scampered to safety and the Rebels looked desperately for another opportunity to achieve a breakthrough. The opportunity almost emerged when Confederate scouts reported that the smaller of the two rocky hills, Little Round Top, was both accessible for climbing and not occupied by Federal troops. Unfortunately for the

Confederates, Meade's chief engineer, General G. K. Warren, had just arrived on top of the hill and realized the same thing. Warren, on his own authority, quickly dragooned every infantry regiment and artillery battery that he could locate at short notice and sent them scurrying up Little Round Top to meet a Rebel attack that was just about to open. The result of this race was one of the bloodiest confrontations of the war.

One Union regiment scrambled up the side of the hill only seconds before a Confederate regiment scrambled up the other side. One of the bluecoats involved insisted, "It was not an attack in line, it was not a chase, it was a carnival of death. Men hewed each other's faces, they grappled in close embrace, with murder as the major thought to all." During this melee, "a Union colonel sprang forward and with one hand snatched a rebel battle flag from an enemy soldier while with the other hand he discharged the contents of his revolver in the Confederate's face. At the same instant, a bayonet thrust from a rebel in the rear gave him a mortal wound and he fell to the earth, holding his life bought flag

> ## It was not an attack in line, it was not a chase, it was a carnival of death.
>
> — AN EYEWITNESS DESCRIPTION OF THE FIGHT ON LITTLE ROUND TOP.

Joshua Chamberlain became famous for his stand at Little Round Top, but fought throughout the Civil War from Fredericksburg to the final surrender at Appomattox.

> *. . .There they lay as they fell, three brave men and the flag drenched with their common blood.*
>
> — BATTLE ON LITTLE ROUND TOP, GETTYSBURG.

close to his heart with a death grip while the rebel too dropped instantly by an avenging bullet from a patriot's hand and there they lay as they fell, three brave men and the flag drenched with their common blood."

In one of the most dramatic episodes of the battle, Colonel William Oates managed to maneuver two regiments around the extreme left flank of the Federal army and pushed toward the summit of Little Round Top only moments after Union Colonel Joshua Chamberlain's under-strength 20th Maine deployed along the tree line. A year earlier Chamberlain had been teaching about ancient battles in his course at Bowdoin College and now it was possible the fate of his own country was in his hands. One of Chamberlain's officers, Lieutenant Hiram Melcher, described the drama that ensued: "The rebels opened a murderous fire on our unprotected line as we had no time to throw up breastworks. We had 308 men in line to resist a furious assault of more than 1,000 rebels. When 130 of our men were down and only 178 remained and each man had fired the 60 cartridges he carried, the time had come when it must be decided whether we should fall back and give up the key to the whole field of Gettysburg or charge and try and throw off the foe. Colonel

Attackers lie dead at the foot of Little Round Top. The picture shows the rocky and wooded nature of the terrain.

Chamberlain gave the order to 'fix bayonets' and almost before he could say 'charge' the regiment leaped down the hill and closed with the foe whom we found behind every rock and tree." During the brief, bloody confrontation that followed, over 300 Confederates including one of their regimental commanders surrendered, but fewer than 100 Federals were still standing to take them prisoner. The Union line held and the battle of Gettysburg was destined to enter a third, decisive day.

Lee was convinced that Meade had stripped the center of his line on Cemetery Ridge in order to counter the attacks on his left and right flanks on July 2, so the Confederate commander insisted that the main thrust on Friday should be on what was probably an undermanned Yankee center. At just past 1 P.M. on July 3 the stillness of the sultry afternoon was broken by the roar of 140 Confederate cannons pouring devastation into the Federal lines. Then suddenly the deafening noise was stilled and 26 graycoat regiments built around General George Pickett's division marched out from the cover of woods on Seminary Ridge and, to the cheers of the Rebel gunners, began a purposeful advance toward a small grove of trees at the center of the Yankee line almost a mile away. The Confederate commander had been correct that Meade had certainly reduced the number of men holding this stretch of Cemetery Ridge, as only about 5,000 bluecoats were at the point of the planned attack, but they were supported by hundreds of Union cannons that the Rebel bombardment had barely affected. Thus as the mile-wide, gray tide closed in on the clearly visible clump of trees, a giant scythe of iron balls swept through the Rebels and began tearing enormous gaps in the advancing ranks. The effect was much the same as if a gigantic shotgun had fired again and again at almost 12,000 men who were caught in an open field without a hint of cover. After the Federal gunners had dropped hundreds of Pickett's men, Yankee riflemen jumped up from the cover of a low stone wall and poured successive volleys into a rapidly crumbling secessionist line. Here and there, small parties of Confederates jumped over the stone wall and engaged in a brutal

> *. . .The time had come when it must be decided whether we should fall back . . . or charge and try and throw off the foe.*
>
> LT. HIRAM MELCHER ON THE BAYONET CHARGE OF THE 20TH MAINE AT LITTLE ROUND TOP.

George E. Pickett's name is forever associated with the charge of July 3, 1863, although he was one of several Confederate commanders on the scene.

General, I have *no* division!

— PICKETT'S ANSWER TO GENERAL LEE'S INQUIRY ABOUT HIS TROOPS AFTER THE NOW FAMOUS CHARGE.

hand to hand contest with the defenders as clubbed muskets, bayonets, and even fists determined control of this vital real estate. One of Pickett's brigade commanders, General George Armistead, nephew of the defender of Fort McHenry in 1814, leaped over the wall only to be shot in the stomach seconds later. The mortally wounded Virginian was lying only a few yards from the spot where his best friend in the pre-war army, General Winfield Scott Hancock, was sprawled, almost as seriously injured. Armistead's charge was later called the "High Water Mark of the Confederacy," but only about 300 men followed the general over the wall and within a few moments most of those men were dead or prisoners. By the time the hail of cannon fire and rifle fire ended, over 7,000 Confederates were killed, wounded, or captured, and when Lee asked Pickett about the status of his division, the younger officer responded, "General, I *have* no division!" When Meade rather wisely scuttled the idea of a "reverse Pickett's charge" against Lee's forces on Seminary Ridge, the Confederate army limped back across the Potomac after suffering the loss of 28,000 men while the Federals, minus 23,000 men, savored a hard-won victory. As Pickett's dazed survivors limped back to their lines on this momentous Friday afternoon, hundreds of miles to the west an equally decisive drama was reaching its climax.

By early July of 1863, Ulysses Grant's army had tightened the siege lines around Vicksburg to the extent that the average Confederate soldier was now subsisting on one moldy piece of hardtack a day and circular letters signed by hundreds of defenders were virtually demanding of Pemberton "if you cannot feed us you had better surrender us," a scenario that the Pennsylvania Confederate was now increasingly inclined to accept. On the afternoon of July 3, Pemberton began negotiating with his Federal counterpart who promptly offered generous capitulation terms including parole of the entire Confederate army. The next day, Independence Day, the United States flag was raised over the main public buildings, and as the telegraph lines relayed the stunning news to delirious crowds all over the North, a grateful Lincoln insisted "the Father of Waters now runs unvexed to the sea." Within 24 hours the Confederacy had suffered two devastating defeats from which it would never completely recover. When a temporary Southern comeback after a solid victory at Chickamauga was more than negated by Grant's brilliant victories at Lookout Mountain and Missionary Ridge, the last days of the decisive year of 1863 became a period of mourning in the South and a time of increasing optimism throughout the North.

In March of 1864, Abraham Lincoln summoned Ulysses Grant from his Western command, promoted him to lieutenant general, a rank held previously only by George Washington, and entrusted him with command of the entire 600,000-man Federal army. Grant refused to set up his headquarters in the national capital and instead determined to exercise command from the front of the Army of the Potomac, while his completely trusted deputy, General William T. Sherman, took charge of Western operations. Grant's plan to defeat the Confederacy was enthusiastically approved by Lincoln, who had finally found a general with whom he could be totally comfortable. While medium-sized Federal armies threatened key Confederate defenses in Mobile, Alabama, the Shenandoah Valley, and the James River, the two main Union armies, each well over 100,000 men in strength, would advance on Lee's army covering Richmond and Joseph Johnston's army screening the vital rail center of Atlanta. All armies were to begin operations on the same day with the premise that the Confederates couldn't stop five offensives at once. While the three smaller Union drives at least temporarily unraveled, the two major Yankee armies under Grant and Sherman began unrelenting drives within hours of one another. In the first week of

Philip Sheridan was brought from the West by Grant to command the Union cavalry. Below he is shown with his generals (left to right: Wesley Merritt, David M. Gregg, Sheridan, Henry E. Davies, James H. Wilson, and Alfred Torbert). In front of the tent is his personal standard, which some claim he waved to rally troops at the battle of Winchester.

May 1864, the climactic campaign of the Civil War dominated the headlines of Northern and Southern newspapers.

As the Confederate armies under Lee and Johnston prepared to meet the first fully coordinated threat to the South, the prospect of continued independence was, although substantially reduced, not completely eliminated. The Rebel armies were badly outnumbered and a number of key points were already under Federal control, but the very democratic nature of the American experiment was, ironically, the best hope of secessionists in the spring of 1864. Lincoln's four-year term as president was coming to an end, and in November millions of Northerners would go to the polls to either substantiate or repudiate the president's conduct of the war. If Yankee voters went to the polls in the middle of a bloody stalemate with no end of the war in sight, it was quite likely that a Democrat amenable to a negotiated peace would take the oath of office next March 4. Thus if Lee and Johnston could hold the Federals at bay for six months, the Confederacy might yet emerge as a permanently independent republic.

At midnight on May 4, 1864, Union engineers waded through waist-deep water to begin construction of pontoon bridges over the Rapidan River at Germanna Ford and Ely's Ford. By midmorning five bridges had been thrown across the river and 100,000 blue-coated soldiers were beginning to enter the eerie, almost haunted twilight world of the Wilderness. This 50-square-mile stretch of dense concentrations of trees and underbrush had played a prominent role in the defeat of Hooker's army at Chancellorsville almost exactly one year earlier, and as the Yankee soldiers marched along the narrow roads, the ghastly sight of unburied skeletons frequently greeted the troops. Grant had no desire to confront Lee in a region where his superior numbers and better cannons would be useless, but for these very reasons, the Virginian was determined to engage the Federals before they emerged into the open, rolling country to the south. Just as Grant was breathing a sigh of relief that Lee had not contested the river crossing, Confederate troops attacked the lead elements of the more than 8,000 wagons creeping through the dense foliage. Yankee

The volleys were so regular and incessant that they echoed throughout the Wilderness like pealing thunder.

— A UNION OFFICIER'S ACCOUNT OF THE BATTLE IN THE WILDERNESS, MAY 1864.

guard units fired back against largely unseen antagonists and massive firefights erupted throughout the Wilderness. As one participant noted of this weird form of large-scale bushwhacking, "no men saw or could be seen, it was a battle of invisible against invisible." An additional horror emerged when musket fire ignited tinder-dry underbrush into deadly fires that frequently incinerated men too badly wounded to crawl out of the path of the advancing flames. Combat continued even as the sun fell and one Union officer insisted, despite his fears, "it was a sublime spectacle in that forest, when the gloom of night enveloped it, to witness the flash of scores of thousands of guns, as invisible combatants hurled this leaden storm against each other. The volleys were so regular and incessant that they echoed throughout the Wilderness like pealing thunder."

Friday, May 6, dawned brightly with cloudless blue skies in stunning contrast with the green of the luxuriant forest. Lee had been handicapped in the first day of the battle by the absence of James Longstreet's corps which had been stationed some distance from the Wilderness. Now Lee's "Old Warhorse" arrived with his men, and his scouts quickly located an abandoned railroad cut that provided a covered approach to the very flank of Winfield Hancock's corps. Thousands of Rebels emerged from the unexpected direction and even Hancock admitted "rolled us up like a wet blanket." However, just as Longstreet was organizing a devastating assault, the burly Georgian was mistakenly shot by his own men as he emerged from a grove of trees, and while he ultimately survived his wounds, unlike Stonewall Jackson, the steam ran out of the Rebel offensive and Hancock quickly cobbled together a final defense line.

By nightfall, Grant had lost 18,000 men while inflicting only 8,000 casualties on the Rebels, and the normally taciturn gen-

★ ★ ★

One scene I now remember, that I can imperfectly relate. While a detail of us were passing over the field of death and blood, with a dim lantern, looking for our wounded soldiers to carry to the hospital, we came across a group of ladies, looking among the killed and wounded for their relatives, when I heard one of the ladies say, "There they come with their lanterns." I approached the ladies and asked them for whom were they looking. They told me the name, but I have forgotten it. We passed on, and coming to a pile of our slain, we had turned over several of our dead, when one of the ladies screamed out, "O, there he is! Poor fellow! Dead, dead, dead!" She ran to the pile of slain and raised the dead man's head and placed it on her lap and began kissing him and saying, "O, O, they have killed my darling, my darling, my darling! O, mother, mother, what must I do! My poor, poor darling! O, they have killed him, they have killed him!" I could witness the scene no longer. I turned and walked away, and William A. Hughes was crying, and remarked, "O, law me; this war is a terrible thing." We left them and began again hunting for our wounded. All through that long September night we continued to carry off our wounded, and when the morning sun arose over the eastern hills, the order came to march to Missionary Ridge.

—SAMUEL R. WATKINS, 1ST TENNESSEE

★ ★ ★

★ ★ ★

In connection with this sad event, I will record also the death of my classmate and friend in boyhood, General McPherson, which occurred the same day, and the announcement of which caused me sincere sorrow. Although in the same class, I was several years his junior, and, unlike him, was more wedded to boyish sports than to books. Often, when we were cadets, have I left barracks at night to participate in some merry-making, and early the following morning have had recourse to him to help me over the difficult portions of my studies for the day. Since we had graduated in June, 1853, and had each been ordered off on duty in different directions, it had not been our fortune to meet. Neither the lapse of years, nor the difference of sentiment which led us to range ourselves on opposite sides in the late war, had lessened my friendship; indeed the attachment, formed in early youth, was strengthened by my admiration and gratitude for his conduct toward our people in the vicinity of Vicksburg. His considerate and kind treatment of them stood in bright contrast to the course pursued by many Federal officers; and his acts were ever characterized by those gentlemanly qualities which distinguished him as a boy. No soldier fell in the enemy's ranks, whose loss caused me equal regret.

—JOHN B. HOOD, GENERAL, CSA

★ ★ ★

eral was so overcome with grief that according to an aide "he threw himself down on his cot and gave himself to the greatest emotion" in a tear-filled breakdown. However, the next morning, as most Yankees expected the now almost traditional order to retreat after a Virginia bloodbath, their officers pointed the men southward toward Richmond, and thousands of bluecoats erupted in wild cheering as they were infused with a new sense of purpose. In subsequent battles at Spotsylvania, North Anna River, and Cold Harbor, thousands of Federals would be killed or wounded but the mauled army would always begin another southward march afterward, and Lee's Army of Northern Virginia would never again fight in the region for which it was named.

While the Army of the Potomac pushed grimly toward Richmond, a group of powerful armies under William T. Sherman advanced through the heavily forested region of northern Georgia with an ultimate destination of Atlanta. Sherman had far more room to maneuver than Grant, and despite relatively bloody confrontations at Resaca and Kennesaw Mountain, by late July the mercurial redhead was just north of the city and Jefferson Davis was furious that Joseph Johnston seemed incapable of stopping him. On July 20, the Confederate president replaced the cautious Virginian with General John Bell Hood, a fearsome fighter who had an arm crippled at Gettysburg and a leg amputated at Chickamauga. Hood was bold and fearless, but often too aggressive for his own good, and within little more than a week he had suffered stupendously high casualties as Rebel forces were thrown against Yankee divisions that had better field positions and more firepower. By the middle of August nearly half the Confederate Army of Tennessee was dead or wounded and Sherman's army was successively cutting each of Atlanta's rail links to the rest of the south. At this point it was get out or starve for Hood's army and on

Grant finally brought the Army of Northern Virginia to bay at Petersburg, where Lee was besieged through the winter of 1864 into the spring of 1865. This Union soldier crouches in a "bomb-proof" of the sort constructed by both sides.

September 2, "General Sherman with a brilliant cavalcade entered the city and telegraphed to the president, Atlanta is ours and fairly won."

By the time the North was celebrating the fall of Atlanta, Ulysses Grant had crossed the James River and pinned Lee's army in a series of trenches and breastworks in front of the town of Petersburg, the main rail center for the Confederate capital. While Grant kept Lee occupied in extended siege operations, Sherman demolished Atlanta's railroad facilities, and much of the city in the process, turned his back on Hood's shadowing army, and plunged into the heart of Georgia with 60,000 supremely confident men who were beginning a march to Savannah and the sea. While Confederate newspapers frantically published Jefferson Davis's prediction that Sherman's march would rival Napoleon's disastrous retreat from Moscow, and Ulysses Grant sarcastically questioned where the Confederates were going to find the snow that had devastated the French emperor, Sherman's men simply pulverized the industrial and agricultural base of one of the most important regions of the Confederacy and then wreaked even more havoc in a northward drive into South Carolina. By Christmas Day, 1864, Hood's army was staggering southward from a devastating defeat on the outskirts of Nashville, Lee's soldiers were gradually starving in the trenches of Petersburg, and much of Georgia was a smoking ruin.

★ ★ ★

In one of these charges, while the shells were flying, I peeped up to see the approaching Federals. Just in front of me there suddenly appeared something like a black buzzing bee. It was a shell. I knew what it was, and down I ducked behind the breast-work. The shell struck the breast-work, right in front of me, and covered me with dirt all to my protruding legs. I was pulled out, and my head bandaged where a piece of the shell had struck me. It was my duty to report the casualties. I did not report myself. "How is this?" asked Major Rion. I told it was slight, and I did not want my wife to be unnecessarily alarmed. "Wounds, sir, are honorable to a soldier and his command. A wound is any blood letting. Don't let this occur again." I told him I hoped it would not.

—WILLIAM M. THOMAS DESCRIBES HIS EXPERIENCES WITH THE CONFEDERATES AT PETERSBURG IN THE LAST YEAR OF THE WAR

★ ★ ★

On Tuesday, March 28, 1865, four of the most powerful men in the United States shook hands, and took comfortable seats in the smoking lounge of a passenger steamer that was moored near Federal army headquarters outside of Petersburg. Abraham Lincoln, Ulysses S. Grant, William T. Sherman, and naval chief David Dixon Porter swapped lively anecdotes amid a cloud of cigar smoke and finally got down to the business of planning the final offensive of the Civil War. Sherman's army had now marched into North Carolina and was preparing a new assault on the remnants of Hood's old army which was once again under the command of Joe Johnston. Meanwhile, Grant's army had stretched Lee's lines to the breaking point and a powerful combined infantry-cavalry force under diminutive Philip Sheridan was poised to capture the vital Confederate position at the crossroads known as Five Forks. Soon after Porter returned to his fleet and Sherman returned to his own army, the Army of the Potomac surged into motion and Sheridan's

A Confederate soldier lies dead in the trenches of Petersburg as the town fell to the Union in April 1865. Afterward there were no defenders between the Union army and Richmond.

riflemen and troopers slammed into George Pickett's shrunken division at the vital crossroads. A furiously contested battle ensued in which the stubbornly fighting Rebels were gradually overwhelmed and the approaches to Richmond were finally opened to the Federals, who had been waiting since First Bull Run for this moment.

A series of determined rearguard actions held open an escape route long enough for most of the Confederate officials and much of the Army of Northern Virginia to escape the burning, chaotic streets of the Rebel capital. But as Lee's army pushed westward in a desperate hope to link up with Joe Johnston, the reality of the plight of the Confederate troops gradually began to sink in. The Rebel army arrived at each supply point to find that either supplies had never arrived or the Yankees had overrun the railroad depot, and by the evening of Saturday, April 8, as the army approached Appomattox Court House, Lee began to realize that his army was trapped and starving. Admitting that "I would rather die a thousands deaths," the silver-haired Virginian agreed to meet with Grant to discuss surrender terms.

On the chilly but clear morning of Sunday April 9, couriers from the two rival armies carried messages from the respec-

Having fought and marched on empty stomachs for a week, surrendering Confederates at Appomattox are fed by Union soldiers.

The Grand Review in May 1865 as the Army of the Potomac, and a day later Sherman's Army of the Tennessee, marched in triumph through Washington.

tive commanders that set up a meeting in the McLean House in the village of Appomattox Court House. Lee, accompanied by a single aide, entered the parlor of a house that contained over a dozen Union officers, each of whom respectfully saluted their antagonist as he moved toward a small table. Lee, dressed in his best uniform and carrying an impressive sword, made a startling contrast to Grant, who was wearing a mud-splattered uniform decorated only by the three stars on the epaulets on his shoulders. After some friendly conversation about mutual experiences in the Mexican War, the two generals got down to business and the Virginian was immediately gratified that his adversary was proposing extremely generous terms of surrender. The entire Confederate army would be permitted to return to their homes on parole, all officers could keep their horses, pistols, and swords while enlisted cavalrymen and gunners could also keep their mounts. As a relieved and gratified Lee left the McLean House to address his own army, Grant ordered a halt to Federal cheering and artillery salutes as it would embarrass men "who are once again our fellow countrymen."

At daybreak in the cold, wet morning of April 12, 1865, units of the Federal Army of the Potomac lined up to accept the formal Confederate surrender. Union General Joshua Chamberlain, one of the heroes of Gettysburg, was given the honor of accepting the Rebel capitulation. Chamberlain placed his division in three lines to receive the surrender, and the veteran bluecoats watched the approach of General John Gordon of Georgia at the head of Stonewall Jackson's old corps. Gordon's ragged Confederates had no idea what treatment they would receive from their former antagonists at this moment of possible enormous humiliation. However, as Gordon rode through the ranks of bluecoats on either side with

Honor was answered by honor.

— A DESCRIPTION OF THE SURRENDER OF SOUTHERN TROOPS AT THE END OF THE CIVIL WAR.

his view straight ahead, he heard Chamberlain give a single command, a bugle rang out, and the Union soldiers shifted their rifles from "order arms" to "carry arms," the salute of honor. Startled, Gordon looked up, and with almost instant realization, turned to the Union general, dipped his sword in salute and ordered his own men to "carry arms" as "honor was answered by honor." As Chamberlain praised his former foes and asked "should not such men be welcomed back into a Union so tested and assured," Confederate generals responded with equal emotion. One general, insisted, pointing to the American flag waving nearby, "Now that is my flag, and I will prove myself as worthy as any of you." Six hundred and twenty thousand young men in blue and gray had died but a Union was restored; the sons, grandsons, and great-grandsons of those proud men would eventually fight together under that American flag in dozens of locations from Cuba to Iraq.

Teddy Roosevelt and his Rough Riders on San Juan Hill. The unit was an odd but highly effective mixture of cowboys and Ivy Leaguers.

CHAPTER V

America Fights Abroad

On the warm, humid evening of February 15, 1898, Clara Barton sat in her hotel room overlooking Havana Harbor and resigned herself to a long night of paperwork despite the distractions of the pre-Lenten carnival that was in progress just below her window. As revelers wearing colorful masks and costumes danced through the streets, the "Angel of the Battlefield" of the Civil War took a brief look at the imposing superstructure of the floodlit battleship *Maine* as it swayed on its moorings a short distance away. Only a few days earlier, Miss Barton and her staff had been the guests of Captain Charles Sigbee and his officers and the experience had been a memorable one for the founder of the American Red Cross. "Captain Sigbee's launch courteously came for us, his officers received us; his crew, strong, ruddy and bright, went through their drill for our entertainment and the lunch at those polished tables, the glittering china and cut glass, with the social guests around us, will remain ever in my memory."

While the USS *Maine* was officially in Cuba on a "courtesy call" that included numerous invitations for Spanish officials to visit the powerful battleship, the presence of the vessel was also President William McKinley's way of demonstrating to the Spanish government in Madrid the deep American concern at that nation's failure to negotiate a solution to the ongoing war of independence being fought by native-born Cubans to rid the

USS Maine *blows up in Havana Harbor. Although the cause of the explosion has never been fully determined, the incident was enough to bring America and Spain to war.*

"Pearl of the Antilles" of European rule. General Fitzhugh Lee, the colorful Civil War cavalry commander and nephew of Robert E. Lee, was now serving as American consul to Havana, and the former Confederate leader had recommended to McKinley that a powerful warship should be sent off Cuba "as an object lesson and to counteract Spanish opinion of our Navy," and to remind the Spanish that the United States was a potent new power on the horizon.

At 9:40 on this balmy tropical evening, as Miss Barton and her assistant pored over the next batch of paperwork to be completed, the table began shaking under them and "the great glass door opening on to the veranda facing the sea blew open, everything in the room was in motion or out of place." Seconds later "there was a deafening roar such as a burst of thunder as perhaps one never heard before and out over the bay the air was filled with a blaze of lights." The "blaze of light" that Clara Barton observed was actually the explosion of the *Maine.* Lieutenant John Hood, officer

> *There was a deafening roar such as a burst of thunder as perhaps one never heard before and out over the bay the air was filled with a blaze of lights.*
>
> — CLARA BARTON ON OBSERVING THE EXPLOSION OF THE *MAINE*.

of the watch, was sitting on the port side of the ship with his feet up on the rail when a terrific explosion tore through the vessel. "I instantly turned my head and there was a second explosion; I saw the whole starboard side of the deck and everything above it as far as the aft end of the superstructure spring up into the air with all kinds of objects in it."

Captain Sigbee quickly organized an evacuation of the ship by the small number of men who were fortunate enough to be in the upper decks away from the explosion, but while perhaps 100 sailors were able to swim clear of the wreck, 260 other seamen were dead or missing and soon telegraph lines from Havana to the United States were filled with graphic accounts of a disaster that most Americans were convinced was a deliberate act of war by Spain.

President McKinley had served in the Civil War and had participated in some of that conflicts bloodiest battles, therefore he had no desire to engulf a now peaceful and prosperous republic in a new conflict. But as attempts to secure Spanish acquiescence to some form of independence for Cuba failed, Congress moved closer to war, and finally, on April 19, 1898, a war resolution was passed while representatives, many of whom had served in the Civil War, lustily sang patriotic tunes that included not only the "Battle Hymn of the Republic" but "Dixie" as well. This new war against a common European enemy in many respects marked the reconciliation of Union and Confederacy.

The spread of war fever, fanned by the sensationalist newspaper articles of the time, created a situation where there were more volunteers than openings in the army of 125,000 men that President McKinley proposed to organize. Even as new regiments were being organized to sail to Cuba, Commodore George Dewey, a protege of

———— ★ ★ ★ ————

And the rain! There was no wind, and all the water had to do was to come right straight down and find a place to fall on. In Ohio when we have that kind of a rain lasting ten or fifteen minutes, we call it a cloudburst. That rain of July 11 was a cloudburst lasting six or eight hours and tapering off into a respectable shower toward morning. It was phenomenal even for that aqueous latitude. Everybody and everything was in water, or under water, or surrounded by water. The situation, however, was not altogether destitute of humor. Most of the officers, before leaving the States, had been beguiled by the soft blandishments of a young gentleman from Michigan into supplying themselves with an ingenious device for a sleeping place when they reached the hot and humid isle. It was entitled a "hammock." . . . It received its initiation that night. When the rains began to descend the young gentlemen who had hammocks climbed into them, rolled themselves in their blankets, stretched their ponchos over them, embraced themselves for having displayed such foresight, the wet ropes began to tighten up, the pegs slipped out of the mushy ground, and commiserated the rest of us because we were forced to sleep on the ground. Along about ten or eleven o'clock the soil had become thoroughly saturated, and the hammocks began to tumble. From that on at short intervals could be heard the swish of the guys as they pulled the pegs out of the ground, and splash and the scream as some fellow went down into the water, and then the great shout of laughter all over the camp, and the cries of "How's your hammock?"

— CURTIS V. HARD OF THE 8TH OHIO VOLUNTEERS
IN CUBA, 1898

———— ★ ★ ★ ————

The 71st New York Volunteers embark for Cuba. This unit contained a number of capable writers and artists and its service is especially well-documented.

Civil War hero David Farragut, ran past the coastal defenses of Spanish-held Manila Harbor in the Philippines and, with a handful of cruisers, annihilated the large Spanish squadron defending the islands at a cost of exactly one American casualty.

Meanwhile, McKinley and his senior military commanders began developing a plan to force the surrender of the Spanish garrison in Cuba. Most of the meetings were essentially Civil War reunions. Army commander General Nelson Miles had served as one of the youngest generals in that war and had been responsible for guarding Confederate president Jefferson Davis after his capture. Major General William Shafter had held a number of significant commands during the Civil War; while the senior cavalry commander, Major General Joseph Wheeler, had been one of the most daring Confederate cavalry leaders of the war and had been lured away from his position as chairman of the House Ways and Means Committee to add a significant southern presence to this new conflict. The president and his senior commanders agreed that their ultimate objective was the capture of Havana,

George Dewey, who had served in the Civil War as a junior officer, showed great initiative in defeating Spanish naval forces in the Philippines as soon as he received word of the outbreak of war.

but since the upcoming yellow fever season would be a significant threat to the army until September, a relatively small expeditionary force of 17,000 men would embark for Cuba as soon as possible, seize a small port, supply the native rebels, and provide a springboard for a much larger invasion in the fall. While most of the initial expeditionary force would be composed of regular army regiments, a few volunteer units would be permitted to accompany

them. One of these regiments was the 1st United States Volunteer Cavalry Regiment, commanded by colorful Indian fighter Leonard Wood. Wood's second in command was Colonel Theodore Roosevelt, who had resigned his post as assistant secretary of the navy in order to obtain a field assignment with an active unit.

Thus in mid-June, Shafter, Wheeler, Roosevelt, and a variety of regular and volunteer regiments set sail from Tampa Bay headed for the town of Daiquiri, southeast of Santiago. The Americans were soon informed that the Spanish garrison in Cuba was about to receive significant support in the form of Admiral Pascal Cervera's squadron of armored cruisers; the initial plan for merely developing a bridgehead was quickly discarded in favor of a major offensive against Santiago in order to provide a base for an American fleet. However, American operations were complicated almost imme-

American infantrymen land in Cuba after the voyage from Florida. The blanket rolls could be discarded for active operations, but the heavy blue wool shirts were ill-suited for tropical service against modern weapons.

William R. Shafter served in the Civil War and led the 24th Colored Infantry on the frontier for many years. As commander of U.S. forces in Cuba he was a more effective officer than his portly appearance might suggest, but he remains a controversial figure.

diately by the physical ailments of the commanding general. William Shafter was certainly not the sort of general who could be easily missed as he weighed almost 350 pounds and was described by one officer as "like three men rolled in one." Shafter had difficulty moving around in the cool of a New England spring, so when he first encountered the blazing tropical climate of Cuba, he quickly retired to his cabin on the invasion fleet's flagship and remained vaguely "indisposed." General Wheeler assumed field command of the army and "Fighting Joe" quickly displayed the impetuous nature that had earned him his nickname in the Civil War.

It was most confusing country and I had an awful time getting into the fight.

— THEODORE ROOSEVELT ON FIGHTING HIS FIRST SKIRMISH IN CUBA.

The ex-Confederate general started pushing advance units up the road from Daiquiri to Santiago and almost immediately collided with more than 2,000 Spaniards supported by heavy Krupp cannons. On the morning of June 24, Wheeler personally led a force of 1,000 dismounted cavalrymen along a jungle encrusted road to Santiago called Camino Real or Royal Highway, while Colonels Wood and Roosevelt led their "Rough Riders" along the ridge that dominated the valley road below. The Rough Riders were the only volunteer regiment fortunate enough to be armed with late-model Krag bolt-action rifles instead of the single-shot, Civil-War-era Springfields that other amateur units carried, but even their weapons were no match for the brand-new Mauser smokeless rifles carried by the Spaniards. Thus when the volunteers collided with a large force of enemy defenders, the Americans' black smoke quickly gave away their positions in the lush tropical wilderness while the Spanish troops remained almost invisible. Roosevelt insisted later that "the enemy

Joseph Wheeler commanded the Cavalry Division, whose men served dismounted during the campaign in Cuba. A former Confederate, Wheeler is said to have referred to the Spanish as "Yankees" in the heat of battle.

bullets made a rustling sound like ripping silk as everyone went down in a lump." The dismounted troopers spread into a skirmish formation but there was very little coordination among the units and Roosevelt admitted, "It was most confusing country and I had an awful time getting into the fight." However, the beleaguered volunteers, taking heavy casualties all the way, finally advanced to a crossroads that linked up with the valley road and when the two American forces united, Wheeler was able to force the defenders to pull back toward Santiago as the old Confederate screamed in delight, "We've got the damn Yankees on the run!" In a one-hour battle, 70 Americans had been killed or wounded compared to Spanish losses only half as large. However, the Americans had gained a psychological victory by forcing the enemy to withdraw.

American troops raise their Krag-Jorgensen rifles near San Juan Hill. The newly issued bolt-action Krag was a modern weapon, but was inferior to the Mausers wielded by Spain's unenthusiastic troops.

Wheeler's aggressiveness had provided an emotional lift for the American troops but the newly captured Royal Highway was too narrow to allow an adequate flow of supplies to be transported from the Daiquiri beaches to the advancing army. Shafter, who had now more or less reassumed command, realized that the army had only two choices—fall back to the coast and wait for fall or capture Santiago and its abundant supplies. The corpulent general chose the latter course and ordered an immediate advance as he admitted, "There would be no attempt at strategy and no attempt at turning their flanks. It was simply to be going straight for them." The American soldiers under Shafter's command would soon pay dearly for this unimaginative solution.

The commander of the Spanish garrison at Santiago, General Arsenio Linares, had been forced to scatter his 10,000 defenders along a number of possible American approach avenues, but his most heavily fortified position was on the most likely route of advance, San Juan Heights. Linares had deployed his

Before the moon rose again, every sixth man who had slept in the mist that night was either killed or wounded.

— RICHARD HARDING DAVIS ON THE MOVE TOWARD SAN JUAN HEIGHTS.

★ ★

William O'Neil

The first man to volunteer for the war with Spain, William O'Neil was appointed a captain in the Rough Riders and given command of Company A. He developed a considerable reputation for courage and selflessness, beginning on the first day of American landings in Cuba, when he jumped into the choppy sea to try to rescue two soldiers who had fallen in. His final day, too, was marked by a show of bravery that in the end may have led to his death.

When war broke out with Spain, O'Neil volunteered right away. On the very first day of the American landings in Cuba, June 22, 1898, the sea off Daiquiri was choppy, with strong swells running onshore, and the transports had to stand well off the coast. As the longboats came bobbing and rolling alongside the transports the troops jumped in, carrying their equipment. To land, the men had to repeat the process in reverse, jumping up out of the boats as they rose and fell in the sea, onto the pier, which was well above sea level. It was dangerous business.

O'Neil landed safely along with the rest of the Rough Riders and then lent a hand supervising the landing of other troops. Suddenly two men, Corporal Edward Cobb and Private John English, "Buffalo Soldiers" of the famed 10th Cavalry, missed their footing. As they fell into the sea, O'Neill jumped from the pier after them, followed by several others. It was to no avail. Weighted down by their rifles and accouterments, the two sank quickly, drowning before they could be pulled to safety.

At Las Guasimas, O'Neil was in the forefront of the fighting when the Rough Riders, forming one of two columns advancing against the enemy, got into a hot little battle with Spanish outposts. Over the next few days, as the American forces closed in on the Spanish defenses about Santiago, O'Neil was always at the front in several skirmishes that developed between Spanish rear guards and American scouts.

Early on July 1, 1898, the Rough Riders and the other dismounted cavalry regiments in the army, got into position for the assault on the heights of San Juan, the key to the defenses of the city of Santiago. At about 10 A.M., Company A, on the regiment's exposed right flank, began taking heavy fire.

To steady the men, the popular O'Neil decided to light a cigarette and walk around in a hail of bullets. For nearly an hour, as his men urged him to take shelter, he stood exposed to enemy fire. Then, as he was making light of the danger, he was suddenly struck in the mouth by a Spanish bullet, which killed him instantly. Greatly mourned by his comrades, O'Neil, who left a wife and a child, was eventually buried at Arlington National Cemetery.

★ ★

best infantry and heaviest artillery pieces along this high ground, and this was precisely the approach line that his American counterpart had chosen. Thus from their heavily fortified breastworks on San Juan Hill and Kettle Hill, elements of six regiments of Spanish troops aimed their cannons and rifles at a nearby clearing that would be the exact approach route of the Americans. Richard Harding Davis, a famous writer and war correspondent, chronicled the American advance on the night of June 30 as they moved toward San Juan Heights: "Twelve thousand men, with their eyes fixed on a balloon, moved slowly through the mud as they stumbled and slipped down the trail. The lines passed until the moon rose. They seemed endless, interminable, there were cavalry mounted and dismounted, artillery with cracking ships and cursing drivers, Rough Riders in brown, and regulars, both black and white, in blue. Three miles away, across the basin of the mist, we could see the street lamps of Santiago shining over the San Juan Hills. Above us, the tropical moon hung white and clear in the dark purple sky, pierced with millions of white stars. Before the moon rose again, every sixth man who had slept in the mist that night was either killed or wounded."

Shafter's less-than-imaginative battle plan was weakened even further by his obsession with the small village of El Caney that featured a fort which seemed capable of threatening the flank of the American attack. The enormous general sent almost 7,000 men, nearly half his total force, to reduce a fort held by only 500 Spaniards, with the expectation of a quick victory that would allow the assault force to link up with the rest of the army in order to attack San Juan by 10 A.M. on July 1.

Though the American commander had dispatched plenty of men to assault El Caney, they were supported by a tiny artillery

---

————★ ★ ★————

During that period of sickness and death and burials the good qualities of the men who had hearts under their blouses came out strong. Great big, husky, bearded, rough-looking men ministered to their sick comrades as tenderly and devotedly as a mother with her helpless child, and without tears, but with as much gentleness, stood by or aided in the burial. A thousand times daily as this devotion was displayed came up the thought, 'Greater love than this hath no man.' Chaplain Campbell arrived in camp on the morning of August 3 and thereafter took charge, of course, of all matters of this kind. Although personally known to only a few of the officers and men he received a hearty greeting. After a hurried introduction and a brief explanation of the situation, he pulled on his rubber boots and rubber coat and started out in the rain and mud to cheer the sick and get acquainted with the well. Inside of two or three hours he had said something to every man, and from that time until the end of his service he was busy caring for the sick, comforting the dying, and burying the dead.

— Curtis V. Hard, 8th Ohio, stationed in Cuba, 1898

————★ ★ ★————

———————★ ★ ★———————

We marched to Yauco and on to Ponce, finding those towns surrendered. We had camped in a wooded ravine two nights. After the first two or three hours of mosquito bites, sleeping in our underwear and barefoot, we put on our pants, wool shirts, and socks, for all of the moist heat. They were mosquitoes of the type you say "One could kill a dog, two could kill a man." They were large, ravenous, pitiless. "They came with bugles sounding mess call," said one man with a swollen face. At mess, at roll call, whatever was doing, you kept slapping your hands and face, I had one eye closed by the swellings around it. There were fellows had both eyes closed. On the second night I followed others in wrapping my rubber poncho around my head. After an hour I would wake with an aching head from foul air breathed over too many times. I would throw the poncho off, beat away the mosquitoes, wrap the poncho around my head again, then sleep till awaking with a headache—and repeat.

— Carl Sandburg, serving with the 6th Illinois in the Puerto Rico Campaign

———————★ ★ ★———————

force of only four light guns that inflicted little damage on the Spanish fortifications. On the other hand, the defenders were able to blaze away with much more modern cannons and rifles and dozens of Americans fell dead or wounded. As one officer noted, "It soon became evident the Spanish were prepared to make a stubborn resistance . . . they took up position in a blockhouse where it was almost impossible to reach them effectively with rifle fire." One of the volunteer regiments, the 2nd Massachusetts, made a desperate assault on the fort, but the single-shot, black-powder Springfields were no match for the defenders' firepower. Finally, a force of men from General Ludlow's brigade of regulars located a sunken road so familiar to men who had fought in the Civil War. Using this position as a fire base, the bluecoats entered into a vicious duel with the defenders of the block-house. While American and Spanish riflemen engaged in this firefight, the men of the 25th Infantry Regiment, one of the African-American units in Shafter's force, swept forward. Lieutenant James Moss, an officer in this unit, described the advance: "The men advance through a grass field and, crossing a lane, enter a pineapple patch. It is raining lead! The line recoils like a mighty serpent, and then, in confusion advances again! Men are dropping everywhere! The bullets are cutting the pineapples under our very feet—the slaughter is awful." Finally, as a huge, yellow balloon manned by army Signal Corps personnel floated far above the assault force, the Spanish defenders fired the last of their dwindling ammunition and withdrew through the lush fields, leaving their commander, General Vara del Rey, and dozens of their comrades dead or dying in the grass. The Spaniards had lost 350 of their 500 men killed, wounded, or captured, but the American column had lost 81 killed and 360 wounded to capture a single, relatively unimportant village.

The United States in the war with Spain continued its tradition of raising a largely volunteer army on short notice in wartime. Regular units, such as the 16th Infantry shown here near San Juan Hill, provided valuable stiffening for the inexperienced volunteers.

Meanwhile, the rest of Shafter's army had been deployed at the base of San Juan Heights and the Americans spent the morning taking a terrible pounding from Spanish cannons and sharpshooters. Brigadier General Hamilton Hawkins, commander of the 6th and 16th Infantry Regiments, had been on the Union line at Cemetery Ridge at Gettysburg, and the general insisted that his men received fire comparable to that endured by the Confederates at Pickett's Charge. The 6th Regiment lost one-fourth of its men in less than 10 minutes and yet the unit had not advanced an inch. Finally, Lieutenant John Parker arrived with a battery of Gatling guns that could fire 3,600 rounds a minute, and as the primitive machine guns peppered the Spanish lines, Lieutenant John Ord, son of a famous Union general, begged Hawkins for permission to lead a charge, insisting, "We can't stay here, can we?" The general finally relented by merely saying, "God bless you and good luck!" and Ord ran forward with a pistol in one hand and a saber in the other yelling, "Come on! We can't stop here!" Richard Harding Davis, observing the bluecoat charge, insisted, "It seemed as if someone had made an awful and terrible mistake. The thing that impressed me the most was that they were so few."

While the American infantry pushed through a withering fire toward the crest of San Juan Hill, a supporting force of dis-

Come on! We can't stop here!

— Lieutenant John Ord leading a charge at San Juan Heights

★ ★

Carl Sandburg

An aspiring journalist from Illinois, Carl Sandburg enlisted in the 6th Illinois, which was being raised for the war with Spain. Within days the regiment was assigned to the newly formed II Corps at Camp Alger, near Dun Loring, Virginia, and began an arduous round of training, involving drills, marches, marksmanship, and other exercises, including sham battles.

Assigned to the invasion of Puerto Rico, Private Sandburg and men of the 6th Illinois boarded their ship at Hampton Roads on July 7, 1898. They spent 18 days aboard the hot, crowded, inadequately equipped transports. Four days were taken up steaming to Guantanamo Bay, Cuba, then 10 days swinging at anchor offshore waiting for the navy to organize an escort, for despite the hardships, keeping the men aboard ship was safer than landing them in fever-ridden Cuba. They were at sea another four days, until they landed at Guanica, Puerto Rico, on July 25.

The 6th Illinois formed part of a column that advanced northward from Ponce, on the south coast, turning a rough mountain track into a practical road as it moved. By the time an armistice brought the war to an end on August 13, the column, though burdened with heavy construction equipment, had made surprising progress. They advanced an average of one mile a day while building a road across the difficult mountainous spine of Puerto Rico in heavy rains.

Of his experience as a road-building soldier, Sandburg observed that he lost eight pounds in those few days, and he later wrote "the shovel is brother to the gun" in reference to the importance of fatigue duties in war.

★ ★

mounted cavalry began an equally bloody climb toward the top of nearby Kettle Hill. Colonel Leonard Wood had been promoted to command a brigade and now Theodore Roosevelt was leading his Rough Riders in a momentous battle. The volunteers began to advance along with the regulars of the 1st, 3rd, 9th, and 10th Cavalry Regiments, all of whom were focused on an enormous iron kettle at the top of the hill, a device used for sugar refining.

At this point in the charge, Roosevelt was the only man on horseback, and the future president wove back and forth in the lines urging forward both volunteers and regulars. Ironically, virtually all of the senior officers of the regular regiments, who were advancing on foot, were killed or wounded at the beginning of the advance, leaving the former assistant navy secretary to direct an increasingly intermingled group of attackers. When the colorbearer of the 3rd Regiment went down, his counterpart in the 10th Regiment grabbed the colors and advanced clutching both banners. Roosevelt enthusiastically insisted, "We were all in the spirit of the thing and greatly excited by the charge, the men cheering and running forward between shots. I galloped toward the hill passing shouting, cheering and firing men."

When the survivors of the charge up Kettle Hill reached the summit, Roosevelt quickly ordered his men to begin covering fire for the infantry moving up San Juan Hill. Suddenly the seemingly broken fragments of the blue-coated infantry gathered together for a final push, and with a sudden burst of speed, overran the Spanish trenches. Lieutenant Ord leaped over one trench and just as he jumped, a wounded defender fired a shot that instantly killed the young American officer. As American flags began waving over the two crucial hills, Lieutenant John J. Pershing of the 10th Cavalry noticed the new unity that had come from the charge as "white regiments, black regiments, Regulars and Rough Riders, representing the young manhood of the North

Theodore Roosevelt emerged from the Spanish-American War a national hero. Over the course of the war he served both as assistant secretary of the navy and commander of the 1st Volunteer Cavalry (Rough Riders).

> *We were all in the spirit of the thing and greatly excited by the charge, the men cheering and running forward between shots.*
>
> — THEODORE ROOSEVELT ON THE CHARGE UP KETTLE HILL.

The United States Army did not have an organized nursing corps until 1901, but Clara Barton and others organized medical volunteers during the war with Spain. Far more American soldiers died from disease than enemy action during the war.

and the South, fought shoulder to shoulder, unmindful of race or color, unmindful of whether commanded by an ex-Confederate or not, and mindful only of their common duty as Americans."

The relatively small force of Americans that had charged up San Juan Heights had suffered severely, as 124 men were killed and 817 wounded compared to a much smaller loss among the defenders of 58 killed and 170 wounded. However, Shafter's men had the Spanish blockaded in Santiago, and since neither of the opposing army commanders greatly desired a bloody repeat of the battle for San Juan, the contest between the American and Spanish fleets became the focal point of the campaign.

Two days after the American ground assault, Admiral Cervera decided that Santiago was now untenable for the Spanish fleet and determined to risk a daring sortie in broad daylight to sprint past the American blockades and make a dash toward Havana. The commander of the American squadron, Admiral William Sampson, had little idea that the Spanish would spring into action on this peaceful, hot Sunday morning and he had divided the fleet by sending the *Massachusetts* and the *Suwanee* to Guantanamo to refuel, while sailing aboard the *New York* to a meeting with General Shafter at Daiquiri. The remaining three battleships, two cruisers, and two armed yachts steamed outside Santiago Harbor with only a few of their boilers in operation. The senior American officer remaining with the squadron, Commodore Winfield Scott Schley, was not one of Sampson's favorite officers and the two men were barely on speaking terms on that languid July morning.

Schley was at first totally surprised by Cervera's daring gambit, and the courage and spirit of the Spanish crews offered a possible counterpart to the Americans' superior firepower. The Spanish admiral ordered his whole fleet of four major ships to swing to the east together, where only the cruiser *Brooklyn* blocked their passage. However, Schley had made his headquarters on the *Brooklyn* and when the captain of the ship exclaimed, "Commodore, they're coming right at us!" the American commander responded calmly, "Well, go right for *them!*" The single American ship was heavily outgunned, but the vessel slowed down the charging Spaniards long enough for the Yankee battleships to join the fray. Schley noted that "all four of the Spanish ships and the fort were firing at the same time; from that moment, the next ten or fifteen moments were the most furious part of the entire combat . . . there were jets of water ahead and astern, the roar of projectiles was one of the things that can be heard once in a lifetime."

The Spanish ships had a daring commander and a gallant crew, but they were also carrying large amounts of defective ammunition, were not heavily armored, and were loaded with wood decks and ornaments that would turn into lethal splinters in an explosion. The powerful American ships, the *Texas, Iowa, Oregon*, and *Indiana*, began unleashing huge broadsides that initially focused on Cervera's flagship the *Maria Theresa* and turned it into a burning hulk. As the ship erupted in a torrent of fire and American sailors began to cheer, the captain of the *Texas* called out, "Don't cheer boys!

★ ★ ★

As for history, Theodore Roosevelt summed it up in a speech at the Stockyards Pavilion in Chicago which I covered for a newspaper. He happened to mention the Spanish-American War and added with a chuckle and a flash of his teeth, "It wasn't much of a war but it was all the war there was." There was history with a light extravagant touch in John Hay, Ambassador at London, writing to Theodore Roosevelt: "It has been a splendid little war; begun with the highest motives, carried on with magnificent intelligence and spirit, favored by that fortune which loves the brave."

—CARL SANDBURG

★ ★ ★

Those poor devils are dying." Another officer noted, "It was a magnificent, sad sight to see those beautiful ships in their death agonies." Within less than an hour the entire Spanish squadron was annihilated with a loss of 357 men. Now the former enemies, the Americans, who had lost only one man killed and one wounded turned into rescuers as they dispatched every rescue craft available and fished almost 2,000 Spanish sailors from the water.

Don't cheer boys! Those poor devils are dying.

— CAPTAIN OF THE USS *TEXAS* AS THE SPANISH SHIP *MARIA THERESA* SANK.

The official armistice ending the Spanish-American war would not be signed for another six weeks, but the land battle of July 1 and the sea battle of July 3 essentially ended the conflict with a stupendous American victory. A war that was shorter than the 1898 baseball season had pulled the United States from a traditional isolationism that had dominated affairs since the time of George Washington. However, America's new role in the world would have a price, and that price would begin to be apparent less than two decades after this conflict that many Americans called "The Splendid Little War."

★ ★ ★

Just as the sinking of the *Maine* propelled the United States into war with one European nation, the destruction of another ship 17 years later lit the fuse for a far larger confrontation. On Friday afternoon, May 7, 1915, a number of American passengers were getting their first view of the Irish coast from the deck of the magnificent eight-year-old Cunard liner *Lusitania*. These Americans were approaching a continent that had been engaged for almost a year in a monumental conflict that was already being called the "Great War," and the "World War." Britain, France, Russia, and their smaller allies were embroiled in a life or death struggle with the forces of the German and Austro-Hungarian empires. Germany had recently introduced a new weapon called the "U-boat" or submarine which was being used to sink ships approaching Britain or France with desperately needed war materials. Newspaper advertisements taken out by the German embassy in the United States warned that British passenger liners such as the *Lusitania* could be used to carry munitions and other war supplies and thus would be considered a legitimate target for submarine attack. Americans were warned to avoid taking passage on vessels of the Allied powers. However, a large number of potential passengers believed that a huge oceanliner was too large and too fast to be sunk by the relatively primitive U-boats and they largely ignored this warning.

At just past 2:00 on this clear, sunny May afternoon, *Lusitania* passengers such as American millionaire Alfred Vanderbilt strolled around the deck as they emerged from their lunch and pointed out the bulk of Old Head of Kinsale in the distance. Suddenly, the whole ship shook violently from a torpedo fired by the German submarine *U-20* which very well may have mistaken the *Lusitania* for her twin the *Mauretania* which was being employed as a British troop ship. A Toronto newspaperman on deck noted, "I was chatting with a friend when suddenly we saw the track of a torpedo followed almost instantly by an explosion. Portions of splintered hull were sent into the air and the ship immediately began to list." Passengers pushed toward the stern and jumped 50 feet into the water as the ship began to fall on her side so quickly that most of the lifeboats could not be properly loaded. Eighteen minutes after the torpedo hit, the *Lusitania* foundered, taking with her almost 1,200 of the 1,900 people aboard, including dozens of children and 128 Americans.

News of the destruction of the *Lusitania* turned millions of Americans, who had been more or less neutral in

———— ★ ★ ★ ————

I ordered the men to travel three on each side of me and to do as I did as closely as possible. I cleared the trench in the rear by a good margin and ran smack into a mortar emplacement. This tallied exactly with my map and we made a turn here directly to the right and within 200 yards came to new dirt which turned out to be the connecting trench we were looking for. While we had been getting to this point, enemy flares from the front line in back of us kept going up at regular intervals. We laid on this bank for about ten or fifteen minutes but no Boche came along. I finally got the men down into the trench and told them to follow at five pace intervals, to stop when the man in front stopped and to wait for further orders to be passed along. I moved at the head of the group and in a few minutes came to a lookout post at the edge of a trench all nicely fixed up but 'nobody home.' I proceeded on around the next traverse and found another lookout post but nobody was in this one either. I figured that around one more traverse we would surely run into an occupied Boche outpost. We could hear them setting flares and talking. Suddenly I heard footsteps. It sounded like a relief of from three to five men. I grouped three men on the off-side of each turn in the trench and took my position between them, ordered the men not to fire or make a move until I did and to let the relief get to me and then close in.

The sounds of the relief party grew closer. Suddenly they were on us—Sergeant Duncan could not contain himself longer and slugged the first Boche that reached him. This was poor business but we had to make the best of the situation. I jumped on the man and wound one of my spiral puttees around his neck and face. The others in the enemy group beat it. The prisoner was the most scared looking mortal I have ever seen.

— MEMOIRS OF TRENCH WARFARE,
CHESTER D. HEYWOOD, 371ST INFANTRY,
SEPTEMBER 9, 1918

———— ★ ★ ★ ————

the European war, into war hawks who wanted the United States to punish Germany for its barbarism. While the German suspension of unrestricted submarine warfare eased tensions temporarily, Americans gradually drifted toward war. Finally on January 31, 1917, the German ambassador to the United States announced that American ships in the "war zone" around France and Britain would be sunk on sight, and President Woodrow Wilson began making active preparations for war. On the rainy evening of April 2, 1917, the president drove through the drizzle to the capitol, whose dome was floodlit from the ground for the first time. Wilson condemned the German government for "warfare against mankind" and asked Congress to declare war. On April 6, after both houses voted overwhelmingly for hostilities, Woodrow Wilson signed the resolution and headlines throughout the United States proclaimed that the United States had entered the Great War.

The American republic was entering a war that had become a three-year bloodbath with no clear end in sight. The introduction of magazine rifles, machine guns, fast-firing cannons, and poison gas to the battlefield had produced casualty totals that staggered the imagination. Most of the major powers already counted their losses in the millions, the French army was on the brink of mutiny, and Russia was engulfed in revolution against the czar. The British and French governments, now reduced to using young boys and older men to fill the huge gaps in their ranks, increasingly saw the American forces as their last, best hope for victory. The focal point for that hope soon became the newly appointed commander of the American Expeditionary Force, John J. Pershing. The 57-year-old veteran of the Spanish-American War was still recovering from the tragic death of his wife and three daughters in a recent fire in the family home in San Francisco, and the taciturn general, named "Black Jack" for his command of African-American regiments, jumped at the opportunity to ease his bereavement through massive responsibility.

On May 30, 1917, Pershing and a small group of aides boarded the passenger liner *Baltic* and sailed from New York for Liverpool. The general was met by King George's private railway carriage and transported to Buckingham Palace for lunch with the king and Prime Minister Lloyd George. Two weeks later, Pershing arrived in Paris and was stunned at the outpouring of emotion at his presence. One of his aides insisted, "Though I live a thousand years, I shall never forget that crowded hour. One may easily believe that not quite the same emotions have swayed a Paris throng since the first years of the 19th century." However, while cries of "Lafayette, we are here" echoed through the streets, in reality, it would be more than a year before Americans could enter combat in numbers large enough to make a significant impact on the outcome of the war.

Pershing's basic plan was to utilize the rest of 1917 and all of 1918 in the development of a powerful American army of about 4 million men backed by hundreds of new weapons such as tanks and airplanes. Then, in the

John J. Pershing commanded American forces in France during World War I. In addition to military duties, he waged a successful campaign to keep the U.S. Army intact and not divided up to replace British and French losses.

spring of 1919, this immense, fresh army would be unleashed on the Germans and smash its way to Berlin. However, this plan began to unravel early in 1918 when the surrender of Russia allowed the German high command to redeploy hundreds of thousands of soldiers from the Eastern front to the trenches of France. At 4:40 A.M. on March 21, 1918, 10,000 German guns opened fire along a 40-mile stretch of the British lines and five hours later newly trained German storm troopers swept through the smoldering ruins of the enemy trenches. Suddenly it became apparent that Pershing could no longer enjoy the luxury of waiting for 1919 to employ his army, the crisis moment of the war had clearly arrived.

Throughout the spring and early summer of 1918, Pershing was faced with the dilemma of attempting to mass a powerful army along the American sector of responsibility on the right flank of the Allied lines while simultaneously using fire brigade tactics to rush available units to plug gaps in the punctured French and British lines. The first large-scale action occurred in the small village of Cantigny on May 28, 1918. At 6:45 A.M.

Troops of the 137th Infantry Regiment fire the Chauchat light machine gun. This unwieldly and unreliable French machine gun was widely criticised, but was the only support weapon available to the Americans prior to the arrival of the Browning Automatic Rifle (BAR) late in the war.

the men of the 28th Infantry Regiment, commanded by Colonel Hansen Ely, a former West Point football star, moved out in perfect alignment to capture a German-held ridge outside the town. Three waves of khaki-uniformed doughboys swarmed into the village and engaged in a furious house-to-house fight with the gray-green clad defenders; then the Yanks swept up the ridge in a formation reminiscent of the Civil War as German defenders on the crest mowed down the front ranks with machine-gun fire. The Americans pushed the enemy troops from the ridge by early afternoon, but as the sun went down waves of storm troopers swept forward in a counterattack that ended in a massive confrontation with rifle butts, trench knives, and bayonets. Well-placed American artillery took a fearsome toll of Germans as they approached the battlefield, but Ely's men were barely able to hold the ridge in a brutal all night battle for which the Americans were not fully prepared. Finally, at dawn, the attackers withdrew to the main German line after suffering an enormous loss of 800 dead, 500 wounded, and 250 captured. At a cost of 199 men killed and 667 men wounded, the Americans had successfully engaged a major German unit and scored a significant victory. However, this small triumph did little to slow down the German offensive which was now lurching dangerously close to a major psychological prize—the city of Paris.

The author of the massive German offensive, General Eric Ludendorff, had originally intended a drive on the French capital as a diversionary movement to pry Allied attention away from his real target, the British army in Flanders. The German commander intended to first drive Sir Douglas Haig's British Expeditionary Force into the sea, then swing west and annihilate the French army with a flank attack. This would leave the largely untested American Expeditionary Force facing the bulk of the German army virtually alone with no allies to either defend or come to their aid. However, Ludendorff gradually became more enamored with turning his diversionary drive on Paris into the real thing, and the newly appointed supreme commander of Allied forces, Marshal Ferdinand Foch, pleaded with Pershing to rush all available American troops to block the enemy drive on the City of Light.

The American commander immediately responded with two of his best units, the regulars of the 3rd Division and the mixed army and Marine force of the 2nd Division. These troops passed through thousands of defeated French troops and haggard civilians fleeing from the advancing German army as they approached the Marne River, about 50 miles from Paris. The Americans dug in around the town of Chateau-Thierry, a small riverside community, and waited for the advancing Germans to strike. The commander of the 2nd Division, short, dapper Major General Omar Bundy, was one of Pershing's worst command appointments and the soldiers and Marines would soon pay dearly for his incompetence.

———— ★ ★ ★ ————

As I have told you before, aviation de chasse resembles in many respects other kinds of hunting; for instance, the pursuit of the festive duck. I have noticed that successful Hun hunters often owe their success to the same qualities which go to make a successful duck hunter, that is, patience and knowing where the birds use, so to speak. I know that many of the best chances I have had I have gotten at the same time of day, the same altitude and approximately the same locality; chances at machines which I had noticed tried to do a certain kind of work, such as taking pictures when the light was most favorable. I went and laid for them, and wish I could have the same chances over again, for I think I could bring down some of them which in my first attempt I hit, but let get away from me. Reminds me again of my beginnings of shooting on the river, and how well I remember the fine shots I used to make a bungle of. When I get to our new sector I shall try to find out something of the habits of these birds and go up and lay for them when the weather is favorable. . . .
Father in his letter wonders if it is very cold high in the air at this time of year. It is bitter, and you notice the difference between now and summer time, although it is not nearly so pronounced as on the ground. Any water jumping out of your radiator, for instance, freezes at once, although it will also do this in summer very high up. I have never suffered from cold, however, as my rig is very good and entirely covers my face. The Spad, which I have always flown on the front, is probably as warm as any machine, particularly the new model, which is so arranged as to give you the benefit of much of the heat from the motor.

— MAJOR CHARLES J. BIDDLE, ON
AIR WARFARE, DECEMBER 24, 1917

———— ★ ★ ★ ————

American cemetery at Belleau Wood, where both U.S. Army and Marine units stemmed the German advance.

On the afternoon of June 1, 1918, the German storm troopers smashed into companies of Marines defending the town. As one Marine insisted, "Our fire was too accurate and heavy for them, they fell by the score covering the poppies and wheat growing in the field." An American machine gunner exclaimed, "I always thought it was a fearful thing to take a human life, but I felt a savage thrill of joy and I could hardly wait for the Germans to get close enough." However, Bundy had failed to deploy any troops on the most dominant hill in the area and the tenacious Germans quickly dragged every available artillery piece to the top of the ridge and pummeled the Marines with high explosives. When a mixed force of soldiers and Marines were ordered to push their tormentors from the hill, the result was near annihilation. The Americans had been trained to advance in ranks that were amazingly similar to Civil War formations and German machine gunners swept the fields over and over. One Marine battalion lost 334 men in 10 minutes and although sheer weight of numbers eventually took the ridge, the cost was enormous.

The capture of Hill 142 still left the Germans in command of nearby Belleau Wood, a 1,000-yard-wide and 3,000-yard-long forest preserve honeycombed with rifle pits, machine-gun bunkers, and mortar emplacements. At 5 P.M. on the afternoon of June 6, as a late afternoon sun beat down on the rows of poppies and wheat, the marines rose up and in four successive ranks advanced toward the woods in an environment reminiscent of Virginia 50 years earlier.

I always thought it was a fearful thing to take a human life, but I felt a savage thrill of joy and I could hardly wait for the Germans to get close enough.

— AMERICAN MACHINE GUNNER IN FRANCE, JUNE 1918.

Within minutes, the fields were covered with dead or dying leathernecks while the surviving Marines pushed through heavy tangled undergrowth, ravines filled with creeks, and formations of rocks and boulders that shielded German riflemen. Major Edward Cole of the 6th Machine Gun Battalion insisted that "The troops started out in beautiful deployment in a perfect line, it was one of the most beautiful sights I had ever seen." Colonel Albertus Catlin, commander of the 6th Marine Regiment noted, "The battalion pivoted on its right, went sweeping across the open ground in four waves, as steadily and correctly as though on parade; they walked at a regular pace, because a man is of little use in a hand-to-hand bayonet struggle after a hundred yard dash." By nightfall on this long, summer day, the southern end of Belleau Wood was in American hands, but 1,087 men were dead or wounded and the Germans held the remainder of the position. The capture of Belleau Wood would require an incredible 20 additional days of grueling combat in which 6,000 more Americans were added to the casualty list. The doughboys were making a significant effort in helping to blunt the German drive for Paris, but the unsophisticated American tactics were creating chillingly long casualty lists to be sent home to the United States.

By late summer Ludendorff's gamble to win the war in 1918 was obviously failing and the Allies once more thought in terms of their own offensive in 1919. Pershing now had 1.4 mil-

> *The troops started out in beautiful deployment in a perfect line, it was one of the most beautiful sights I have ever seen.*
>
> — MAJOR EDWARD COLE OF THE 6TH MACHINE GUN BATTALION IN BELLEAU WOOD.

American troops occupy German second-line trenches in the Argonne Forest. Troops arriving in France were issued a British-style steel helmet. These troops also wear British-style puttees in place of American canvas leggings, which were in short supply.

★ ★

Fiorello La Guardia

A congressman from New York at the outbreak of World War I, Fiorella La Guardia joined the army without resigning from Congress, putting aside his devotion to pacifism to secure a commission in the Air Service. La Guardia went on to train American pilots in Italy, surviving three crashes, and led several bombing raids on the Adriatic.

Assigned as second-in-command to a bomber squadron at Foggia, Italy (his father's hometown), La Guardia learned to fly the Italian Caproni heavy bomber, while training new American pilots. Between training and operational accidents, he survived three crashes. He made several bombing raids against Austro-Hungarian naval installations on the Adriatic, and his aircraft received damage twice from enemy fire.

In mid-1918 he was transferred to the Intelligence Service, which made use of his linguistic abilities and political skills for various assignments, including a delicate diplomatic mission to Spain. He became personally acquainted with Italian King Vittorio Emanuele III, whom he called "Manny," and General John J. Pershing, and he made numerous speeches throughout Italy promoting the Allied cause.

The army authorized La Guardia to return to the U.S. so that he could campaign for reelection in 1918. A certified war hero and one-man balanced ticket—aside from his linguistic skills (Italian, Spanish, German, Yiddish), his mother was Jewish while he was an Episcopalian—he was handily returned to Congress and later went on to become mayor of New York. He also served as national director of Civilian Defense during World War II.

Knowing of his immense pride in having served his nation, La Guardia's closest friends referred to him as "Major" for the rest of his life. La Guardia died in 1947.

Congressman (later Mayor) Fiorello La Guardia

★ ★

The "Lost Battalion" of the 77th Division fought on after being surrounded for five days by the Germans in the Argonne Forest. Becoming one of the greatest American legends of World War I, the survivors were still numerous and in good health at this reunion in New York on September 24, 1939.

lion troops in France with thousands of additional men arriving each week, and the American commander was rapidly developing a plan for a limited offensive that would serve as a springboard for the major push the following spring. The American commander's two major objectives for a fall offensive were to clear out a German salient near the town of Saint-Mihiel and then push through the Argonne Forest to threaten the main German east-west supply route along the Western Front. The attack on Saint-Mihiel was of marginal strategic value at this point in the war. Pershing should have concentrated all available units on the Argonne offensive, but the American commander insisted he could perform both missions, and on September 12, 1918, the first major American offensive of the Great War lurched into motion.

Three thousand American cannons pierced the night air as nine divisions of assault troops prepared to smash into the German lines around Saint-Mihiel. A squadron of light tanks under Colonel George Patton screened a line of infantrymen, who rushed up to the German barbed-wire emplacements with wire cutters and Bangalore torpedoes and cut or blew gaps in the enemy line. The advancing troops were brave and energetic, but coordination among assault units was still deficient

Henry Johnson

Henry Johnson, a member of New York's black National Guard regiment, distinguished himself by launching a nearly unbelievable one-man assault on a handful of Germans when they overran an American camp near the Aire River in 1918, despite the fact he had two broken legs.

One April night in 1918, Johnson and Needham Roberts, both privates, were manning an outpost near the Aire River, keeping watch while their corporal and two others napped. Roberts heard a noise, like someone clipping barbed wire. He alerted Johnson and the two went to investigate. Again came the sound of wire being clipped. Suddenly the sky lit up with illuminating rockets.

A swarm of Germans came out of the darkness hurling grenades. Both men were hit and went down, crippled for life. Roberts got into a sitting position and began firing methodically with his French Lebal rifle at three rounds to the clip, while Johnson struggled to his feet despite two broken legs and began firing as well, getting three Germans with three rounds, the last at a muzzle's length.

As Johnson reached for his bolo knife, a fourth German leaped, Luger in hand, over the body of the third. Bludgeoning his attacker with his rifle, Johnson was surprised to hear him cry out in English, "The little black son-of-a-bitch has got me." Johnson replied, "Yes, and this lil' black son-of-a-bitch is going to get you again if you get up." The German stayed down.

Meanwhile, two Germans had overpowered Roberts and were carrying him away. Unsheathing his bolo, Johnson hobbled after them. He split the skull of the nearest, which discouraged the other, who promptly fled. The clubbed German decided to rejoin the fight, and rose, firing his pistol. Hit, Johnson went down on his hands and knees.

As the German approached to finish him, Johnson swung his bolo upwards, disemboweling the man. Then he struggled to his feet again and hobbled in pursuit of the survivors of the raiding party for nearly a half-mile, alternately hurling grenades and taking swings with his bolo.

The French rewarded Johnson with the Croix de Guerre, their second highest decoration, and one general framed the cap that had belonged to the German whose skull Johnson had split. From his own country, Johnson received a pension, but little recognition. Attempts to have him awarded a Medal of Honor are still made from time to time.

Henry Johnson   *Needham Roberts*

Why the Signal Corps is a combat branch—U.S. signalman hit while close to the front lines in World War I. Telegraph and primitive radios and telephones were available, but extensive use was also made of carrier pigeons.

and the majority of German defenders were able to escape through the gaping holes in the American line of advance. However, 13,000 German soldiers and 500 cannons were captured in the offensive and the stage was set for the climactic American offensive of the war, the Meuse-Argonne offensive.

Pershing's plan was to push a huge American assault force through the Argonne Forest toward a major German defensive position on Barricourt Heights, a ridge line about 12 miles inland from the Meuse River. If the Americans could push past this high ground, they would be able to threaten the whole communication and transportation network of the left flank of the German army and force the Kaiser's troops to abandon most of occupied Lorraine province. Then, in the spring of 1919, the American Expeditionary Force would drive into Germany itself on a war-winning offensive.

> ## *The men were tired when they went into the fight.*
> — COLONEL GEORGE MARSHALL, IN THE ARGONNE FOREST, SEPTEMBER 1918.

The American commander's strategic concept was sound, but the Argonne Forest was laced with over 1,000 heavily concealed German artillery pieces along with hundreds of machine gun nests, barbed wire entanglements, and tank traps, all rolled up into four mutually supporting defensive lines throughout the gloomy region. The permanent German garrison in the region was a relatively modest 50,000 men, a force that could probably be overwhelmed by the

Dear Mother,
I skipped a couple of days in writing, and I hope you will excuse me because I was in no mood to write. I had a spell of homesickness and I felt blue. The grind of the daily routine seems to get me, I just can't get my heart into this war business and I don't think I ever will. The wounded that came back from the front the last couple of days made me sick. Everyone was bandaged, some their legs, some their arms and many were bound up around the head. The sickening part was the blood-soaked bandages. It made me shiver, and made me feel like a coward for a moment. I had desperate thoughts, figuring how I could get out of this some way. . . .
Well, I gradually came to my senses and realized that, being a non-com, I couldn't and mustn't think that way. I have to set a good example for the rest of the men. All I can do is to carry on and trust in God. It seems terrible to pray for one's own safety alone, I include all soldiers in my prayer, the enemy as well as all of the Allies, but it's foolish, I suppose, because the wounded still keep coming back. There are so many of them now, that there aren't enough ambulances and they use the motor trucks and pile them on. The trucks come along at almost a snail's pace and yet the wounded men cry out, "Slower! Don't drive so fast!" Each pebble you ride over must seem like a rock when you are wounded. It's simply awful the way they whimper and groan. A lump was in my throat.

— PRIVATE CHARLES F. MINDER,
306TH MACHINE GUN BATTALION,
MAY 18, 1918

———— ★ ★ ★ ————

600,000 men that Pershing was planning to utilize in the assault. However, the key to success was absolute surprise and swiftness in carrying Barricourt Heights, as American intelligence officers projected that the enemy could throw an additional 15 divisions into the forest within 72 hours, a reinforcement that would probably turn the operation into a bloody stalemate.

At 11 P.M. on the evening of September 25, 1918, 4,000 American guns opened fire as nine divisions of doughboys moved into position to advance. Colonel George Marshall observed the men as they swung into line: "The men were tired when they went into the fight, they had been held in the woods in wet clothes and wet feet for a week or more then made a long march without any sleep." At 5:30 A.M. the next morning the order "Fix bayonets!" was made along the line and for 15 miles between the Meuse River and the Argonne Forest olive-clad Americans wearing British-designed helmets and backed up by French-designed artillery advanced almost shoulder to shoulder in one great brownish-green panorama. For a few precious moments the assault force was protected by a thick fog which had reduced visibility to 40 feet, but then the German guns opened up and chaos began. An American general noted, "The fields were covered with barbed wire, men could not get through. The men were disorganized and were under heavy shrapnel fire. As soon as the sun rose, the men were cut to pieces by machine gun fire."

The doughboys, many of them only weeks from basic training, were confused, deafened by the noise of the guns, and blinded by the smoke and fog as friends and comrades

U.S. troops go over the top into combat during one of the offensives in 1918. The soldiers carry the excellent 1903 Springfield rifle, although some troops carried British or French weapons when supplies were short.

dropped to the ground around them. There was little room to maneuver in the dense, wooded terrain and most units made only modest gains during the first day of the offensive. By nightfall three divisions of German reinforcements were deploying in the woods while the Kaiser's troops dropped hundreds of gas shells on American positions. After two additional days of inching forward, Pershing called a temporary halt to the offensive while tallying a total of 45,000 casualties, a figure that approached the combined Union and Confederate dead and wounded at Gettysburg.

A few days later a fresh offensive lurched into motion and gifted young commanders such as Colonel George Patton and Brigadier General Douglas MacArthur provided significant local gains. However, by October 10, two weeks into the offensive, a mind numbing 100,000 casualties had been suffered while an additional 100,000 men had simply disappeared from their units as they drifted back through the rear echelons. The Meuse-Argonne offensive, developed as a swift, surprise assault, had degenerated into one of the worst battles of attri-

Gas masks at the ready on their chests, four Americans carry a wounded German back from the front. Due to the difficult terrain and the need to carry casualties over long distances under fire, four stretcher bearers were used in World War I in place of the two of earlier wars.

tion in American history, and Pershing's major response was to simply throw in thousands of fresh soldiers and continue the battering against the German lines. The United States Navy brought up huge, 14-inch naval guns to provide fire support while the American Expeditionary Force launched its first large-scale gas attack on the Germans. For three weeks the assault force inched forward through the gloom and mist of the forest. Finally, on the afternoon of November 1, advanced American units cleared the forest and broke out into the open countryside beyond. The survivors were now reorganized and resupplied for the next phase of the offensive, an assault on the German-held strong point of Sedan, one of the most powerful fortresses in France. However, as the new attack gained momentum, events in Germany were far outpacing Pershing's troops. In a climactic 11 day period, the Kaiser abdicated and fled to Holland, riots and uprisings broke out throughout Germany, and the new German government requested an armistice. At exactly 11 A.M. on November 11, 1918, all firing along the Western Front ceased and Woodrow Wilson proclaimed the victory of the Allied cause.

The campaign to make the world "safe for democracy" ultimately cost the lives of 79,658 American soldiers while an additional 200,000 men had been seriously wounded, mostly in a single ghastly period of about 16 weeks in the summer and autumn of 1918. These casualties paled in comparison to the millions of men lost in Russia, Germany, France, and Britain, each of which had suffered the virtual annihilation of a generation of their young men. Yet when the carnage had finally ended, little had been permanently settled. A draconian peace imposed on Germany merely set the stage for a return engagement of global conflict. As one French general noted, "We have not a peace, but merely a twenty year truce," a prophetic statement that would send the next generation of Americans into an even larger and more far-ranging conflict.

American infantryman on Guadalcanal in January 1943. The helmet, metal "dogtag" identification discs, and M-1 Garand rifle were standard issue throughout the war. The canvas leggings, two-piece twill fatigues, and long bayonet were somewhat antiquated, but still to be seen in some units at war's end.

CHAPTER VI

The Arsenal of Democracy

At 7 A.M. on the beautiful, balmy morning of December 7, 1941, Privates Joseph Lockard and George Elliott were preparing to end their duties for the army's Aircraft Warning Service in the American territory of Hawaii. The two men were operating a newly developed radar set at Opana Point on the northernmost tip of Oahu Island, and they normally conducted training sessions from 4 A.M. to 7 A.M. each morning. However, Elliott, recently transferred to this position, wanted more experience with the sophisticated machine and was still peering into the oscilloscope several minutes later when an enormous blip appeared on the screen. While the duty officer at the Information Center at their headquarters politely informed them that they were viewing an incoming flight of American bombers, the two khaki-clad soldiers were actually observing the approach of 183 attack planes of the Imperial Japanese Navy on their way to bomb the main American naval base in the Pacific Ocean—Pearl Harbor.

Less than an hour later, Commander Mitsua Fuchida, the Japanese mission commander, radioed fleet commander Admiral Chuichi Nagumo a coded message of *"Tora Tora Tora"* ("Tiger Tiger Tiger"), which meant that the assault force had reached Hawaii undetected. At 7:55 A.M., the first of several V-formations of Japanese planes peeled off one by one and began dropping their lethal cargoes on the unsuspecting

Despite impressive-looking damage sustained at Pearl Harbor on December 7, 1941, the USS West Virginia *and many other ships were eventually repaired and returned to active service.*

American ships below them. Their major target was Battleship Row in Pearl Harbor where eight powerful battleships were riding at anchor in their role as a deterrent to Japanese aggression in the Pacific. Now that deterrent force was about to be annihilated. The battleship *Oklahoma* was hit by four torpedoes in less than a minute and capsized, taking 400 of her crew with her. On the *West Virginia,* Captain Mervyn Bennion sank to the deck with his stomach ripped open from a bomb fragment. Bennion would be dead in minutes; his ship would sink soon after. The *Maryland,* moored next to the *Oklahoma,* was safe from torpedo attacks, but Japanese dive-bombers smashed the ship, a fate similar to the *Tennessee.* The *California* was wreathed in flames from both bombs and torpedo hits and sank at its berth. A squadron of dive-bombers peeled over a nearby drydock facility and pummeled the *Pennsylvania* which was undergoing repairs. The *Nevada* was actually able to get underway and begin moving slowly down the blazing channel, but then luck ran out and the battlewagon was beached after numerous torpedo and bomb hits. While the casualty list on these crippled or sinking ships was enormous, none would come close to matching the fate of the men onboard the *Arizona.* A flight of Japanese torpedo planes miraculously missed the dreadnought with every weapon fired but then the ship's luck ran out. Five bombs from high-level bombers all struck their marks and one bomb hit the magazine where almost a ton of gunpowder had been stored. This explosion quickly ignited much larger amounts of ammunition in forward compartments and the *Arizona* seemed to leap out of the water in the middle of a tremendous blast of fire and debris as over 1,000 died with the 33,000-ton ship.

While part of the Japanese assault force struck the ships, other planes focused on Hawaii's most important air bases where planes had been dutifully parked wing tip to wing tip to avoid attacks by saboteurs. Japanese pilots couldn't believe their luck at this total lack of dispersal, and as one American plane ignited and exploded, it often took several more with it to fiery destruction. Army nurse Lieutenant Monica Conter was stationed at Hickam Field on this climactic morning and her shock at the attack mirrored most other Americans' surprise: "While drinking coffee and tomato juice I heard some planes real low, one sounded like it might crash on the hospital . . . just as I jumped up from my desk I heard a terrible noise and ran out on the screened porch overlooking Pearl Harbor. I saw planes so low they looked as if they might be landing in the Harbor. I never heard so much noise in my life, bombs, some 500 pounds, machine guns and our anti-aircraft guns . . . then came a second attack, we all fell face down on the wounded in the halls, operating room and heard the bombers directly over us. . . ."

A tiny number of American pilots were able to get their planes airborne amidst the explosions and fires and a few attacking planes were shot down or badly damaged; however, when this "Day of Infamy" was over 18 American ships had been sunk or badly damaged and 2,403 Americans were dead. Despite this seemingly one-sided victory, the Japanese empire had gained much less than it initially appeared. While the attack had almost annihilated the battleship segment of the Pacific fleet, none of the three almost irreplaceable aircraft carriers in the Pacific had been in harbor on this December morning and thus the most powerful naval weapon in the upcoming war was still intact. The attackers had

> *I never heard so much noise in my life, bombs, some 500 pounds, machine guns and our anti-aircraft guns . . .*
>
> — LIEUTENANT MONICA CONTER, PEARL HARBOR, DECEMBER 7, 1941.

also failed to destroy such crucial targets as drydocks, petroleum stores, and submarine facilities, all of which were vital to the functioning of the American navy. Finally, the surprise attack on Pearl Harbor had unified a disunited people into a single community focused on a single purpose of annihilating the nation that had launched this premeditated assault. As one admiral noted as he surveyed the burning wreckage of Pearl Harbor, "When this war is over, the only place the Japanese language will be spoken is in Hell."

Americans, very much like a generation earlier, were now involved in a World War that had already been underway for some time. The French general's prediction of a mere 20-year truce at the end of the Great War had been remarkably accurate as the harsh terms imposed upon Germany at the Treaty of Versailles had set the stage for the rise of fascism under Adolf Hitler. Hitler's Nazi regime aggressively expanded the borders of the Third Reich until the German attack on Poland forced France and England to enter a conflict which initially went almost totally against the democratic Allies. By the fall of 1941, France and most of the rest of western Europe were conquered by the Germans, Britain was being pounded by Luftwaffe bombers, and huge Nazi tank formations were roaming through

General Douglas MacArthur was American commander in the Philippines at the time of the Japanese attack. He abandoned his command to organize the Allied resistance in Australia only after receiving a direct order from President Roosevelt.

the recently invaded Soviet Union. The preoccupation of European colonial powers with the war with Hitler had allowed an increasingly aggressive and militaristic Japan to conquer large segments of China, French Indo-China, and other territories while Imperial leaders also set their sights on the wealth and resources of Singapore, Indonesia, and numerous other territories that now seemed ripe for the taking. The only significant obstacle to this expansionist impulse was the only other significant nation not yet involved in the World War, the United States. When it became increasingly apparent to Japan's militarists that the American government under Franklin Delano Roosevelt was highly unlikely to accede to the empire's territorial demands, the move toward open warfare became inexorable. The attack on Pearl Harbor was only one element in an ambitious and violent plan to create a "Greater East Asia Co-Prosperity Sphere" that would make Japan the dominant force in the Pacific world.

The Japanese plan to neutralize American power in the Pacific region was essentially based on eliminating two major centers of possible resistance. One was the naval and air power based in Hawaii and the other was the substantial American presence in the Commonwealth of the Philippines. The U. S. Congress had already passed legislation authorizing the total independence of the Philippines to become effective on July 4, 1946, but in 1941 the islands still served as a linchpin in the strategy of checking Japanese aggression. However, the commonwealth's defenses, under the command of former Army Chief of Staff General Douglas MacArthur, were more impressive on paper than in the field. MacArthur had recently mobilized over 100,000 Filipinos into a national militia and was expecting substantial American air and ground reinforcements during the spring of 1942. But when Pearl Harbor was attacked, his only first line forces were a single regiment of American regulars, a few units of elite Philippine scouts, and about 135 modern fighters and bombers. A devastatingly effective Japanese air attack a few hours after Pearl Harbor virtually eliminated the air component of his force, and by Christmas of 1941 a Japanese invasion force was approaching the capital city of Manila while the surviving American and Filipino units were retreating into nearby Bataan Peninsula for a final stand.

Douglas MacArthur, who would develop a generally positive record of leadership in future campaigns, was the architect of disaster in this first full-scale ground confrontation between Imperial and American troops. The general's obsession with destroying the Japanese attackers on the beaches had caused him to inadequately provision Bataan for a long siege, so that when the Americans and Filipinos withdrew into the peninsula, they ended up defending a region that provided almost no food. While the haggard, emaciated men, who called themselves the "Battling Bastards of Bataan," grimly hung on through increasingly severe Japanese offensives, MacArthur, known derisively as "Dugout Doug" to the ground troops, sequestered himself in a tunnel on the nearby fortified island of Corregidor and only visited Bataan once during the three-month battle.

★ ★ ★ ★ ★ ★ ★ ★ ★ ★ ★ ★ ★ ★ ★ ★ ★ ★ ★ ★

Richard Sakakida

A Japanese-American from Hawaii, Richard Sakakida was drafted in early 1941 and sent to intelligence school, after which he was sent to the Philippines to spy on the Japanese. Sakakida began his spying career with another young Japanese American, and both men were disguised as merchant seamen who had jumped ship. The pair arrived in the Philippines in April 1941, and they were soon active in various Japanese organizations.

Information provided by Sakakida and his colleague proved useful in rounding up Japanese agents and freezing Japanese assets in the Philippines after Pearl Harbor. Called to active duty after Pearl Harbor, Sakakida and his colleague served in Army Intelligence on Bataan and Corregidor, interrogating prisoners of war, translating documents, and helping decode Japanese messages. Sakakida's colleague was among those evacuated in the closing weeks of the first Philippine campaign, and he wound up on General MacArthur's staff in Australia. Sakakida gave up his place on the aircraft to another man and remained behind.

Captured by the Japanese, Sakakida managed to convince them that his services as a translator and interrogator had been forced through torture. By mid-1943 he had been released to become a civilian employee at Japanese headquarters in Manila. From this position he was able to supply information to Filipino guerrillas, who passed it on to MacArthur's headquarters, and he was instrumental in bringing about the Bismarck Sea victory.

On one occasion Sakadida engineered the release of a large number of guerrillas by disguising himself as a Japanese officer. After the liberation of the Philippines began, Japanese headquarters withdrew from Manila into Northern Luzon in early 1945, and Sakakida went with it. Shortly after the surrender of Japan he made contact with American troops. Save for about 180 days when he was on active duty on Bataan and Corregidor, he had been undercover for more than 1,600 days.

After the war Sakakida served as a prosecution witness in the trial of General Yamashita and in the trial of a Japanese-American resident of the Philippines who had collaborated with the enemy. He remained in the army, retiring in 1975 as a highly decorated lieutenant colonel.

★ ★ ★ ★ ★ ★ ★ ★ ★ ★ ★ ★ ★ ★ ★ ★ ★ ★ ★ ★

Finally, on April 3, 1942, Good Friday morning, the Philippines campaign reached its climax. MacArthur had been ordered to escape to Australia a few weeks earlier, and Lieutenant General Jonathan Wainwright, the newly appointed commander of American troops in the Philippines, knew his men were unlikely to stop a full-scale offensive. While the total of American regulars, Philippine scouts, and the Filipino militia on Bataan still totaled an impressive 80,000 men, widespread disease and malnutrition left only 27,000 men capable of even standing upright, and of these men, 75 percent were suffering from malaria. These walking skeletons were now attacked by 50,000 fresh Japanese troops under Lieutenant General Masahuru Homma, who was supported by over 150 heavy guns and an air force that had complete control of the skies. The result was a predictable disaster.

The Japanese offensive sliced through the American lines at an ever-accelerating pace and defenders began pulling back desperately toward the tip of the peninsula about 10 miles from the front lines. In the main hospital on Bataan, nurses and corpsmen quickly cut traction ropes so wounded men could roll out of bed during severe air raids. Fleets of small boats carried a fortunate few hundred survivors across the channel to Corregidor, but on April 9, 1942, exactly 77 years to the day after Lee had surrendered to Grant at Appomattox, 70,000 Filipino and American troops surrendered to Japan in the largest capitulation in United States history. However, the "Battling Bastards" nightmares were only beginning, as a combination of Japanese incompetence and cruelty resulted in the ensuing Bataan Death March. Thousands of soldiers were marched in the tropical heat with almost no water towards distant prison camps. Men who fell were often bayoneted, shot, or even run over with trucks or tanks. Of the 70,000 men who started the Death March, only 54,000 ever reached prison camps, while a lucky few escaped into the jungle. More than 10,000 men died on

A U.S. Marine holds a shell for a 76mm pack howitzer during the battle for Tarawa. His helmet had stopped an enemy bullet a short time before.

Colonel James Doolittle had participated in many pre-war air races and exhibitions. On April 18, 1942, he led the first bombing raid on Japan, utilizing a daring plan to transport B-25 bombers on an aircraft carrier which could barely accommodate them.

route as Japanese soldiers exhibited their contemptuous attitude toward soldiers who surrendered instead of killing themselves. But as a handful of prisoners escaped and eventually made it back to the United States with their incredible tales of brutality, Americans became even more united in their desire for revenge on Imperial Japan. The first element of this revenge was about to begin.

While Japanese gunners were deploying siege guns on the tip of Bataan to bombard the doomed garrison on Corregidor, an American army air force colonel prepared his B-25 Mitchell bomber to take off from the rolling deck of the carrier *Hornet*. Shortly after dawn on April 18, 1942, Colonel James Doolittle led a squadron of 16 bombers on a daring mission into the heart of the Japanese empire—the capital city of Tokyo. Shortly after lunchtime, the American bombers flew low over a city that had just finished an air-raid drill and most Tokyo residents merely assumed that the approaching planes were part of the exercise. Children in schoolyards and people in a baseball stadium waved at the passing planes, mistaking the Mitchells for Japanese aircraft. A few minutes later bombs began to fall on a number of military targets with the Imperial Palace scrupulously avoided. Then the planes roared toward China where they would land. When the president was asked by newspapermen the origin point of the dramatic raid, he blithely answered, "Shangri-La," the mythical kingdom of a recent best-selling book and film. However, the military and naval leaders of Japan very much knew the attack had come from an American carrier, and they were determined that this embarrassing situation would never occur again.

Admiral Isoroko Yamamoto, the energetic Japanese fleet commander who had engineered the Pearl Harbor operation, quickly responded with a complex plan to force the remnants of the American Pacific fleet into a showdown battle by invading and capturing the vital island of Midway, 1,000 miles east of Hawaii. Yamamoto knew that he could deploy almost 200 ships of all types against the less than 50 vessels available to the new American Pacific fleet commander, Admiral Chester Nimitz. However, the enormous Japanese advantage was whittled down by a number of factors. First, Yamamoto dramatically reduced the size of his attack force by orchestrating a huge diversionary attack on the Aleutian Islands at the tip of Alaska, and then compounded the error by dividing his Midway assault fleet into several smaller squadrons. Thus, of 10 carriers available for action, only four of these critical ships would actually be involved in frontline operations. An equally important disadvantage was that American intelligence services had broken the Japanese codes, so that Nimitz knew early enough that Midway would be attacked to allow him to concentrate every available ship and plane in the right place at the right time.

Admiral Chester Nimitz commanded U.S. naval forces in the Pacific. He is shown here wearing the insignia of the new rank of fleet admiral, authorized December 19, 1944.

On the morning of June 4, 1942, slow-moving, cumbersome Catalina Flying Boats confirmed that the Japanese fleet was closing on Midway as 36 fighters and 72 bombers launched from four carriers droned through the tropical skies. A squadron of Marine fighters, mostly composed of obsolete, slow Buffalos along with a handful of more modern Wildcats roared from Midway's airfield and rose to challenge the vastly superior enemy Zeroes. Seventeen of 25 Marine planes hurtled into the sea within moments, but several American fighters penetrated the Japanese escort long enough to shoot down enemy bombers, and when the Imperial planes arrived over Midway itself, accurate antiaircraft guns put up a ferocious fire. The Japanese strike force failed to cause decisive damage to the island's defenses and almost half of the attack force was shot down or damaged; the result was a call for a second assault, a request that would eventually turn the tide of the battle.

While Midway Island was under attack, the commanders of the two American carrier task forces, Admiral Frank Jack

I could not be happy ashore at this time. My place is here with the fight.

— LIEUTENANT COMMANDER JOHN WALDRON IN A LETTER TO HIS WIFE FROM MIDWAY ISLAND.

Fletcher and Admiral Raymond Spruance, ordered the *Yorktown*, the *Enterprise*, and the *Hornet* turned into the wind, and fighter, torpedo, and dive-bomber squadrons launched into the air. The coordination of units left much to be desired, and the first squadrons of slow-moving torpedo planes arrived over the Japanese fleet with no sign of their covering fighters. The result was the virtual annihilation of several American squadrons. The most dramatic and costly engagement occurred with the arrival of the 15 planes of the *Hornet's* Torpedo Squadron 8. The unit commander, Lieutenant Commander John Waldron, was an energetic aviator from South Dakota who was part Sioux. His men were encouraged to carry several pistols and hunting knives in case they landed in enemy territory. The night before the squadron went into action, Waldron wrote his wife, "I love you and the children very dearly and I long to be with you. But I could not be happy ashore at this time. My place is here with the fight." The next morning, all 15 planes pushed in at full throttle as they arrived over the four Japanese carriers in clear sight below them. However, without fighter cover, about 30 Zeroes began to chop the squadron to pieces, until, one by one, all 15 planes crashed into the ocean. Only one of the 30 men in

A U.S. Marine aviator sits in the cockpit of a Grumman Wildcat on Guadalcanal. By this point in the war the aircraft, flown by several different pilots, had accounted for 19 enemy aircraft.

Troops of the 1st Marine Division land at the beginning of the long Guadalcanal campaign in August 1942. Due to the priority given the European theater, many Marines were still carrying the 1903 Springfield rifle, highly accurate but operated by bolt action.

the squadron, Ensign George Gay, survived the attack, and the young Texan barely escaped with his life as his damaged plane sank into the Pacific. Gay hid under the seat cushion of his plane as it bobbed in the water and watched most of his comrades from the squadron meet a worse fate.

At 10:20 A.M. on June 4, 1942, it appeared that the Japanese navy was about to win the battle of Midway as most of the attack planes launched by the Americans had either been shot down or missed their targets. Then, a relatively small force of dive-bombers from the *Yorktown* and the *Enterprise* flew over the Japanese fleet and, to their amazement, discovered virtually no fighter defense. The sacrifice of the earlier attack squadrons had not been in vain, as their assault had pulled most of the Japanese fighter cover away from the carriers. Then Lieutenant Commander Maxwell Leslie and Lieutenant Commander Clarence McClusky led their squadrons in a steep dive, and in one of the most critical five-minute periods in military history, left the *Akagi*, the *Soryu*, and the *Kaga* writhing in flames. This left only Admiral Tamon Yamaguchi's *Hiryu* to deal with the three American carriers. Yamaguchi, a graduate of Princeton who had traveled widely in the United States, sent a scratch force of 24 planes hurtling into the American fleet, and although almost every plane was shot

★ ★ ★ ★ ★ ★ ★ ★ ★ ★ ★ ★ ★ ★ ★ ★ ★ ★ ★

Benjamin O. Davis Sr.

For 20 years, from 1916 to 1936, Benjamin O. Davis was the only black line officer in the regular army. His military career was distinguished beyond that—he became the first black general in the Army—despite the limitations imposed by prevailing racial attitudes.

A native of Washington D.C., Davis was born in 1877 and entered Howard University in 1897, intending to become a teacher. In July 1898, he volunteered for service in the Spanish-American War and was commissioned a second lieutenant in the 8th Volunteer Infantry, one of 10 regiments composed of men supposedly resistant to various tropical diseases, four of which were composed largely of black troops.

After occupation duty in Cuba, Davis was mustered out in March 1899. He shortly enlisted in the 9th Cavalry, one of the regular army's four black regiments. Davis served in the Philippines, where he earned a commission in 1901, and began rising in the army. He served variously as military attaché to Liberia, as ROTC instructor at various black colleges and universities, such as Tuskeegee and Wilberforce, and as a technical advisor to black National Guard units. In the late 1930s he was appointed the first black commander of New York's famous 369th Infantry Regiment, "The Harlem Hellfighters," by which time he had risen to colonel.

In October 1940, Davis was promoted to brigadier general, the first black general in the army. In January 1941, he was given command of a brigade of two black cavalry regiments in the 2nd Cavalry Division. There he became the first black officer in the U.S. Army to directly command whites, since most of the officers in black regiments were white. General Davis reached the mandatory retirement age of 64 in June 1941, and was placed on the retired list. He was immediately recalled to active duty, in a move that Republicans claimed was motivated by Franklin Roosevelt's desire to cater to black voters.

For the next five years, Davis served in various staff assignments, essentially as an inspector general of black troops and an advisor on black affairs to the War Department, duties which he performed with a good deal of success, greatly influencing policies toward black troops and their employment. In mid-1945 his name was placed on a list of officers to be promoted to major general, but with the surrender of Japan all promotions were canceled. General Davis retired for a second time in 1948, shortly after the official integration of the armed forces. In retirement he lived in Washington and Chicago and was active in civic affairs until his death in 1970.

In addition to having been the first black general in the army, Davis held several other distinctions. One of the oldest officers on active duty during World War II, he was one of the last generals not to have graduated from college, one of the few to have not attended any of the army's professional schools, and at the time of his retirement was the oldest man on active duty in the army.

★ ★ ★ ★ ★ ★ ★ ★ ★ ★ ★ ★ ★ ★ ★ ★ ★ ★ ★

down, the *Yorktown* was mortally wounded. But an American counterattack soon pulverized the *Hiryu* and the otherwise powerful fleet of Japanese battleships and cruisers now had no air cover. Yamamoto was forced to call off the operation and the battle of Midway entered the history books as the decisive turning point of the Pacific war.

Several weeks later, the victorious Americans were launching their first offensive of the war on the little known island of Guadalcanal in the Solomon chain, a green hell of overgrown jungle, poisonous insects and snakes, and intolerable weather conditions. The American high command initially had little interest in this uninviting piece of real estate, but when intelligence reports confirmed that Japanese engineers were constructing an airfield that could threaten a number of Allied positions, the 1st Marine Division was given hurried orders to hit the beaches and capture the airstrip.

At 2:00 in the morning on August 7, 1942, an American invasion fleet rounded Cape Esperance at Guadalcanal's northern tip and the Marines on deck stared at Savo Island rising from the humid mist. At daylight, destroyers opened fire, landing craft were lowered, and the first American amphibious landing of the war got underway. The lead elements of Major General Archer Vandergrift's division quickly defeated a small force of Japanese construction troops at the airfield and the Americans rapidly set up a defensive perimeter. However, Japanese rein-

A U.S. Marine sniper on Gaudalcanal. Older rifles were highly effective in the sniping role and were still being used even in Korea.

U.S. Marines on the march on Gaudalcanal in October 1942, after several grueling months of combat. Marine at right carries the Browning Automatic Rifle (BAR), an infantry squad's main support weapon.

forcements were soon pouring onto the island and 19- and 20-year-olds from Osaka and Yokohama were soon engaged in mortal combat with their counterparts from Detroit and New York. The vast majority of soldiers from both armies had grown up in the temperate climates that dominated both countries and this totally alien, totally hostile environment initially shocked both forces. The control of the airstrip allowed the U.S. Marines to dominate daylight operations, but at night large numbers of Japanese troops would launch "banzai" attacks as they screamed threats and curses, often in surprisingly good English, at the grim Americans manning the defense lines.

Meanwhile in the adjoining waters, soon to be nicknamed "Ironbottom Sound," American and Japanese naval squadrons slugged it out in a six-month sea campaign which cost both sides dozens of major vessels. Gradually, as additional Marine and army units disembarked and dozens of new planes landed on Henderson Field, renamed for one of the Marine pilots killed at Midway, the Americans pushed further inland and forced the Japanese into a series of futile, bloody assaults. As the year 1942 approached its end, the Japanese government was forced to admit that Guadalcanal would have to be evacuated. The Americans had made the first giant step toward Tokyo.

★ ★ ★

While American and Japanese forces were dueling for control of Guadalcanal, another major amphibious assault force was preparing to land almost at the other side of the globe. Nearly a year after Hitler had joined Japan in a war against the United States, American and German ground forces had yet to engage in a battle and President Roosevelt was desperate to find some point in which the relatively inexperienced troops could fight the vaunted Wehrmacht on something like equal terms. While a number of senior American generals, including Chief of Staff George Marshall, were advising the president to stage a showdown with the Nazis through a cross-Channel invasion into France as soon as possible, Roosevelt tended to accept British Prime Minister

Allied commander Dwight D. Eisenhower observes with concern a U.S. training exercise in March 1944. These exercises frequently used live ammunition and resulted in a considerable number of casualties.

Winston Churchill's advice that an early assault on the powerful German forces in France would be a bloodbath; Churchill was convinced that American troops would be far more valuable, and more likely victorious, in the North African deserts where British troops were already fighting a desperate battle to keep Egypt and the Suez Canal from Hitler's armies.

Roosevelt essentially agreed with his British counterpart's strategic thinking and the president gave orders for the initiation of Operation Torch, the American invasion of French Morocco and Algeria. At 4 A.M. on November 8, 1942, the first of 34,000 assault troops clambered into bobbing landing craft and made their way towards the coast of North Africa. The beaches were not defended by German soldiers, but by the forces of General Philippe Petain's French government that had been allowed to function after Hitler had seized most of the country. The Frenchmen initially put up stiff resistance, but a series of negotiations set up by American Commanding General Dwight Eisenhower eventually transformed the Frenchmen from enemies to allies and allowed the United States forces to move into position to confront the Germans.

The U.S. P-51D of 1944 was a considerable improvement over earlier models. It could accompany bomber formations far into Germany and took a heavy toll among attacking Luftwaffe fighters.

By midwinter 1943, American army units were deployed along a series of ridge lines in central Tunisia, while Field Marshal Bernard Montgomery's British Eighth Army was gradually pushing German Field Marshal Erwin Rommel's Afrika Korps westward through Libya after a spectacular English victory at El Alamein. At this point, Hitler, who currently had a huge German army being cut off by the Soviet army at Stalingrad, chose to intervene further in the North African campaign. He rushed 100,000 reinforcements to hold the ports and airfield of northern Tunisia and ordered the local commander, General Jürgen von Arnim, to crush the American troops who were clinging to the steep, bare hills to the south.

While both talented German field commanders, von Arnim and Rommel, planned offensives against the newly arrived American forces, the United States troops were being led by one of Eisenhower's poorest choices for command, Major General Lloyd Fredendall. The irascible, 59-year-old general had flunked out of West Point twice and then risen to high command through administrative talent rather than bravery or intelligence. When the American II Corps of three divisions was deployed in Tunisia, Fredendall had immediately employed 200 engineers to blast out an underground command post inside a tunnel which in turn was at the rear of a canyon 40 miles from the front lines. Thus the American troops would soon confront the legendary German "Desert Fox" commanded by a general who seemed interested only in his own personal safety.

In late January 1943, Rommel turned over command of his operations against Montgomery to a subordinate, Italian General Giovanni Messe; taking 12,000 of his best troops and 160 powerful tanks he headed west to smash into Fredendall's divisions. While the Desert Fox pushed toward the American lines, von Arnim launched his own attack from the north and smashed into American armored and infantry units covering the vital crossroads town of Sidi-bou-Zid on the morning of February 14. Two German panzer divisions, covered by waves of Stuka bombers and Messerschmitt fighters, separated the American infantry from their armored support and killed or captured 3,000 defenders while destroying over 100 tanks. Then Rommel's column swept forward and drove for the huge American supply base at Tebessa, 35 miles west of a mountain pass called Kasserine.

Kasserine Pass was a good place to fight a defensive battle as the main road was dominated by scrub-covered hills that rose 2,000 feet and allowed defenders to rake anything that attempted to penetrate below. However, Fredendall botched the deployment of defensive forces and, under cover of a fierce artillery barrage, five German armored battalions plunged through the haphazardly organized defenders and seized the pass. At this point Eisenhower sacked Fredendall and replaced him with 2nd Armored Division commander Ernest Harmon. Harmon quickly concentrated every available man and gun in the town of Thala, 12 miles west of Kasserine, and in a rare desert sleet and snowstorm parried each of Rommel's thrusts. American artillery matched German tanks, and by nightfall of February 22, the Desert Fox pulled his tanks back through the icy roads of Kasserine and rejoined the rest of the Afrika Korps in its duel with Montgomery.

The Kasserine campaign had cost the American army 5,000 men, but Rommel had not been able to inflict a crushing defeat on the newly arrived enemy, and in the wake of this operation

★ ★ ★ ★ ★ ★ ★ ★ ★ ★ ★ ★ ★ ★ ★ ★ ★ ★ ★ ★

Charles E. Kelly

Acknowledging his "fighting determination and intrepidity in battle," Charles E. Kelly was awarded a Medal of Honor for his critical role in the defense of an ammunition dump under attack by the Germans. At one point, Kelly is described as hurling 60mm mortar rounds as if they were hand grenades, before he covered the withdrawal of his comrades, using a bazooka and automatic rifle, later slipping away himself to rejoin his unit.

Kelly was born in 1920 to a working-class Irish family in Pittsburgh, Pennsylvania. After holding a variety of jobs, he was inducted into the army and volunteered for airborne training. Much to his embarrassment and the ridicule of his friends, who claimed that he was obviously "not tough enough," he washed out of the program and ended up in the infantry. Assigned to the 143rd Infantry of the Texas National Guard in September 1943, Kelly took part in the landings at Salerno in Italy.

On September 13, 1943, in the face of heavy German counterattacks that threatened to drive the Allies back into the sea, Kelly volunteered for a patrol that sought to locate and neutralize several enemy machine guns in the vicinity of Altavila, focus of some of the heaviest fighting. No sooner had he returned from this task than Kelly once again volunteered, this time to establish contact with an American infantry battalion that was believed to be on a nearby hill. Proceeding under heavy enemy fire, Kelly reached the hill only to find it occupied by the Germans. He then returned to apprise his commander of this important information.

Shortly after his return, two previously undetected German machine guns began taking elements of the 143rd Infantry under fire. Although he had already twice performed hazardous missions beyond the call of duty, Kelly once more volunteered, and with several other soldiers undertook the difficult task of destroying both the guns. By this time he had exhausted all of his ammunition, as had many of the other troops, so he requested permission to go to the rear to pick up a fresh supply.

As Kelly approached the regimental ammunition dump in an old ruined building, he discovered that it was under attack by the Germans. The defending troops made Kelly welcome, loaded him with ammunition, and assigned him to defend the rear of the ammo dump, lest the Germans attack from that direction too. He held this position until dawn, when the Germans attacked the storehouse.

As enemy pressure became overwhelming, it became clear that the place could not be held much longer. Kelly volunteered to cover the withdrawal of the other defenders, and when the last of the defenders managed to escape, Kelly himself got away.

When Kelly was awarded a Medal of Honor, it was proof enough that he was indeed "tough enough."

★ ★ ★ ★ ★ ★ ★ ★ ★ ★ ★ ★ ★ ★ ★ ★ ★ ★ ★ ★

one of the most colorful, controversial commanders in American history was pushed to the forefront. The less than spectacular leadership in much of this campaign encouraged Eisenhower to appoint a new field commander in Tunisia, General George Patton. The arrival of the opinionated, energetic, egocentric Patton injected new vigor into the somewhat shaken American troops as spring came to North Africa, and a series of increasingly dramatic offensives pushed the Italian and German armies closer and closer to the shores of the Mediterranean. By the afternoon of May 7, the British and American troops had captured the key cities of Bizerte and Tunis and almost 240,000 Axis troops were now prisoners. For the first time, Hitler had been evicted from an entire continent, and now Europe was clearly in sight as an Allied objective.

As the Allies prepared to attempt to knock Italy out of the Axis through an invasion of Sicily and then the Italian mainland, the original American plan for a cross-Channel invasion in 1943 was postponed until the following year. Therefore, it became apparent that for the immediate future, the main assault on Hitler's Germany would come from the air, not from the ground. During the spring and summer of 1943 dozens of squadrons of huge American heavy bombers arrived at newly constructed bases in England and the pilots and crews of the Flying Fortresses and Liberators prepared to do battle with the vaunted Luftwaffe.

★ ★ ★

The air war over Europe was a study in contradictions. The pilots, navigators, bombardiers, and gunners who manned the B-17s and B-24s of the army air force lived in conditions that their infantry counterparts could only dream about. Clean sheets, fresh food, and festive dances

─────── ★ ★ ★ ───────

March 13.—Flew on mission 14. Target past Leghorn broke 4:45 time. Can low on fuel. Came home without formation. Not a milk run, lot of flak, but thank God it was inaccurate. I'd hate to go back there next month. Hit target. Bridge. 1000 lbs. Saw coast of France.

March 14.—Made mission 15. Target- Rome marshalling yards. 100 per cent concentration of bombs. Good job. Made 5:05 time. Cook's tour of Italy.

March 15.—Made mission 16. Flying almost every day is tough. Target- Cassino. Right on front line. We were only one of 16 Bomb Groups to hit the town. When we got over it, there was nothing left of Cassino. Only a hole in the ground. Loads & loads of trucks going to the front. It was a sight I'll never forget. The town was only dust. Captain Tate asked me to write up my impressions of the raid for the squadron book. I did so. Capt. Tate said I did swell. Tonight is my first braodcast on the group radio program. Made the broadcast Quite successful except that I read the news too fast, but with a little experience might do right well.

March 16.—Flew spare. Saw two ships collide and explode. Chet Angell, V.E. Miller & Wise. My buddies all dead. Flew back to field. Sick. 13 good men dead. Can't stand it much more. Guess I'm a sissy.

— DIARY OF TECHNICAL SERGEANT HARRY SCHLOSS, 17TH BOMBER SQUADRON, 1943

─────── ★ ★ ───────

★ ★

Ernie T. Pyle

Ernie Pyle began his career as a war correspondent from London in 1941. Unlike many correspondents, who frequently spent most of their time in bars, Pyle reported from up front with the troops. Rather than matters of policy, strategy, and command, he focused on the daily routine of the soldier's life, the stress of combat, the simple pleasures and pains. But as did all correspondents, he left much of the misery and horror of combat unsaid. Nevertheless, as can be seen in his first published collection, *Here is Your War* (New York, 1943), it emerged very clearly. He won a Pulitzer Prize in 1943 for his sensitive reporting.

As a war correspondent, Pyle covered operations in North Africa, Sicily, Italy, and France, before going to the Pacific, where he reported from Iwo Jima and Okinawa. Pyle was killed by a Japanese machine-gunner on Ie Shima on April 18, 1945. On the site was erected a simple monument, originally just of wood and paint, but later replaced in stone, "On this spot the 77th Division Lost a Buddy, Ernie Pyle."

★ ★

★ ★

Maurice Rose

After enlisting following high school, Maurice Rose went on to brigadier general and led troops on D-day and during the Normandy campaign. In 1945, while arranging to personally supervise the attack on Paderborn, Germany, he was killed by German soldiers.

Late on March 30, 1945, Rose, a general who commanded "from the front," was driving forward to supervise the attack on Paderborn, when his party was taken under fire by enemy forces. In the gathering darkness, Rose and his comrades attempted to escape, but a German tank rammed their jeep, pinning it against a tree. A German soldier popped out of the turret with a machine pistol in hand.

What happened next is unclear, as his aides unbuckled their pistol belts, Rose went for his pistol, though whether to attempt to shoot it out or to surrender the weapon cannot be determined. He was killed instantly by a burst of machine pistol fire. The highest ranking American Jewish officer ever killed in action, Rose was posthumously awarded a Silver Star.

★ ★

were all readily available staples of an airman's existence. On the other hand, during the minimum of 25 missions that had to be completed before an aircrew could return home, the odds were actually better than even that a crewman would be killed or captured. While infantrymen could always run away from enemy fire that seemed impossible to confront, airmen were trapped thousands of feet in the sky with no real escape route. The airmen were also victims of a horrendous miscalculation on the part of their generals. The so-called "bomber barons," who had directed the development of American heavy bombers, had been convinced that a four-engined airplane bristling with machine guns and flying in a mutually supportive formation could easily defend itself against the attack of enemy fighters. However, the two most advanced German interceptors in 1943, the ME-109 and FW-190, were so fast and so maneuverable that they could slash bomber flights to pieces before the massed machine guns could fully take effect.

Audie Murphy, above receiving the French Legion d' Honneur, was the most decorated American soldier in World War II.

By the summer of 1943, German military leaders had deployed a stupendous force of 900,000 personnel in the operation of a multitiered defensive system designed to decimate each intruding American bomber mission. The air battle would open when twin-engined German "Destroyers" would stand off from the approaching bomber stream and launch volley after volley of air-to-air rockets designed to bring down some bombers while disrupting the tight formation of surviving planes. Then the Messerschmitts and Focke-Wulfs would peel down with machine guns and cannons tearing jagged holes in the bombers as American gunners fired back with turret guns, belly guns, side guns, and tail guns. Then 14,000 heavy flak guns and 35,000 medium guns arranged in successive defense belts would roar into action firing up to 5,000 shells a minute at any point in the bomber stream. This lethal gauntlet would send plane after plane hurtling earthward as keyed up crewmen in surviving bombers counted how many parachutes, if any, emerged from the doomed aircraft.

As the war raged in Europe, U.S. forces continued to advance in a less publicized campaign across the Pacific. The double column formation allowed troops to quickly clear a road when under attack or to allow vehicles to pass.

A typical, frenzied, bloody air battle occurred on August 17, 1943, when 315 American bombers flew deep into Germany to attack the ball-bearing plants at Schweinfurt and the Messerschmitt aircraft factory complex at Regensburg. As the American bomber squadrons flew across the English Channel into France, they were initially escorted by fighters, but the escorts lacked range to enter Germany and the Luftwaffe planes merely bided their time until the bombers were alone. Then, for six hours, German fighters slashed through the army air force formations and knocked down 60 planes carrying 600 men while losing 27 of their own aircraft. German war industries received fairly significant damage, but unless American air commanders discovered a way to significantly reduce the rate of losses, the air offensive against Germany simply could not continue.

★ ★ ★

While Americans on the home front were increasingly shocked at the casualties among air crews in the skies over Germany, the last major Pacific operation of 1943 produced equally ghastly losses. In order to provide protection on its flank for a proposed drive through New Guinea, the Philippines, and Formosa to Japan, the American navy planned to attack and conquer a series of island chains from the Gilberts to the Marianas. The first target was the three-square-mile island of Betio in the Tarawa atoll defended by 5,000 Japanese troops under Rear Admiral Keiji Shibasaki. The Japanese commander had deployed a vast assortment of weapons ranging from dozens of light machine guns to 8-inch coastal guns dragged in from the captured British base at Singapore, and most of these pieces were concealed in a vast network of pillboxes and blockhouses that dotted the island.

At 3:30 on the morning of November 20, 1943, the battleships *Maryland* and *Tennessee*, both of which had been raised from the bottom of Pearl Harbor and put back into action, began a savage bombardment of Tarawa in conjunction with another battleship and a powerful fleet of cruisers and destroyers. However, the massive firepower of the battlewagons had little impact on the almost impregnable Japanese bunkers and the 10,000 Marines of the V Marine Amphibious Corps were exposed to a still fully functioning enemy defense network.

The American assault commander, Major General Holland "Howlin' Mad" Smith, had been particularly concerned with the combination of irregular tides and an extensive, shallow coral reef which would play havoc with American landing craft. Part of this problem was supposed to be addressed by the use

A U.S. Marine receives medical treatment on the beach at Tarawa in December 1943. Most of the medical personnel attached to the Marines were in fact members of the U.S. Navy.

I was stationed at an evacuation hospital in New Guinea. On the moonlit night of April 23, 1943, a sudden roaring over our wood frame building where I live drew me outdoors.

The sky was filled with white aircraft bearing the Japanese insignia. Bombs began dropping like rain. The airstrip about five miles away was their target.

My heart pounded as I was overwhelmed with a feeling of helplessness being confined to the ground with no place to hide. We were sitting ducks!

I immediately thought of the numerous patients in the hospital tents on the hill. I ran in that direction, intending to reassure them, only to discover that they, too, were watching the attack and worrying about the nursing staff.

Thereafter, every full moon brought a subsequent attack.

— PHYLLIS T. GALEAZ, WAC STATIONED ON NEW GUINEA

of 125 newly developed "Amtracs," which were amphibious tracked vehicles that could ferry troops and supplies across water and land alike. But as the strange looking new vehicles pushed through the reef, hidden Japanese batteries began a devastating barrage which knocked out two dozen Amtracs in a few minutes and ultimately destroyed 90 of them. Thus hundreds of Marines were soon wading through the lagoon to distant beaches with Japanese machine guns cutting a huge scythe through them. The camouflage-suited sea soldiers were pushing through a half-mile stretch of waist-deep water in a sort of water-logged version of Pickett's charge that was soon running up enormous casualty lists while the advancing troops couldn't even fire back at their tormentors.

By nightfall, about 5,000 Marines had been landed, but at least 1,500 of them were dead or wounded and even an impressive array of strafing attacks had failed to significantly reduce the enemy defenses. The next morning, 2nd Division commander General Julian Smith began releasing large numbers of infantry reserves and artillery batteries but the Japanese commander had concealed dozens of snipers and machine gunners in an innocuous-looking, rusting hulk sitting in the lagoon and these defenders opened up a devastating fire. Marines were forced to engage in a bloody deck-by-deck shootout on the vessel while the remainder of the reserve force staggered onto the beaches. All day on November 21 the surviving Marines poured cans of gasoline down the vents of Japanese bunkers and used flamethrowers to immolate defenders of pillboxes. Using these techniques, the attackers were able to split the Japanese defenders into ever smaller pockets while a steady stream of American reinforcements lengthened the odds against Shibasaki's men. Finally, on the morning of November 22, the third day of the battle, the surviving defenders sent a defiant radio message to their homeland and launched a suicidal charge that ultimately left only 146 men

A U.S. Marine armed with a carbine brings forward a belt of machine gun ammunition during the fighting on Tarawa in December 1943. He has reversed his helmet for increased visibility in close-quarters fighting.

alive. Tarawa was now in American hands, but a small piece of coral in the middle of the Pacific had cost the lives of 1,000 Marines with 2,000 more seriously wounded.

By the end of 1943, the United States had in many respects avenged the humiliation of Pearl Harbor and Bataan and had established itself in Roosevelt's phrase as "The Arsenal of Democracy." However, both Japan and Germany still controlled most of the territories they had conquered early in the conflict and the roads to Tokyo and Berlin would contain some of the most desperate battles in the history of the American republic.

Men of the 28th Regiment, 5th Marine Division celebrate after raising the American flag on Iwo Jima. They all have the M-1 rifle and the more efficient short bayonet.

CHAPTER VII

The Great Crusade

*B*y January of 1944, the United States had been fighting the Axis powers for two years and had inflicted a number of substantial, though not necessarily decisive, defeats on the armies and fleets of Germany and Japan. The mobilization of America for war was now in high gear, and the United States could now field an impressive armed force of 11.3 million men while over 200,000 women had also joined the colors. However, the nation was also faced with the unenviable prospect of fighting two separate wars on opposite sides of the world while also supplying enough skilled workers to keep the enormous array of war factories operating 24 hours a day. American forces were now everywhere on the offensive, but according to traditional military theory, the attackers were expected to outnumber the defenders at least 3 to 1 to have any reasonable chance of success. Yet the requirements of war production, air operations, and naval operations had forced the nation to engage two powerful enemies with the relatively modest total of about 95 army and Marine divisions, a situation that meant that American ground troops would frequently be entering battle actually outnumbered by enemy defenders. Only superior productivity and technology could compensate for this critical shortage of men on the front lines of battle.

As both Axis and Allied military and political leaders studied their maps and charts in the early months of 1944, each side discovered both opportunities and challenges. For the Allies, 1943 had been a year of substantial progress as victories at

U.S. troops land in Normandy on June 7, 1944, probably at Utah beach. The Germans have been driven from the vicinity and the troops are no longer directly under fire as they land.

Guadalcanal, Tunisia, Sicily, Stalingrad, and Kursk had clearly put the Axis on the defensive. However, German forces still held excellent defensive positions in central Italy, a large Nazi army had been deployed in France, and the Japanese still held their most important conquests. Thus it readily became apparent to both sides that 1944 would most likely be the climactic year of the war.

The most dramatic event of this dramatic year was Operation Overlord, the Allied invasion of Normandy. However, the assault on France could not begin until the attackers controlled the skies, and at the beginning of the year this accomplishment seemed to be a distant event. Two significant developments completely turned the balance of power before the onset of summer. First, the army air force finally received a fighter plane that could escort the bombers to Germany and keep the Luftwaffe interceptors at bay. The P-51 Mustang, a beautifully designed, powerfully armed fighter, was fitted with auxiliary fuel tanks that dramatically extended the range of this lethal, silver aircraft. Now the German fighter pilots, the "Jaegers," had to get through the incredibly fast Mustangs before they could intercept the bomber

> *If you look up in the sky and see a plane, it will be one of ours.*
>
> — ALLIED COMMANDER DWIGHT EISENHOWER TO HIS GROUND UNITS ABOUT TO INVADE EUROPE ON D-DAY.

stream, and hundreds of these Luftwaffe planes crashed and burned before they ever got the chance. In turn the arrival of the Mustangs released hundreds of much heavier, slower Thunderbolts from escort duties to turn to a ground attack role. Now P-47s, armed with multiple heavy machine guns, bombs, and air-to-ground rockets, roamed France shooting up German troop trains, ammunition convoys, and airfields, totally disrupting much of General Erwin Rommel's defense plan. Thus by the eve of the D-day landings, Allied commander Dwight Eisenhower could tell his ground units, "If you look up in the sky and see a plane, it will be one of ours."

On the overcast morning of June 6, 1944, the greatest armada in history, 5,000 ships ranging from small landing ships to enormous battleships, made the final stage of the Channel crossing from England to France. Flying overhead were the lead elements of 12,000 Allied airplanes that would be put into the skies over the invasion beaches. However, the ultimate decision of whether this "Longest Day" of the war ultimately became an Allied or German victory belonged to the 150,000 Allied soldiers who nervously clambered into bobbing, pitching, landing craft and headed toward Juno, Gold, Sword, Utah, and Omaha beaches. The majority of these men had never been in combat, and on this gray Tuesday morning they were about to face German defenders including significant numbers

U.S. troops move inland from Utah Beach. By a fortunate accident, troops had landed on the wrong Beach, which was much less heavily defended.

who had fought in Russia, North Africa, and on other battle-fields. As the American invasion forces approached their two assigned beaches, Utah and Omaha, two very different battles erupted. The 4th Division's landing at Utah Beach started off on a sour note when it landed south of the designated site. However, American paratroopers dropped during the night had succeeded in blocking major German reinforcements, and the assault force was able to land several platoons of amphibious Sherman tanks which provided the firepower to blast the Germans from their defensive positions. By nightfall, at a cost of fewer than 200 men, Americans were flooding across Utah Beach and pushing onto causeways leading to the Contentin peninsula.

Omaha, on the other hand, was a different matter. The men of the 1st and 29th Divisions entered a sandy killing field. First, through an incredible blunder, the 32 amphibious tanks assigned to Omaha were placed in the water three miles out from the beach and almost all of them sank like rocks taking

I took a head count and there were only eleven of us left, from the thirty on the craft.

— A SERGEANT RECOUNTING THE D-DAY LANDING.

their startled crews with them. Most of the landing craft carrying supporting artillery also capsized in the rough seas, while 10 infantry landing craft also foundered, killing 300 assault troops before the beach was even in sight. As soon as the jaws of the landing craft opened, German machine gunners occupying a ridge line above the beach poured thousands of bullets into the emerging Americans and shots penetrated far enough to hit even men who had ducked into the water to avoid the hailstorm of lead. One sergeant recounted the terror of hitting the beach at Omaha: "We yelled to the crew to take us in, we would rather fight than drown. As the ramp dropped we were hit by machine gun and rifle fire. I yelled to get ready to swim and fight. We were getting direct fire right into our craft. My three squad leaders in front and others were hit. Some men climbed over the side. Two sailors got hit. I crawled to hide behind a steel beach obstacle. Bullets hit off it, others hit more of my men. I took a head count and there were only eleven of us left, from the thirty on the craft."

When the 29th Division's assistant commander, Brigadier General Norman Cota, arrived on the beach he found a chaotic

U.S. troops land in Normandy on June 12. Although not in danger from enemy fire, they prudently wear inflatable life preservers around their waists.

situation with Americans bunched together and offering the defenders a perfect target. Cota quickly realized that if the men stayed where they were they would be annihilated; only by getting over a nearby seawall would the Americans have a chance of survival. One admiring lieutenant noted, "Exposing himself to enemy fire, General Cota went over the seawall giving encouragement, directions and orders to those around him. Finding a belt of barbed wire inside the seawall, General Cota personally supervised placing a bangalore torpedo for blowing the wire and was one of the first three men to go through the wire." At a cost of almost 3,000 casualties, the assault force on Omaha Beach finally got a foothold on French soil and by nightfall on this climactic Tuesday, Hitler's Atlantic Wall had been breached.

> *We yelled to the crew to take us in, we would rather fight than drown. As the ramp dropped we were hit by machine gun and rifle fire. I yelled to get ready to swim and fight.*
>
> — A SERGEANT ON THE LANDING AT OMAHA BEACH ON D-DAY.

★ ★ ★

While one enormous Allied invasion was penetrating the defenses of Hitler's "Fortress Europe" an equally impassive American armada was about to smash into the inner ring of the Japanese Empire. Admiral Chester Nimitz had organized Operation Forager, the invasion of the Mariana Islands, to pro-

———— ★ ★ ★ ————

I'd like to tell you something about the Beach at Grandville, if I knew the right words. As you lie on top of the cliff looking down over miles of white sand and water almost as blue as Bermuda and the sun warm and clear. To go swimming in that water and to lie in that sand were experiences long to be meminisced. You forget, at a time like that, that the water is probably mined in places, that there are still Germans on that pretty little island that lies about six miles off shore, that along the road where you walked down to the beach a man was blown to death a few short days ago.

Then there is another sensation which comes later as you prowl through a deserted German dugout where the Nazis sat and waited for D-Day to come. That is the sensation of fear. The piles of ammunition which have been collected—all of it deadly stuff that I want no part of. And I say prayers when Hallowell and Antonelli throw hand grenades that they all may be duds. The good Lord heard my prayers and they were duds. The German trenches which they had fortified against the invasion. The coops in which they kept their police dogs to be used in coastal defense, like those I saw on peaceful Nantucket this time last year. The rounds and rounds of shell fire stored away, but also with that not-yet-de-booby-trapped look and I didn't want to linger one little bit.

And I shall try to tell you what I thought about as we rode along the dusty roads of France that sunny Sunday morning. The French people in their well-worn clothes on their way to church. The church in one town we went through which had been just about cut in half and still the steeple stood. The cathedral at Coustances—or is it a cathedral? And why don't I know more about the places I am seeing? And you realized the eternal wrongness of war. God made the countryside green and beautiful and even when men insist on tearing it up with shells and bombs and flak, God goes right to work on healing the wounds; and the grass and the flowers grow there and the trees spread their boughs to cover the open places.

— ANNE McCAUGHEY, A U.S. ARMY RED CROSS AIDE ON UTAH BEACH AUGUST 15, 1944

———— ★ ★ ★ ————

vide both advanced naval bases for the next leap toward Japan and airfields for the new B-29 "Superfortress" bombers to attack the Japanese mainland. The seriousness of this threat was readily apparent to Japanese premier General Hideki Tojo, who quickly began diverting significant army and navy units to the commander of Saipan, Lieutenant General Yashitsugu Saito. However, Saito's initial garrison of 21,000 men could be only modestly reinforced as American air and submarine attacks smashed most of the transport ships attempting to supplement the defenders' numbers, with over 8,000 men killed and thousands of others forced to return to more secure bases.

At dawn on June 16, 1944, ten days after the invasion of Normandy, the first units of a 130,000-man force of American Marines and soldiers climbed into over 700 landing craft and began closing in on Saipan Island. They were supported not only by a vast array of battleships, cruisers, and destroyers, but also by the most powerful concentration of aircraft carriers and planes ever seen, 15 carriers deploying 1,000 planes were present to discourage any Japanese interference with the invasion, and, hopefully, get a crack at the combined Japanese fleet which had not been fully deployed since Midway two years earlier.

Combat units from the 2nd and 4th Marine Divisions braved Saito's expertly deployed cannons, mortars, and machine guns, while 160 American dive-bombers and fighters swept over the beach areas bombing and strafing any defenders that dared to expose themselves. While Saito threw away far too many infantry units in poorly coordinated counterattacks, his gunners deftly shifted from position to position and inflicted heavy casualties on the attackers as over 2,000 Americans were killed or wounded by the end of the first day.

The furious land engagement quickly set the stage for a monumental naval confrontation as Admiral Jisaburo Ozawa, commander of the Japanese Mobile Fleet, sallied forth to contest the American landings. Ozawa's fleet was still a powerful force to be reckoned with as it included 9 carriers, 5 battleships, 13 cruisers, and 28 destroyers, but Admiral Raymond Spruance's Saipan covering force not only boasted 15 carriers but also 7 brand-new battleships, 21 cruisers, and 69 destroyers, a fleet that dwarfed the vessels available at Midway.

Ozawa was able to locate Spruance's fleet before the Americans could locate him, and in four attack waves launched during the morning and early afternoon of June 19, 373 planes were thrown at the American fleet with the primary target being the 15 carriers. American fighters and antiaircraft guns simply massacred the oncoming Japanese planes, and by sunset almost 310 of the attackers had been shot down with many of the remaining aircraft too badly damaged to fly again. While American gunners called this aspect of the battle of the Philippine Sea "the Great Marianas Turkey Shoot," American submarine crews were having an equally profitable time. The undersea boats fired deadly torpedo spreads at Ozawa's flagship, the carrier *Shokaku*, and another carrier, *Taiko*, and both flattops were sent to the bottom of the Pacific. Then, American carrier scouts finally sighted the Japanese fleet and dozens of dive-bombers and torpedo planes peeled off to get a hit. When

Admiral Raymond Spruance made able use of carriers and naval aircraft during the Pacific campaigns. He effectively destroyed the Japanese carrier capacity at the battle of the Philippine Sea.

As the war drew closer to the Japanese home islands, attacks by kamikaze pilots increased. This wounded U.S. pilot has been forced to land on an American carrier set aflame by a kamikaze. Both the pilot and the carrier were saved.

the air attack was over, the carrier *Hiyo* was sunk, the *Zuihaku* and the *Chiyoda* badly damaged, the battleship *Haruna* crippled, and two supporting vessels sunk. The only negative side to the American attack was that the assault was launched at extremely long range and it would be difficult for the victorious planes to return to their carriers. The night of the attack, every American ship was lit up like a Christmas tree to guide the pilots home, and search and rescue missions operating without letup found most of the air crew who had been forced to ditch. During this incredibly one-sided naval battle, only 20 American planes were lost in actual combat while Japanese losses passed the 400 mark. However, on Saipan itself, the casualty rate was far less advantageous to the American attackers.

As the battle of the Philippine Sea reached its climax, two Marine divisions and the army's 27th Division were engaged in a deadly sweep through the northern end of Saipan which was soon nicknamed "Death Valley." While the foot soldiers pushed ahead through withering fire, and Marine and army generals feuded over proper battle tactics, 3,000 defenders found a gap in the American lines and launched one of the largest banzai attacks of the war, decimating two army battalions and pushing down the west coast of the island until they were pulverized by artillery fire. This failed assault soon drove General Saito to commit suicide, but the death of the field commander did not end the bloodletting as thousands of Japanese civilians residing on the island threw themselves from cliffs into the sea below rather than surrender to the advancing Americans. By the time this carnival of death was over, 3,000 Americans, 24,000 Japanese troops, and 8,000 Japanese civilians were dead, and 13,000 additional Marines and soldiers were wounded. Even as the final stage of the battle was raging, engineers were preparing Saipan's airfields for the B-29s to rain fiery havoc on Japan.

The whole theory of mobility that we had been taught, of our racing across the battlefield, seemed to have gone up in smoke.

— AMERICAN CORPORAL IN NORMANDY 1944.

★ ★ ★

While one American army pushed grimly through the swamps and caves of the Marianas, another force of Yanks was confronting the equally nightmarish topography of Normandy. The region of France chosen for the Allied invasion had confused the Germans sufficiently to tie up many of their best units waiting for a landing in Calais, but the bocage country of Normandy was a difficult spot to begin the liberation of Europe. The local farmers had spent centuries developing a series of giant hedgerows to contain their livestock, and now these maze-like hedges were crawling with German soldiers who were capable of bringing the entire Allied advance to a

The key French town of St. Lô was all but destroyed during the Normandy fighting. Allied units were equipped with armored bulldozers to clear rubble-clogged streets.

halt with slender forces of their own. Soldiers dressed in field gray would pre-sight machine guns and cannons and then pulverize any American unit that tried to maneuver its way through the hedged-in fields. As the long summer days were spent inching forward from one German strong point to another, one American corporal noted in exasperation, "we were stuck, something dreadful seemed to have happened in terms of the overall plan. The whole theory of mobility that we had been taught, of our racing across the battlefield, seemed to have gone up in smoke." However, the same entrepreneurial spirit and ability to improvise that had made the United States such an awesome industrial power now emerged on the battlefield. American corporals, sergeants, and lieutenants tinkered and experimented and produced tanks with huge metal tusks, new forms of bangalore torpedoes, and other weapons specially designed to rip or blast through the hedges. Finally, with a sense of relief that must have matched that of the Army of the Potomac as it cleared through the Wilderness of Virginia, the American First Army pushed its way into the clear and prepared to engage the Germans in the rolling countryside that led towards Paris.

In mid-July of 1944, General Omar Bradley, who was now the

American soldiers in a victory parade through Paris on August 26, 1944. The war was going well but each soldier had a gas mask slung on his left hip in case the retreating Germans should turn to acts of desperation.

American ground commander serving under Eisenhower's overall authority for the invasion, developed a plan code-named Cobra which was designed to use the massive American superiority in airpower to its fullest extent. Bradley's plan was to use a massive saturation bombing of the German-held side of the St. Lo-Perriers road to knock the enemy senseless, and then, when the dust settled, use infantry divisions to hold open the shoulders of the gap while American armored units penetrated far into the Nazi rear. On July 25, a vast armada of fighter-bombers, medium bombers, and heavy bombers began one of the heaviest tactical air strikes of World War II. Unfortunately, poor visibility and a mix-up of orders resulted in many of the planes hitting friendly units. Over 600 Americans, including Lieutenant General Leslie McNair, were killed in the attacks, but much of the deadly German armor was also made rubble and Bradley's forces were now well on their way to Paris.

During most of the remainder of the summer of 1944 the most mobile army the world had ever seen to this point was finally able to operate almost exactly the way it had been trained. Vast numbers of Mustangs and Thunderbolts roamed the skies, pouncing on German infantry, trucks, tanks, and trains. One of their victims was Erwin Rommel, the Desert Fox, who was badly wounded in a British strafing attack. American Sherman tanks were no match for German Tigers or Panthers on a one-to-one duel, but the Yankee tank destroy-

Our platoon bivouacked in an apple orchard and I tried to pitch a pup tent in an ice-encrusting sleet storm but was thwarted by the mud, the wind and the cold. When I awakened in the morning, I found the tent blown down on top of me. But it mattered little—I was by then too exhausted to care much about anything, much less a tattered GI pup tent whose pegs wouldn't hold firm in the soft Dutch earth.

The date was November 11, 1944—Armistice Day back home—and the first snow of winter was falling heavily.

After a few days, the rest of the Army caught up to us and we received mess-kit hot chow again.

In the field, when finished eating, soldiers dumped unfinished portions of food into a swill barrel and then sloshed mess kits in a barrel of soapy hot water.

While dumping my uneaten food into the barrel the first day, I was overrun by several undernourished Dutch children from nearby Heerlen who darted up to the garbage bucket and frantically scraped handfuls of garbage up and gorged them down. Then they scraped the sides of the pail with small spoons trying to get every last remaining scrap of food. As fast as they had appeared, they were gone again, bolting away through the apple trees. The sight was pathetic.

During the ensuing days, the platoon began beckoning to those urchins whenever they reappeared and offering them mess kits full of hot food. As long as we were in the orchard, we were determined not to let these babies scrape garbage barrels again to stay alive, at least not in front of us.

From the company field kitchen, I "liberated" sugar, flour, butter and coffee and, with my weekly ration of cigarettes swapped for candy bars, was able to supply my newly adopted children with items they had not seen during the five-year German occupation.

— PRIVATE ROSCOE C. BLUNT JR.

★ ★ ★

★ ★

The Four Chaplains of the Dorsetshire

In one of the most dramatic moments of World War II, four men of God, of different faiths but one cause—all chaplains on the army transport *Dorsetshire*—helped save hundreds of men when the ship was torpedoed in the Davis Strait. They distributed life jackets and helped men over the side, frequently having to coax and encourage the fainthearted. Toward the end, each gave his own lifejacket to a frightened young soldier. Then, as the ship went down, they were seen standing side-by-side in prayer. Their story once was known to all Americans.

It happened about 1 A.M. on Wednesday, February 3, 1943, when the Europe-bound ship carrying 902 men was torpedoed, just 20 miles off Greenland. Struck amidship, slightly aft on her starboard side, the ship began going down fast, and there was no chance it could be saved. "Abandon Ship!" was ordered.

Panic developed, for many of the troops aboard had disobeyed instructions to sleep in their life jackets. In the midst of the chaos and fear, the four chaplains stood out as pillars of strength. The ship went down only 25 minutes after the torpedo had hit. Only 230 of the men aboard *Dorsetshire* survived, the ship taking hundreds down with her, and others perishing in the icy cold waters. No one knows how many of those who survived did so because of the heroism and self-sacrifice of the "four chaplains":

George Fox, a native of Pennsylvania, was born in 1900 and lied about his age in 1917 to enlist in the army. He served in the Ambulance Corps at St. Mihiel and in the Meuse-Argonne, where he was wounded, leaving him partially disabled. After the war he attended the seminary, became an itinerant Methodist minister, married, and eventually settled down as minister to a small church in Vermont. Shortly after Pearl Harbor, his son joined the Marine Corps, later seeing combat in the Pacific, and Fox decided to become a military chaplain.

Alexander Goode was born in 1911 in Brooklyn, but his family later moved to Washington, D.C., before settling in York, Pennsylvania. The young man was active in his synagogue and in B'nai B'rith. In the mid-1930s, he married and had several children, became a rabbi, and pursued an academic career. He joined the army as a chaplain in early 1942.

Clark V. Poling, born in 1910, was a native of Ohio, the son of a prominent Reform clergyman and publisher of a widely circulated religious magazine. The younger Poling naturally gravitated to the ministry, attending Yale Divinity School. He served in several churches during the 1930s, married, and on the outbreak of World War II was minister of a church in upstate New York. He joined the Chaplains' Corps shortly after Pearl Harbor.

John P. Washington was born in 1908 to a working-class Irish-American family in a tough section of Newark, New Jersey. An outstanding athlete, after college he entered the seminary, and was ordained a priest in the Roman Catholic Church in 1935. He worked in various parishes, and joined the army as a chaplain in early 1942.

The heroic sacrifice of the four chaplains greatly moved the American people, who took it as symbolic of the very meaning of America and as an outstanding example of interfaith cooperation. It was proposed that they each be awarded the Medal of Honor, but under prevailing army regulations the medal could only be awarded for deeds committed in direct combat with the enemy (a situation which has since changed). They were each awarded the Distinguished Service Cross and after the war an interfaith chapel was dedicated to their memory.

★ ★

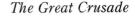

*An American soldier stand-
ing amid the rubble of
bombed out buildings, cap-
tures a surrending German
soldier. One of many such
scenes in the autumn of
1944.*

ers were expected to confront the Panzers while the seemingly
limitless number of Shermans went for the vulnerable Nazi
infantry and transport units. Soon the rapidly advancing
American First Army was joined by General George Patton's
newly authorized Third Army, and the two armies of GIs raced
in concert with Montgomery's Tommies to liberate Paris and
then close in on Hitler's main defenses on the German border.
At a cost of 210,000 Anglo-American casualties, including
40,000 men killed, the Allied campaign for France had resulted
in the loss to the German Reich of 450,000 men, 20,000 trucks,
3,500 cannons, and 1,500 tanks. However, the final push into
the German heartland would be far more lengthy and brutal
than anyone could have conceived in the golden, early autumn
days of September 1944.

The German army in France had been smashed, but Hitler's
forces still held excellent defensive positions along the borders of the Reich itself. Also, as the Allied army in Europe
grew to ever larger levels, and advanced deeper into the
Continent, the supply system became an ongoing nightmare.
Most importantly, there simply wasn't enough fuel being
unloaded from the captured ports to enable the huge number
of Allied vehicles to keep moving forward indefinitely. The
result of these complicating factors was an enormous letdown
to Allied hopes to end the war before the end of 1944. A number of stunning disappointments occurred in rapid succession.

A Stuart light tank from an armored headquarters unit covers captured German paratroopers at Bastogne as more heavily armed Shermans continue the advance. The extreme youth of most of the Germans is very evident in the original photograph.

First, Bernard Montgomery's essentially solid plan to secure a bridgehead over the Rhine River through a daring combined armor-airborne offensive in Holland collapsed through a combination of poor timing and worse luck. Operation Market-Garden was based on pinpoint coordination between British and American tank units and paratroopers. However, while paratroopers from the American 82nd and 101st Airborne Divisions were able to seize a number of key bridges leading to the crucial span over the Rhine in the town of Arnhem, their British counterparts essentially parachuted into the middle of a powerful German tank force from which British armored units were unable to extricate them. Adding insult to injury, much of the fuel used for this ill-fated offensive had been siphoned from supplies designated for George Patton's Third Army drive to the south, and as vital gasoline shipments slowed to a trickle, the American tankers were virtually halted in place just short of the main German defenses. Finally, a third eastward drive between Montgomery and Patton's advance smashed into the gloomy Hurtgen Forest, in which American tank and air superiority were rendered virtually useless and GIs and Germans fought a gruesome ground battle that was little different from Civil War battles such as Chancellorsville and the Wilderness. As Christmas of 1944 approached, it became increasingly obvious that the war against Hitler would extend well into the next year and, perhaps, even further.

A wounded soldier is treated on Okinawa. U.S. Army units were used in the more extensive land operations required to subdue New Guinea, the Philippines, and Okinawa.

★ ★ ★

While Americans on the home front sensed a frustrating stalemate developing through newspaper accounts of the war in Europe in the fall of 1944, headlines from the Pacific theater were far more spectacular during this season. The highlight of the war against Japan during late 1944 was a titanic clash between the Imperial and American fleets which ultimately decided the outcome of the naval war in the Pacific.

The mammoth confrontation that would go down in history as the battle of Leyte Gulf was set in motion as General Douglas MacArthur prepared to return to the Philippines that he had been forced to leave in the spring of 1942. As the American general had prepared to leave Corregidor, he promised the Filipino people they would not be left indefinitely under Japanese occupation and proclaimed, "I shall return!" Now the controversial general was about to redeem that promise as 160,000 American soldiers, covered by the most powerful fleet in the history of naval warfare, closed in on the island of Leyte in the first step in the liberation of the Philippines. The Japanese naval high command knew the Americans were coming and the admirals had devised the daring SHO-GO plan to throw every last element of Imperial naval power into a

Admiral William Halsey commanded the Third Fleet for much of the Pacific War. Visible here are his naval pilot's wings, which he had gained in 1935 at age 52. Halsey's aviation experience helped make him an effective commander as the sea war became dominated by aircraft carriers.

Fulfilling a vow made early in the war, General Douglas MacArthur returns to the Philippines, landing on Leyte, October 20, 1944.

I shall return.

— GENERAL DOUGLAS MACARTHUR ON LEAVING THE PHILIPPINES UNDER JAPANESE CONTROL IN 1942.

showdown with the Pacific fleet. Japanese strategy developed by Admiral Ozawa planned to use Japan's seven remaining aircraft carriers as bait to lure Admiral William Halsey's powerful covering force away from the Leyte invasion beaches. Then two Imperial surface fleets would slip through Surigao Strait and San Bernadino Strait and fall upon the lightly defended American transports with the fury of some of the world's most powerful warships. Once MacArthur's supplies were cut off, the Japanese army defending the Philippines would launch a huge offensive designed to drive the invaders into the sea.

The battle of Leyte Gulf opened on October 23, 1944, when American submarines spotted the advanced elements of the Japanese fleet approaching the Philippines. A combination of torpedo attacks and air strikes from some of the impressive American carrier force that now deployed 17 major flattops demolished the 73,000-ton battleship *Musashi*, one of the two largest battleships in the world, and also annihilated a number of Japanese cruisers. However the carrier USS *Princeton* was sunk by Imperial land-based aircraft in this exchange and Admiral Kurita's strike force was able to pull out of range to prepare for a renewed approach to Leyte the next day. The next day Admiral Jesse Oldendorf's powerful surface force of six battleships, eight cruisers, and twenty-eight destroyers collided with another wing of the Japanese attack fleet, Admiral Nishimura's two battleships, one cruiser, and four destroyers. In the last World War II engagement settled by heavy guns alone, Oldendorfs ships performed the classic "crossing the T" maneuver dreamed about by admirals for centuries and threw the combined weight of all their broadsides against the badly outgunned Japanese. In 15 minutes, with virtually no loss to the Americans, the Imperial squadron was annihilated with only one damaged destroyer limping away.

At this point in the battle the American fleet was on the verge of a huge one-sided victory, but now Ozawa's plan began to pay dividends as Admiral Halsey took the bait and sailed full-steam ahead after the Japanese carriers to the north. The American fleet commander could deploy almost 800 warplanes to attack an Imperial force that could barely put up 100 of its own aircraft, and in a running battle all day on October 25 three Japanese carriers were sent to the bottom of the Pacific. However, most of the heavy units screening the American transports unloading at Leyte had now been drawn away, and the most powerful element of the Japanese surface fleet was almost within sight of its highly vulnerable target. Four battleships, including the super-battleship *Yamato*, nine cruisers, and fifteen destroyers were approaching an American support fleet that was now protected only by a collection of destroyers and tiny escort carriers, which were actually converted merchant ships with virtually no weapons or protection beyond their small detachment of planes. In one of the most one-sided engagements in naval warfare the "baby flattops" and the destroyers mounting 5-inch guns went head-to-head with the enormous 18-inch broadsides of the Japanese batttlewagons. Destroyers made suicidal torpedo attacks on the *Yamato* while the planes from the escort carriers kept diving on the Imperial ships even when ammunition and bombs were gone. As the destroyer *Johnston* dodged the 3,500-pound shells fired by the Japanese battleship, the vessel was surrounded by a whole squadron of enemy destroyers that simply pulverized the ship in a ring of fire. Even the Japanese officers were impressed by the *Johnston's* heroic last stand and they stood at attention and saluted the enemy warship as it dipped below the waves with most of the crew.

The lightly armed American screening vessels were taking a

U.S. paratroopers drop from C-47 transports over Southern France. The Anvil-Dragoon landings made the German situation in France even more desperate.

terrible pounding from the much heavier Imperial ships, but their unrelenting attacks convinced Admiral Kurita that he was being led into an ambush of much larger American ships just over the horizon. Thus, after sinking two destroyers and two escort carriers, Kurita issued a withdrawal order and the Japanese fleet turned back just before closing in on the vulnerable transports. The battle of Leyte Gulf was now effectively over and more than 10,000 Japanese and 1,500 American sailors were dead or dying. At a cost of one carrier, two escort carriers, three destroyers, and three submarines, the United States Navy deprived the Imperial fleet of four carriers, three battleships, ten cruisers, eleven destroyers, four submarines, and almost the entire remaining complement of carrier aircraft. Japan's fate now rested on its remaining army divisions and a new breed of suicide pilots called "the men of the divine wind," the kamikazes.

★ ★ ★

The same spirit of a final roll of the dice that pervaded the conference rooms of the Japanese high command in the autumn of 1944 was evident in the gloomy confines of Hitler's Wolf's Lair headquarters. As the multiple Allied offensive ground to a halt, the German dictator began developing a daring plan to launch a massive counteroffensive exactly where and when the Allies least expected it. Hitler decided to concentrate every spare plane, tank, and man he could find for a massive thrust through the Ardennes Forest aimed at the Meuse River and eventually, the key port of Antwerp. If this drive was successful the British army would be cut off from the American army and the two Allied armies could be annihilated individually.

As darkness fell on the Ardennes Forest on December 15, 1944, 30 divisions of German infantry and tanks deployed to drive against a region held by only four American divisions, two of them bled white from earlier fighting and two others just in from the United States.

The next morning I left the hospital and with a convoy of soldiers who could not be broken in spirit, started back to the division.

— MEMOIRS OF A PRIVATE STATIONED IN FRANCE IN DECEMBER OF 1944.

The Ardennes area was viewed as the safest spot in the line and few Americans had any inkling of what was massing a short distance away. At 5:30 the next morning German officers all along the misty, snowcovered line blew whistles and thousands of soldiers in camouflage white parkas moved westward. The American 28th Infantry Division was strung out along the River Our and entire companies were virtually annihilated as 2,000 German guns smashed into their lines. In the Eiffel region of the forest, two entire regiments of the 106th Infantry Division were outflanked and surrounded, and their capitula-tion represented the single, largest haul of American prisoners by the Germans in the whole war. Meanwhile, German Colonel Otto Skorzeny was directing a daring infiltration operation in which hundreds of English-speak-ing soldiers outfitted in GI battle gear swarmed through the rear lines, cutting telephone lines, changing direction signs, and generally sowing panic as no American soldier was now quite sure who was a friend and who was an enemy. By nightfall on this short, wintry day, a huge bulge was developing in the American lines and dozens of American units were outflanked or surrounded. However, the extremely tight German schedule of attack was already begin-ning to unravel.

During May of 1940, a somewhat similar

American generals Omar Bradley, Dwight Eisenhower, and George Patton confer in the ruins of a bombed-out French village. Bradley is dressed strictly regulation, Patton in a flamboyant cav-alry-style uniform, and Eisenhower is in-between.

★ ★

PRESIDENT GERALD R. FORD JR.

Shortly after Pearl Harbor, a young Gerald Ford applied for a commission in the navy. In April 1942, he was commissioned an ensign. After an abbreviated basic training course at Annapolis, he was trained as a physical fitness instructor pending flight training. In 1943, he requested transfer to the Pacific fleet.

Ford served as the *Monterey's* athletic director and as gunnery officer for its 40mm antiaircraft guns. He saw extensive service in operations from the South Pacific to the final missions off Japan, earning 10 battle stars. Ford's most notable service occurred during the great typhoon of December 17 and 18, 1944, which struck as the fleet lay off the Philippines.

Several aircraft in the ship's hangar deck broke loose and began careening across the deck, crashing into each other. This set off a series of fires and small explosions that threatened the safety of the ship. As it heaved and rolled in the storm, Ford plunged into the flames to cut away wreckage so that it could fall into the sea, with some crewmen holding onto him by means of rope around his waist, and while others sprayed a firehose on him, a feat for which he was decorated.

Of the 41 men who have served as president, 29 have seen military service.

★ ★

German offensive against France had ripped through much of the same region and French units simply disintegrated under the blows of combined infantry-tank-airplane assaults. However, the Americans holding these lines four years later were far less willing to concede superiority to the Germans than their Gallic predecessors, and units from divisions down to squads simply hunkered down in the snow and made the Nazis pay dearly for each mile of advance. The extent of this American determination is seen in the memoirs of an infantry private who noted, "On December 17 the hospital staff informed us that if you can walk or crawl, you will have to go back to your division as soon as possible. The next morning I left the hospital and with a convoy of soldiers who could not be broken in spirit, started back to the division." By that evening this soldier was a squad leader fighting doggedly in the snow to stem the German tide.

22 December 1944

To the German Commander:

NUTS!

The American Commander

— LETTER FROM GENERAL ANTHONY McAULIFFE TO THE GERMAN COMMANDER WHO HAD DEMANDED HIS SURRENDER.

One of the most dramatic episodes of the Ardennes campaign occurred in the small crossroads town of Bastogne, Belgium. The defense of the town was entrusted to the 101st Airborne Division which carried no heavy artillery or tanks and yet was surrounded by a steel ring of three German panzer divisions that massively outgunned the paratroopers. However when General Fritz Bayerlein, the German commander of the besieging forces, demanded surrender from American leader General Anthony McAuliffe, the paratroop general sent one of the most famous responses in military history, the single word "Nuts!", which summarized the attitude of the defenders.

Hitler's last gamble began to unravel when clearing weather brought out thousands of Allied planes to hammer away at German tanks and infantry. Meanwhile, George Patton, who had been advancing with his Third Army in a totally different direction, managed the incredible feat of breaking off one major battle with the Germans on his front, switching the army to a whole new axis of advance, and pushing through snow and ice covered roads under enemy fire to smash the Nazi flank near Bastogne. While Patton's tanks were pushing through the

An American gunner hangs out of a B-29 bomber 25,000 feet over Tokyo after an attack by a Japanese fighter in January 1945. He was rescued after 15 harrowing minutes.

frozen countryside, at 3 A.M. on Christmas morning the Germans tried one last massive offensive against McAuliffe's paratroopers. The airborne troopers used the last of their meager antitank weapons, and the bravery of a small reinforcing column of Sherman tanks, to smash wave after wave of white-clad infantrymen and the accompanying panzers. Later, a combination of American air power and Patton's well-timed arrival pulverized an already staggering German offensive.

Before Hitler's Ardennes offensive, General Eisenhower's greatest concern was the difficulty of rooting out the Germans from the imposing West Wall defenses that the enemy had constructed. Once Eisenhower and his lieutenants recovered from the initial shock of the German offensives, Eisenhower realized that his prayers had been answered; the enemy was now out in the open where the massive Allied superiority in tanks and aircraft could be fully utilized. Within hours after the dazed and bleeding German columns pulled back to their start line, the Americans were lurching forward in a drive that continued to gain momentum all the way to the Rhine River.

The last major barrier between the American army and the German heartland was pierced on March 7, 1945, when a company of soldiers arrived on the west bank of the Rhine and noted to their amazement that the bridge leading to the town of Remagen on the east side of the river was still intact. Within hours of this discovery, American infantry units and tanks were pouring across the Rhine despite the furious efforts by

German heavy artillery and new jet fighter-bombers to halt the procession which would drive the final nail in the coffin of National Socialism. Six weeks later, on April 25, 1945, at the town of Torgau on the Elbe River, elements of the 69th Infantry Division linked up with the vanguard of the Soviet 58th Guards Division and the retreating German armies were now fully encircled. Five days later, Hitler, who had started the "Thousand Year" Third Reich, retreated to his private bunker in Berlin and shot himself as Russian troops were advancing through the rubble of the German capital only a few hundred yards away. A week later, the defeated but still arrogant surviving leaders of the Reich capitulated to Eisenhower and his Soviet counterpart and Japan now stood alone as the target of a monumentally powerful American war machine.

★ ★ ★

While Hitler's Reich unraveled during the spring of 1945, Imperial Japan was also crumbling from the powerful blows of American air, naval, and land power. As American tanks swept through Germany in February and March, 60,000 Marines were fighting a gruesome battle on a slag heap of an island called Iwo Jima. This island, also known as Sulfur Island because of its volcanic activity, was 15 square miles of lava beds and ash populated by 21,000 Japanese soldiers who were determined to fight to the death in order to buy time for their countrymen on the mainland only a few hundred miles away to prepare for the inevitable Yankee onslaught. The Imperial troops were not selling their lives cheaply as one Marine assault battalion lost 850 of its 1,000 men on the first day of the battle and some other units approached this level of casualties a few days later.

As the sea soldiers slogged through the volcanoes, one of the participants in the battle described his surroundings, "it never looked more aesthetically ugly than on D-day morning, or more completely Japanese. It's silhouette was like a sea monster, with the little dead volcano for the head, and the beach area for the neck, and all the rest of it, with its scrubby brown cliffs for the body." The first major objective was the capture of Mount Suribachi, the highest spot on the island, from whose top Japanese observation posts were calling down a deadly fire on the advancing Marines. On February 23, 1945, the 2nd

Battalion of the 28th Marine Regiment launched an almost vertical assault up the volcanic hill and one of the attackers broke out a small American flag; soon afterward, an unknown Marine scrounged a much larger flag from a naval landing vessel and an Associated Press photographer snapped a picture of five mud-splattered men planting the banner on Suribachi, an image that would soon rival "The Spirit of '76" or "Washington Crossing the Delaware" in the pictorial annals of American history. However, the "season of hell" on Iwo Jima was far from over as evidenced by the fact that three of the five men in the photograph would be dead or wounded shortly afterward. As one officer noted, "At Tarawa, Saipan and Tinian I saw Marines killed and wounded in a shocking manner but I saw nothing like the ghastliness that hung over the Iwo beach head. Nothing any of us had ever known could compare with the utter anguish, frustration and constant inner battle to maintain some semblance of sanity." Another participant insisted the violence was on a scale beyond imagination as "whether the dead were Japs or Americans, they had one thing in common; they had died with

> *Nothing any of us had ever known could compare with the utter anguish, frustration and constant inner battle to maintain some semblance of sanity.*
>
> — OFFICER ON IWO JIMA IN FEBRUARY 1945.

5th Marine Division troopers inch their way across Iwo Jima. The island's volcanic ash made digging foxholes and trenches difficult.

the greatest possible violence. Nowhere in the Pacific war had I seen such badly mangled bodies."

The grueling advance from one ridge line to the next ultimately resulted in the deaths of five battalion commanders and severe wounds to 14 other colonels, while casualties among enlisted men were equally severe. Finally the leathernecks stormed the main underground bunker of General Tadamichi Kuribayashi who had just been promoted to full general by Emperor Hirohito. The now almost predictable round of ritual suicides ended the battle as only 216 of the 20,000 defenders surrendered. The casualty list of Marines was actually longer as 6,000 men were killed with an additional 20,000 Americans wounded, a stupendous tally for a small piece of volcanic ash. However, the capture of Iwo Jima provided an ideal emerging airstrip for the giant Superfortresses that were now pummeling Japan, and the invasion set up the even larger Operation Iceberg, the assault on Okinawa, only 325 miles south of the Japanese mainland.

U.S. Marine casualties during the early hours of the Iwo Jima landing. Marines were at the mercy of Japanese gunners on the island's higher elevations.

The invasion of Okinawa on Easter Sunday, 1945, was both a logical successor to the Iwo Jima operation and prelude to the invasion of Japan itself, which was scheduled to begin in the autumn. The 60-mile-long island was a marked departure from the coral atolls and tropical jungles that were the main feature of most of the Pacific war. A wooded and mountainous north gave way to a rolling densely farmed south and was defended by a full Japanese army of over 100,000 men. The island's commander, General Mitsuru Ushijima, had no intention of throwing his men away in useless banzai attacks intended to throw the Americans into the sea; instead, he decided to lure the invaders into a series of bloody ambushes that would gradually sap their strength.

The American expeditionary force under General Simon Bolivar Buckner Jr. was one of the most powerful concentrations of the war. Buckner, the son of a famous Confederate general who confronted Ulysses Grant, commanded both a Marine amphibious corps and an army corps and directed a force of 183,000 land troops backed up by almost 1,500 naval vessels.

Colonel Paul Tibbets Jr. stands next to the B-29 "Enola Gay" which was used to drop the first atomic bomb on August 6, 1945.

After the most intensive pre-invasion bombardment of the war, Buckner's troops splashed ashore to a deathly silence; the defenders were not yet ready to reveal themselves. However, within a short time, a ferocious confrontation developed. While Japanese infantry and artillery fired from densely fortified hills, caves, and even hillside burial vaults, the full force of the kamikaze air attacks was also felt. During one, single appearance of the "divine wind" suicide craft, nine American ships were damaged, two of which sank. That night, the Japanese launched a rare airborne counterattack as their paratroopers tried to recapture Yontan airfield which had just fallen into American hands. However, a Marine antiaircraft unit quickly shifted its guns back and forth from firing at enemy planes to shooting at advancing paratroopers and the assault was routed.

On June 17, the American forces began penetrating the last Japanese position, the defense line along Kunishki ridge. As General Buckner watched the grim assault, an enemy shell hit his observation post and 10 minutes later the American commander was dead. Three nights later, General Uskijima committed hara-kiri in his almost captured bunker and the last ground battle of World War II came to its bloody end. The American fleet had paid a terrible price for the slow progress of the campaign. Thirty- six ships were sunk, 386 more vessels were damaged, and 5,000 sailors died, more than twice as many as were lost at Pearl Harbor. Nearly 7,000 Marines and soldiers also died to secure this springboard to the Japanese mainland, while most of the 100,000 defenders joined them in death.

However, as American generals and admirals began final planning for what was sure to be an even bloodier event, the invasion of southern Japan, a single B-29 Superfortress changed the course of the war when it dropped the first nuclear bomb on Hiroshima. When a second atomic explosion annihilated Nagasaki three days later, the normally aloof but now thoroughly shaken emperor finally began to use the authority of his office to call a halt to the bloodletting. On September 2, 1945, General Douglas MacArthur, accompanied by several American and British generals who had surrendered to the imperial army in the dark days of early 1942, watched the humiliation of Pearl Harbor and Bataan come full circle. On the powerful new battleship *Missouri* the representatives of a decimated Japanese empire signed the surrender which officially ended the bloodiest war in mankind's history. However, even as Americans celebrated in a frenzy of emotion, new tyrants and new hostile ideologies would begin to raise their own challenges to the victors of the Great Crusade.

Weary American soldiers in Vietnam bring in a fallen comrade on an improvised stretcher. Two stretcher-bearers are used instead of four to reduce danger from mines.

CHAPTER VIII

Korea to Kuwait

*T*he aftermath of the American victory in World War II produced a curious blend of affluence and anxiety. American citizens enjoyed access to a wide variety of new homes, cars, television sets, and appliances, and the economy of the United States dominated the globe. However, the militarism and fascism of Japan and Germany were merely replaced by the aggressive totalitarianism of the Soviet Union and China, while the armed forces of 12 million men that had defeated Tojo and Hitler had been reduced to barely a million personnel by the fall of 1948. As the American government mothballed warships and deactivated army divisions, the only fully functional shield against aggression became the nation's vaunted nuclear arsenal and the bombers that could deliver these new weapons. Yet these defenses would soon prove utterly useless to meet the challenge of Communist expansionism which began to sweep Asia.

During the five years following the end of World War II, Soviet sponsorship of Marxist coups in eastern Europe and Stalin's blockade of Berlin encouraged most Americans to believe that the first shooting war against the Communists would begin somewhere on the European continent. Thus there was considerable shock and surprise when Americans turned on their new television sets in June of 1950 and were informed by newscasters that the Cold War had turned into open combat not in Germany but in the little-known nation of Korea. This small, poor country had been a Japanese colony until the end of World War II, and eventually had been divided into a Communist-dominated north led by an erratic young Marxist zealot named Kim Il Sung and a southern non-Communist republic led by veteran nationalist Syngman Rhee. While Rhee had regularly made noises about forcibly reuniting the peninsula by invading the north, his small army of 90,000 men had been armed by the United States with only defensive weapons and had no air power, heavy artillery, or tanks. On the other hand, the Soviet Union had lavishly supplied North Korea's 250,000-man army with tanks, heavy guns, and a small tactical air force. Meanwhile when the Communists seized control of China in 1949 Chairman Mao had sent back to Kim several divisions of battle-hardened Korean nationals who had taken part in the long war against the Chinese nationalist government. Now Kim had the men and weapons to forcibly unite the country under the red banner of Marxism-Leninism and in June of 1950 the egocentric, unstable North Korean dictator unleashed his army on the south.

At dawn on Sunday, June 25, 1950, the "liberation" of South Korea began as long columns of Communist troops spearheaded by powerful Russian T-34 tanks poured across the 38th Parallel and Soviet-built Yak fighter-bombers bombed and strafed the capital of Seoul. As Kim's troops approached the

Douglas MacArthur and staff watch the bombardment prior to the Inchon landing. This difficult operation through a narrow waterway was the boldest stroke of MacArthur's career.

Republic of Korea's capital city, President Harry Truman authorized Far East commander General Douglas MacArthur to deploy the first American ground troops in the conflict. By July 4, a slightly bewildered 400 men from the 24th Infantry Division under the command of 34-year-old Lieutenant Colonel Charles Smith, passed through throngs of flag-waiving civilians near the southern tip of the peninsula and moved several miles north of the town of Osan which appeared to be the next target of Kim's advancing army. Most of the men of Task Force Smith were not confident veterans of the war with Japan or Germany, but 19- or 20-year-olds who had received indifferent training and had spent several months on soft occupation duty in Tokyo. They were not only inexperienced but woefully under equipped for stopping an armored thrust, as the only available antitank weapons were two fairly puny 75mm recoilless rifles, two light mortars, and a few obsolete, lightweight bazookas.

Men ran down the hill like jackrabbits, there was no longer platoon organization, just people running. No one wanted to die.

— AMERICAN TROOPS OF TASK FORCE SMITH IN THE 1ST DAYS OF THE KOREAN WAR, JULY 1950.

The tired, disoriented troops deployed along a ridge that covered a highway and a railroad line about six miles above Osan. Smith confirmed the arrival of a five-gun battery of 105mm howitzers a mile behind him as he peered expectantly up the highway for any sign of approaching Communists. Finally, on the rainy morning of July 5, Smith squinted through the mist and observed a column of 33 tanks preceding an enormous line of trucks carrying thousands of North Korean soldiers toward Osan. The colonel quickly called in fire support from the rear artillery battery and the American howitzers managed to disable two T-34s. However, 31 undamaged tanks lurched forward, bypassed the feeble resistance that Task Force Smith could offer, and swept southward. Meanwhile the Communist infantrymen dismounted from their six-mile-long column of trucks and virtually surrounded the badly outnumbered defenders. At this point, lack of training and discipline became increasingly evident as much of the American defense line simply evaporated. One participant noted, "Men ran down the hill like jackrabbits, there was no longer platoon organization, just people running. No one wanted to die." Wounded men were left to the questionable mercy of the oncoming North Koreans

★ ★

Mitchell Red Cloud Jr.

Mitchell Red Cloud Jr., a Winnebago Indian, was recognized posthumously for bravery with the Medal of Honor, and President Harry S. Truman said he had gone to "take his place among the other great Indian warriors who died bravely on the field of battle." Red Cloud gave his own life to save his company from being overrun, permitting it to evacuate its wounded and establish a new defensive line.

Corporal Red Cloud reached Korea with the 19th Infantry in July 1950 and took part in a heartbreaking series of rear-guard actions as American and Republic of Korea forces fell back before the North Korean onslaught, finally establishing a stable front in early August along the Pusan Perimeter. Then came the American amphibious landing at Inchon on the west coast of Korea, deep behind enemy lines, which broke the back of the North Korean forces.

Within days the 19th Infantry was on the offensive, sweeping westward, then northward. As United Nations forces pursued the enemy across the 38th Parallel, the 24th Infantry Division was on the extreme left of the line, up against the east coast of Korea. Red Cloud was involved in all of this fighting. As a combat veteran, he was of great value to his comrades in E Company, as they learned the arts of war in the hardest school. Then, in November, the Chinese Communists intervened, striking hard and with enormous strength.

On November 5, 1950, Red Cloud's company was holding the line near Chonghyon. Armed with the formidable Browning Automatic Rifle (BAR), Red Cloud was posted on a ridge somewhat in front of company headquarters. Chinese infantry began infiltrating through some underbrush toward the company position. When the enemy had reached within about 100 yards from E Company's lines, Red Cloud spotted them as they began to emerge from the brush.

Raising the alarm, he rose to his feet and standing in full view of the attacking enemy laid down a devastating fire with his BAR, checking the initial Chinese attack. As the Chinese recovered, Red Cloud remained standing and continued to pour on a voluminous fire, in which he was joined by his comrades. Suddenly he was hit and fell unconscious, grievously wounded. Recovering consciousness in a few minutes, he refused evacuation, got to his feet, and wrapping his arm around a tree for support, resumed firing.

Red Cloud fought on in this fashion for about five minutes, as the Chinese, despite losses, approached ever closer. Then, as his buddies fell back, he was overwhelmed by enemy troops, who cut him down where he stood.

★ ★

American soldiers and a South Korean guide move up to the front in Korea in July 1950. The men of this headquarters unit are primarily equipped with carbines.

and in some cases officers outran their men to the rear. By the end of this gloomy day after Independence Day, it was obvious that far more than a token American ground contribution would be needed to prevent the entire Korean peninsula from becoming a "worker's paradise," and even the first significant reinforcements of GIs were not able to immediately stem the red tide of Kim's triumphant soldiers.

By early August 1950, General MacArthur had committed most of the forces under his immediate command, the equivalent of three divisions; and this force, combined with the remnants of the South Korean army and modest units supplied by other United Nations countries, had been able to hold a line on the southern tip of Korea centered on the port of Pusan. Lieutenant General Walton Walker, commander of what was designated as the Eighth Army, deftly shifted his few reserve units from one vulnerable spot to another, plugging gaps in the line, and keeping the North Korean army at bay. Meanwhile, MacArthur had devised a daring counter-thrust, an amphibious landing far to the north at Inchon, the main port for Seoul. Inchon offered about every negative feature that an amphibious planner could dream up—erratic tides, high waves, poor landing facilities, and potentially lethal mudflats were all prominent features. But MacArthur insisted that just as General Wolfe had defeated Montcalm at Quebec because he had attacked from an "impossible" direction, a landing force of Marines could secure Inchon because Kim's generals would never suspect an assault at this point on the coast.

On September 15, 1950, as Kim's legions were pounding away on the Pusan line, United States Marines of a joint Marine-army X Corps clambered over a seawall along Inchon beach and began pushing toward the South Korean capital. Almost simultaneously, reserves that Walton Walker had hoarded for just such an eventuality thrust outward from the Pusan perimeter and smashed into overextended North Korean attackers. In an incredibly short time, the whole Communist army began to unravel as it was squeezed between a gigantic pincers, and while thousands of North Koreans surrendered, others simply melted away into the mountainous countryside. Soon MacArthur, encouraged by Truman and the senior American military leaders, was sweeping past the old 38th Parallel border and marching on Pyongyang, Kim's northern capital. A spectacular, complete military victory now seemed within easy grasp, but as MacArthur's forces pushed into the bleak north country during increasingly ominous cold snaps, the entire balance of power on the peninsula was about to shift dramatically.

Chinese Communist leader Mao Tse-tung had watched the American and United Nations offensive with North Korea with

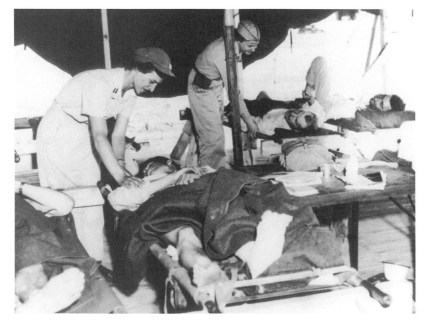

Troops wounded in Korea could be taken to the safety and superior facilities of American hospitals in Japan. These soldiers awaiting evacuation are being tended by officers of the army and air force nursing corps.

Soldiers of the 1st Cavalry Division cross the 38th Parallel and enter North Korea for the first time in October 1950. The war seemed to be going well.

mounting fears that hostile troops might soon be on the Yalu River on the border of the new Marxist Chinese state. Mao quickly committed 300,000 "volunteers" to a counter deployment in Korea, and during early October of 1950 large columns of men with mustard-colored, quilted uniforms streamed south of the Yalu and deployed along the approaches that the X Corps and the Eighth Army would have to take to reach the Chinese border. When Truman and MacArthur met on Wake Island on October 15, both leaders discounted Chinese warnings that they would smash any attempt to penetrate further into North Korea, and the Far East commander was ordered to conclude an advance to the Yalu as soon as possible before the onset of winter severely complicated operations. Ten days after the Wake Island conference, a number of Republic of Korea (ROK) units were ambushed by Chinese forces and a few days later some American regiments noted Chinese troops supporting North Korean units in battle. Then suddenly, all signs of Chinese intervention ended and Allied forces continued to once again push toward the Yalu. In reality, Chinese troops had not pulled back across the Yalu, but had merely deployed in a series of promising ambush positions and MacArthur was now about to fully accommodate them.

While MacArthur's Inchon operation had been a brilliantly conceived campaign, the septuagenarian general had made a major strategic blunder when he had ordered his two main forces, the X Corps and the Eighth Army, to push through North Korea on opposite coasts with a major mountain range preventing mutual support. Now, as the full fury of an early Korean winter set in, Mao's "volunteers" smashed into the two badly outnumbered American columns. Soon after American troops enjoyed an elaborate Thanksgiving dinner in the field, 30 divisions of Chinese troops smashed into the X Corps and the Eighth Army and created as MacArthur insisted, "an entirely new war." General Walker's Eighth Army was suddenly facing more than 180,000 Chinese assault troops on the west coast of the Korean peninsula and these troops worked furiously to set up roadblocks to envelop the Allied forces. However, although Walker was forced to abandon thousands of tons of supplies and equipment, the Eighth Army was able to keep ahead of the Communist pincers and by December 15 American and ROK troops were entrenching in new positions along the 38th Parallel.

The Allied withdrawal from the eastern part of North Korea was far more harrowing. At the time of the Chinese counter-offensive the 1st Marine Division, three battalions of soldiers

General Oliver P. Smith bids farewell to the fallen of the 1st Marine Division in December 1950. Originally commissioned in 1917, Smith had fought on Peleliu and Okinawa.

With no time to wait for medics, a Marine rifle squad brings in a wounded buddy in Seoul just after the Inchon landing. Casualties soon outnumbered stretchers, and doors were pressed into service.

of the 7th Infantry Division, and 41 Independent Commando of British Royal Marines were deployed along the huge, frozen Chosin reservoir north of the towns of Hagoru and Koto-Ri. After using overwhelming numbers to almost annihilate the army battalions that were stretched out near the reservoir, the Chinese troops seized command of a series of ridges that dominated the only road between Hagoru and the American-held port of Wonsan on the coast. Major General Oliver Smith, commander of the Allied forces in the region, determined to break out of this encirclement complete with all of his equipment and guns. When asked about his plan of retreat, he responded, "Retreat, hell! We're just attacking in another direction!"; a statement that had more than a ring of truth to it.

During some of the most frigid weather conditions that American troops had ever fought in, the mixed force of British and American Marines and survivors of the 7th Infantry Division engaged in a running shoot-out with the Communist troops holding the ridges. While ground troops broke up road blocks in bloody hand-to-hand fighting, Marine air units swept over the ridges in dangerous strafing runs that slowed down the Chinese machine guns and mortars pounding the road below. As General Smith noted later, "During the long reaches of the night and in the snow storms, many a Marine prayed for the coming of the day or clearing weather when he knew he would again hear the welcome roar of planes." While

> *Retreat, hell! We're just attacking in another direction!*
> — MAJOR GENERAL OLIVER SMITH

Taken by surprise by a Chinese offensive in December 1950, the fighting retreat of the 1st Marine Division became the most famous feat of arms of the Korean War. These Marines rest in the snow along the road from Changjin to Hungnam.

the Marines and soldiers suffered over 4,000 casualties on the breakout to Wonsan, including over 700 killed, the ground and air forces inflicted almost 40,000 casualties on the Communist besiegers, including nearly 25,000 dead, an accomplishment that eliminated three Chinese corps from the order of battle for months to come.

By Christmas of 1950, the majority of American ground forces had been withdrawn safely back to the old border between the two Koreas, but General Walker, who had organized much of this operation, was killed in a jeep accident during the final stages of the process. Walker's replacement, General Matthew Ridgway, one of the heroes of D-day, almost immediately faced a new crisis as the Chinese launched a New Year's offensive that threw almost 500,000 soldiers at the 200,000 men holding the lines along the 38th Parallel. Trading space for time, Ridgway ordered a withdrawal to a line 40 miles below Seoul as he drew the Chinese attackers to the end of their already stretched supply lines. By late January the American strategy began to pay

During the long reaches of the night and in the snow storms, many a Marine prayed for the coming of the day or clearing weather when he knew he would again hear the welcome roar of planes.

— MAJOR GENERAL OLIVER SMITH, KOREA, WINTER 1950.

dividends, and Ridgway was able to begin a cautious, gradual offensive northward so that by the first day of spring 1951, the American, Korean, and U.N. forces were back on the 38th Parallel. Nine months after Kim Il Sung's initial gambit to forcibly reunify Korea, the main mobile phase of the war had ended in stalemate. Now an exasperating, frustrating, two-year war of position was about to begin and one of the first casualties of this new type of warfare would be Douglas MacArthur.

President Truman and General MacArthur had little love for one another, as the president viewed his general as an egotistical sham, while the Far East commander viewed the commander in chief as a small-time politician who rose to the White House by sheer luck. Now, in the spring of 1951, the two men differed sharply on their view of the future of the Korean conflict. Truman saw Europe as the main battlefield of the Cold War and was genuinely alarmed that the defenses in Western Europe of the United States had been stripped to supply forces to hold the Chinese at bay in Korea. At this point he was more than willing to accept an end to the war in Korea that would merely keep the Communists north of the 38th Parallel. On the other hand, MacArthur saw Asia as the real testing ground in the war against Communism and believed that the Chinese could be decisively beaten if he was permitted to

Veteran airborne leader Matthew Ridgway, in command of the entire U.S. Eighth Army, surveys the front line in North Korea in February 1951. He wore the grenade as a personal identifying mark.

> ───── ★ ★ ★ ─────
>
> *Contrary to what you see in Hollywood movies, not all opposing soldiers killed each other whenever they got the chance. I know of at least four instances when opportunities to kill were passed up. In one amusing case, not involving me, Stan O'Connor had run out of gas and, walking along the road, encountered three Asian mortar men who had built a fire. They had hot water and Stan had packs of coffee, so the four of them drank coffee together and, according to Stan, shared their mutual dislike of war. The next day he encountered the same three men in a prisoner-of-war camp. It turns out that they were Chinese soldiers.*
>
> — WILLIAM D. DANNENMAIER, 15TH INFANTRY, JUNE, 1953
>
> ───── ★ ★ ★ ─────

blockade the China coast, destroy China's war industries through naval and air attacks, reinforce the troops in Korea with Chinese Nationalist forces, and allow Nationalist troops to attack the Chinese mainland. These steps virtually guaranteed a widening of the war, and when MacArthur publicly castigated Truman's failure to implement these proposals, the president relieved the legendary general of his command. MacArthur would return home to a hero's welcome and Truman would fatally damage his prospects for re-election, but the policy of static, limited war triumphed and American forces in Korea settled down to long months of virtual trench warfare.

As the war settled into a stalemate, pressure for negotiations gradually built up on both sides, and by the autumn of 1951 armistice discussions were being held in the tiny settlement of Panmunjon. However, the Chinese and North Koreans were heavily committed to the Communist technique of simultaneously talking and fighting to secure maximum advantage, and negotiations dragged on with only glacial progress accomplished. Finally, the election of Dwight Eisenhower to the U.S. presidency and the subsequent death of Joseph Stalin dramatically changed the leadership of the

A PFC leads a squad of the 25th Infantry Division forward in March 1951. Many of the characteristically barren hillsides had been productive rice paddies before the war.

U.S. Marines read about the impending armistice at Panmunjon in July 1953. By order of President Truman, racial segregation finally came to an end in the U.S. armed forces during the Korean War.

two competing ideologies. When Eisenhower began hinting strongly that failure to sign an armistice might lead to the use of nuclear weapons or a dramatic widening of the conflict, the peace process began to accelerate. On July 26, 1953, General Mark Clark and a delegation of North Korean and Chinese commanders affixed their signatures to an armistice agreement that essentially fixed the borders of the two rival Korean republics at the 38th Parallel. The United States had lost 34,000 men killed and 103,000 men wounded to stop Communist aggression in Korea while China lost almost a million men among their "volunteer" armies that had aided Kim Il Sung. However, while most Americans were frustrated at the failure to produce total victory on the Korean peninsula, they would soon be even more exasperated by events in another Asian conflict.

★ ★ ★

Less than a year after the Korean armistice, a new confrontation with Communist aggression began to emerge in the French colony of Indochina. Led by Ho Chi Minh, a

Communist-dominated revolutionary movement called the Viet Minh waged a struggle for Vietnamese independence from France that culminated in the capture of a large French army in the strong point of Den Bien Phu. After the French withdrew from Indochina in the wake of that disaster, the Communist consolidated control in the northern half of Vietnam while a nationalist leader, the anticommunist Ngo Dinh Diem, assumed leadership of a southern Republic of Vietnam. When Diem, supported by the United States, refused to hold elections for a possible reunification of the country, claiming undemocratic conditions in the North precluded a fair contest, Ho Chi Minh and his military commanders began supporting a southern insurgent movement called the Viet Cong. During the early 1960s these Communist forces conducted a guerrilla war of gradually increasing intensity which became a major threat to South Vietnamese independence after Diem was assassinated during a coup by other anticommunist leaders. By late 1964 Viet Cong strength had reached nearly 100,000 men and Ho Chi Minh was pouring in additional North Vietnamese units with the ultimate intention of cutting South Vietnam in two and then overrunning the severed parts of the country.

The major part of the United States military task [in Vietnam] can be completed by the end of 1965.

— SECRETARY OF STATE ROBERT MCNAMARA, OCTOBER 1963.

On February 7, 1965, most Vietnamese citizens were celebrating the end of their most important holiday of the year, the Lunar New Year's celebration called Tet. At this point over 24,000 American servicemen were deployed throughout the country in a desperate bid to prevent the shaky South Vietnamese government from collapsing under Communist military pressure. At 2 A.M. on that holiday morning while most people slept off the celebrations of the night before, a force of Viet Cong sappers crawled over the barbed wire protecting the American airfield at Pleiku and the nearby helicopter base at Camp Holloway. Suddenly a pyrotechnic display of rockets, grenades, and incendiaries lit up the humid night sky as the Communist infiltrators destroyed or damaged 22 planes and helicopters and killed nine Americans while wounding 128 servicemen. Three days later another Viet Cong force attacked the American enlisted men's quarters at Qui Jhon and killed or wounded 44 men. President Lyndon Johnson, who had already received authorization from Congress to retaliate against Communist attackers when the American destroyer *Maddox* was attacked in the Gulf of Tonkin the previous August, now initiated Operation Rolling Thunder, a retaliatory air offensive against North Vietnamese military installations.

During much of 1965, American reinforcements entering South Vietnam were used primarily to secure airfields and other key military sites; by early fall the Army of the Republic of Vietnam (ARVN) was near total collapse as North Vietnamese regulars poured into the south and inflicted a series of bloody defeats on the increasingly dispirited southern troops. The combination of battle deaths and desertions was costing the ARVN a battalion a week while President Johnson continued to agonize over whether or not significant ground forces should be deployed. Finally, the American president decided to send a significant number of combat units to the hard-pressed country and the total troop commitment would reach 175,000 by the end of the year.

The person responsible for effectively utilizing this massive infusion of manpower was General William Westmoreland, senior American military commander in Vietnam. Westmoreland knew he faced a deteriorating military situation and he resolved to use his new combat units to blunt an expected

William C. Westmoreland was U.S. commander in Vietnam, 1965-1968. Westmoreland's job was made more difficult by the fact that he only had direct control of U.S. army units, but not navy, air force, Marine, and South Vietnamese forces.

★ ★

Roy Benavidez

Roy Benavidez was working as a communications specialist on May 2, 1968, when he received word that a Special Forces team was pinned down under heavy fire. Commandeering a helicopter, he personally went to the rescue, saving eight men while being wounded nine times. Awarded the Distinguished Service Cross, the Army's second highest decoration for valor, the award was later upgraded to a full Medal of Honor.

In 1959, after tours in Korea and Germany, fairly typical assignments for an American soldier during the height of the Cold War, Roy Benavidez took airborne training. For the next six years he served with the 82nd Airborne Division during the successive crises of the early 1960s—Berlin, Cuba, and the rest—while getting married and beginning a family. In 1965 he went to Vietnam as an advisor and was so seriously wounded that he was almost discharged as permanently disabled. With hard work, he requalified for airborne duty and went on to join the Special Forces.

Benavidez, by then a staff sergeant, returned to Vietnam for a second tour of duty in 1968 and was soon assigned to a special reconnaissance detachment that operated in Cambodia, supporting various special operations activities.

It was there he saved the Special Forces team, although he suffered severe wounds during the effort. Benavidez required four major operations over the next few months, but in 1969 was sufficiently recovered to return to limited duty.

Seven years later, the army declared him totally disabled, and he retired as a master sergeant in 1976. Settling in El Campo, Texas, Benavidez found himself battling the Social Security Administration, which was not convinced his injuries were disabling.

Meanwhile, several of his former officers had undertaken a campaign to have him awarded the Medal of Honor. By 1980, sufficient eyewitness accounts had been gathered to permit the army to upgrade Benavidez's Distinguished Service Cross to a Medal of Honor.

Normally awards of the Medal of Honor are made by the president. However, although he signed the appropriate orders, President Jimmy Carter was unable to present the Medal of Honor to Benavidez due to the pressures of the Iran hostage crisis. As a result, the medal was not presented until 1981, by President Ronald Reagan, who personally read the citation, the first time that this had ever occurred. In addition to having been awarded the Medal of Honor, Benavidez was subsequently enrolled in the "Intelligence Hall of Fame" by the National Security Agency.

★ ★

General Westmoreland talks with men of the 18th Infantry Regiment of the 1st Division outside Bien Hoa in August 1965.

Communist offensive. The American general moved a number of units into a defensive arc around the capital city of Saigon, secured bases for the arrival of further reinforcements, and finally began to authorize limited offensives to throw the enemy off balance. Ironically, the first large American unit that would engage in a full scale battle with the Vietnamese Communists was a regiment whose initial claim to fame was a disastrous defeat, the 7th Cavalry. The descendants of the famous cavalrymen who had ridden to glory and annihilation under George Armstrong Custer were helicoptered into the Northern Highlands region called the Ia Drang Valley in November of 1965 and they almost immediately confronted three battalions of North Vietnamese regulars commanded by General Chu Hung Man, an aggressive officer who wanted the glory of winning the first battle against the "Imperialist Yankees."

The battle of Ia Drang was a vicious, bloody encounter between elite units of both armies and American commander Lieutenant Colonel Harold Moore must have had uncomfortable flashbacks to Custer's fate when he realized that General Man was pouring in fresh units and gradually surrounding the cavalrymen. However, these 20th-century troopers were smart, tough, experienced fighters who were able to form a formidable defensive perimeter while they waited for addition-

The 173rd Airborne Brigade, shown here in November 1967, was one of the first large American units to arrive in Vietnam. Although men of the 82nd and 101st Airborne Divisions served in Vietnam as infantry, the 173rd made the only operational parachute drop during the war.

al helicopter-borne units to land and even the odds somewhat. One participant in the battle provided a sample of the intensity of the engagement, "Sergeant Savage hit twelve of the enemy himself during the afternoon but the Communists still almost overran the perimeter." One American platoon lost 20 of 27 men in less than an hour, but the tremendous firepower of the cavalrymen dropped far more attackers. Soon American fighters, artillery, and even giant B-52 strategic bombers were thrown into the fray, and when the Communists broke off the engagement they had lost almost 1,300 men killed compared to 80 American fatalities. However, in an aftermath of battle that would become disconcertingly familiar in this frustrating war, the victorious Americans watched the defeated North Vietnamese survivors retreat into the jungle with no effective way to pursue a force that could slip across the border to Laos or Cambodia, safe havens from American attack.

> *Sergeant Savage hit twelve of the enemy himself during the afternoon but the Communists still almost overran the perimeter.*
>
> — A PARTICIPANT IN THE BATTLE OF IA DRANG.

During the next year, American deployment in South Vietnam rose to 385,000 men but Ho Chi Minh poured enough of his own regulars across the border to raise Communist strength to about 300,000 men, a formidable force for a guerrilla war. By early 1967 General Westmoreland was able to conduct "Search and Destroy" operations with five infantry divisions, two Marine divisions, four independent army brigades, and an armored cavalry regiment backed up by enormous numbers of support troops. The steady stream of reinforcements allowed Westmoreland to conduct a variety of offensive operations that by the end of 1967 were beginning to pay dividends, as Viet Cong and North Vietnamese forces were thrown on the defensive and the South Vietnamese government was given an opportunity to consolidate its hold on significant portions of the countryside. However, this feeling that there was indeed a "light at the end of the tunnel" in Vietnam came to a crashing halt in January of 1968.

By the fall of 1967 Ho Chi Minh and his military advisors conceded that the war in the south was at best a stalemate, and that it appeared that North Vietnam's employment of large units had been unequal to the task of defeating the constantly reinforced American forces. Ho Chi Minh even suspected that the United States might soon invade the north, a move that would force the recall of significant units from southern operations. The Communist response to this dilemma was a plan for a violent, widespread simultaneous uprising in both rural and urban areas throughout South Vietnam timed to begin when the ARVN forces would be least prepared, during the Tet celebrations. The North Vietnamese leaders decided to initiate this offensive utilizing primarily southern Viet Cong units rather than northern regulars, creating somewhat of a hedge against a military disaster if the operation failed, while keeping the regular units ready to enter the battle to exploit any possible success. By the week before Tet, almost 90,000 Communist troops had been infiltrated into assault positions and were merely waiting for the beginning of the holiday to launch their uprising.

On January 31, 1968, the Viet Cong attacked 30 of South Vietnam's 44 provincial capitals and most of the nation's largest cities including Hue and Saigon. While the

Wounded trooper of the 1st Division is treated during an ambush northeast of Saigon, June 17, 1967. The Viet Cong often attacked American units with the real aim of inflicting heavy casualties on troops coming to the rescue.

★ ★ ★ ★ ★ ★ ★ ★ ★ ★ ★ ★ ★ ★ ★ ★ ★ ★ ★ ★

Sharon Lane

Sharon Lane took on the hardest nursing duties in Vietnam. In a civilian ward full of Vietnamese women and children injured in the fighting, she volunteered for the night shift. A few minutes before her shift was due to end on June 8, 1969—on her 43rd day in Vietnam—the hospital came under enemy rocket fire. The civilian ward was devastated, and Lane was struck in the neck by a piece of shrapnel. She bled to death within minutes. She was the only female officer to die in Vietnam due to enemy action.

In May 1968, Lane had reported to Fort Sam Houston in San Antonio, Texas, where she was commissioned a second lieutenant in the Army Nurse Corps. Soon deeply involved in a rigorous training program, she learned to perform minor surgery and treat various types of wounds, as well as basic military subjects, including communications and self-defense. After six weeks she was ordered to Fitzsimmons Army Hospital, near Denver, and was assigned to the tuberculosis ward. Promoted to first lieutenant in August, later that year she was transferred to the hospital's Intensive Care Unit, but she shortly put in for a transfer to Vietnam.

Lieutenant Lane arrived in Vietnam on April 26, 1969, and was assigned to the 312th Evacuation Hospital. An Army Reserve unit from Winston-Salem, North Carolina, the 312th Evac had been activated after the Tet Offensive and arrived in Vietnam in September 1968, to be assigned to Chulai. Like all medical personnel, Lane was soon working 12-hour shifts six days a week to cope with the enormous number of casualties, both military and civilian.

After her death, Lane was posthumously awarded the Bronze Star and Purple Heart, as well as the Vietnamese Gallantry Cross with Palm. In addition, facilities at Fitzsimmons Army Hospital and Aultman Hospital were dedicated to her memory, and a statue of her was also erected at Aultman Hospital, which honored Lane and 110 local servicemen who had died in Vietnam.

★ ★ ★ ★ ★ ★ ★ ★ ★ ★ ★ ★ ★ ★ ★ ★ ★ ★ ★ ★

American military police-men take cover next to their fallen comrades at the U.S. embassy during the Tet Offensive of January 31, 1968. The Viet Cong suffered heavy losses during the offensive, but the psychological impact on American public opinion proved to be decisive.

Communists were primarily targeting areas held by ARVN forces, American units were quickly deployed in a number of the most ferocious engagements and in most cases inflicted devastating defeats on the insurgents. The most intensive, extended battle occurred in the old imperial capital of Hue where the 1st Cavalry and 101st Airborne Division and Marines conducted the most extensive urban campaign of the war, and engaged in a bloody house-to-house and street-to-street battle that destroyed enormous segments of the city. Every night, tens of millions of American viewers watched in fascination and horror as television screens carried the violent images of warfare close-up. While the Marines and soldiers inflicted far more casualties than they received, the sight of dozens of dead and mangled Americans being carried from the battered streets and houses of the flame-wreathed city deeply disturbed the American public.

In a tactical sense, the Tet Offensive was an absolute disaster for the Communists. Forty-five thousand of the 88,000 Viet Cong troops who participated in the general uprising were killed or wounded and the southern-based insurgency movement never fully recovered from this devastating blow. However, the American public focused on images of the Viet Cong storming the American Embassy in Saigon and the carnage in Hue, and questioned the validity of General

Westmoreland's recent assertion that the Communists were nearly defeated. When the American commander requested 206,000 additional troops from President Johnson the political fallout was enormous and the president began to seek a way out of the impasse before the November elections. Finally, after it became obvious that Johnson would have an enormous difficulty securing his party's nomination for the upcoming election, the president coupled his announcement that he would not seek reelection with an order to curtail bombing of North Vietnam as a prelude to peace negotiations with the Communists. America was now committed to disengagement, and the tactical disaster of Tet now emerged as a brilliant strategic victory for Ho Chi Minh.

The Vietnam War was the major issue of the 1968 presidential election, and Richard M. Nixon was able to win the contest in large part through a promise to have "peace with honor" through "Vietnamization," a process through which a gradually shrinking force of American troops would provide a shield for the upgrading and training of the ARVN to eventually take over responsibility for the defense of South Vietnam. The task of carrying out this difficult procedure was given the new commanding general, Creighton Abrams, who succeeded Westmoreland in the summer of 1968, when the former commander in Vietnam moved up to become chief of staff of the

Medics help evacuate a wounded member of the 101st Airborne Division from Hamburger Hill in May 1969. This costly frontal assault, made after the reduction in U.S. forces had already been announced, led to further criticism of American military leadership and tactics.

army. Abrams inherited a force at its peak strength of 543,000 men, but he was under enormous pressure from Washington to minimize casualties while leaving the ARVN in the best possible position when American forces withdrew. While Abrams was able to organize a string of successful offensive campaigns he was increasingly hampered by two major negative developments. First, as it became obvious that the United States had no intention of attempting to win the war, morale in many combat units began a noticeable downward slide. The concept of fighting a prolonged, unwinnable holding action was extremely unappealing to men in the front lines of an already exasperating war, and much of the earlier offensive spirit of the first years of the war was missing in the final years of the conflict. Second, while individual ARVN troops seemed willing enough to fight the Communists, the political and military officials who led them were frequently both incompetent and corrupt, more interested in their personal advancement than defeating the enemy. As American units pulled out of key locations throughout the country, the ARVN units replacing them were of increasingly questionable combat effectiveness.

It is a brutal war.
— Journalist Bernard Fall

By the winter of 1973, American diplomats were able to conclude a series of negotiations that made even the exasperating Korean War peace discussions appear productive. After five years of Communist propaganda and posturing the United States was able to secure the release of American prisoners of war in exchange for a virtually complete military withdrawal from South Vietnam. Almost as soon as the last American units had been withdrawn, the North Vietnamese leaders, who had succeeded the now deceased Ho Chi Minh, began planning a massive offensive against the shaky Thieu government in the south. A combination of questionable military decisions by Thieu and the continued incompetence of many ARVN generals ceded ever larger swaths of territory to the advancing North Vietnamese regulars, until by April of 1975 the Communists were closing in on Saigon itself. American television viewers now watched a final act in the drama as helicopters rescued American Embassy personnel from the roof of the embassy building only moments before enemy troops broke through and raised Communist emblems over the building.

The Vietnam Veterans Memorial in Washington, DC. Designed by artist Maya Lin, "the wall" was controversial at first but has since become the most visited site in the nation's capital.

While this conclusion to the war was not an American military defeat in the strictest sense, since the last United States forces had left the country two years earlier, the nation had lost 57,000 men to support a non-Communist South Vietnam that no longer existed. As Saigon officially became Ho Chi Minh City, American political policy, if not military prowess, appeared to be a total failure in Southeast Asia.

The forcible annexation of South Vietnam by the North Vietnamese government was probably the high-water mark of Communist military aggression. Little more than a decade after the Marxist emblem waved over the American Embassy in Saigon, Communism seemed to be in retreat on a number of fronts. As the Berlin Wall was demolished, the Russian flag replaced the Soviet banner over the Kremlin and even China opened its system of capitalist investment. It became apparent that the Cold War was largely over and in the battle of rival ideologies, the American value system had triumphed. However, President George Bush's proclamation of a "New World Order" in the wake of the end of the Cold War was soon challenged by terrorist bands and outlaw states that threatened American security from a number of directions.

★ ★ ★

The most dramatic of these threats emerged in the summer of 1990 when Saddam Hussein, the ruthless dictator of Iraq, brutally invaded the tiny neighboring state of Kuwait and strongly hinted that Saudi Arabia would soon be annexed as well.

During the autumn days of 1990, President George Bush and the chairman of the Joint Chiefs of Staff, General Colin Powell, entrusted General Norman Schwarzkopf with command of Operation Desert Shield, the defense of Saudi Arabia against Iraqi attack. Both Powell and Schwarzkopf had served in Vietnam as mid-level officers and these leaders were determined that the mistakes of that earlier conflict would be avoid-

General H. Norman Schwarzkopf visits men of an armored unit in Saudi Arabia in January 1991, one week before Operation Desert Storm.

ed in this Middle East confrontation with aggression. The burly Schwarzkopf, nicknamed "The Bear" by his men, oversaw one of the most impressive buildups of military power in the annals of history while coordinating a coalition of Allied forces which included a diverse group of nations ranging from Britain to Syria. When the United Nations gave Saddam a deadline of January 15, 1991, to withdraw from Kuwait, the Iraqi leader entrenched almost 550,000 soldiers along the border with Saudi Arabia and defied the Coalition forces to oust him. While Schwarzkopf could muster a slightly smaller ground attack force of almost 450,000 men, the American commander had

Soldiers of the U.S. VII Corps in gas masks and protective suits at the beginning of Desert Storm. Designed to be worn in a major European conflict, the suits were intended to protect against radiation and all known chemical and biological agents.

As army units fanned out across the desert, the U.S. Marines were assigned the liberation of Kuwait City itself. Several men in this patrol, walking past a burning oil well, carry M16s mounted with the M203 grenade launcher.

the powerful support of almost 200 warships, 1,600 first line combat planes, and almost 2,000 tanks, including the unrivaled latest generation of American armored vehicles.

On Wednesday January 16, as Americans in the eastern sections of the country sat down to watch the evening news, live reports from the Iraqi capital of Baghdad were suddenly interrupted by the wail of sirens and the staccato sound of antiaircraft guns barking into action. They were responding to an armada of unmanned Tomahawk missiles and manned F-4 Wild Weasels, FA-6B Navy Prowlers, and F-18 attack jets that were sweeping across the bleak desert terrain to initiate a lethal attack on Saddam's command and control facilities. Unlike the more random attacks of World War II the use of laser-guided missiles and "smart" bombs allowed the Americans and other Coalition forces to obliterate military targets with minimal damage to other areas of the city, but by the end of the first day of the new offensive, called Desert Storm, it was clear that the expensive, latest-generation of military hardware was about to pay substantial dividends. For the next six weeks an average of 2,000 sorties a day were flown by American and Allied air units, although a substantial number of these attacks had to be diverted to "Scud Busting" as Saddam unleashed flurries of the large, rather inaccurate Soviet missiles at Israel and Saudi Arabia. When the

Americans began deploying Patriot defensive missile systems in the threatened countries, Hussein's most daring gambit was checkmated.

By the middle of February 1991, Schwarzkopf and his advisors were convinced that the air offensive had decimated the Iraqi defenses and the next phase of Desert Storm, the ground assault, was set in motion. The American commander was determined to avoid a head-on offensive against the enemy which might produce a fearsome casualty list such as the 1918 Meuse-Argonne offensive which slaughtered thousands of doughboys. Schwarzkopf developed a more sophisticated assault plan in which Saudi and other Arab forces would drive for Kuwait City protected on their flanks by U.S. Marines on the coast and army mechanized and armored units farther inland, while far to the west the XVIII Airborne Corps would thrust into Iraq itself and drive through a region that Saddam had failed to fortify properly.

At 5:30 A.M. on the cold, rainy morning of February 24, 1991, forward units of the 2nd Marine Division approached the first Iraqi defensive line. As tanks, tracked amphibious vehicles, and newly designed jeep-like Humvees roared ahead, engineer units fired rocket-propelled explosive charges at the minefield that lay ahead. The Marine ground units, protected by chemical-protection suits in case Saddam initiated a gas or chemical attack, dodged Iraqi mortar fire and pushed through several lines of barbed wire and chain-link fences, and then clambered

Soldiers of the 101st Air Assault Division, now primarily a helicopter rather than an airborne unit, land in Iraq on February 25, 1991, far in advance of Coalition ground forces. The Iraqi command had not expected such a long-range deployment under such difficult conditions.

through trenches, foxholes, and bunkers as Iraqi forces fired and retreated through the vast desert behind them. The "Hundred Hour War" had begun and one of the most potent American offensive of the 20th century was already rapidly gaining momentum.

> *The oil well fires were really bad. . . . it would get so dark that I literally could not see the front bumper of the truck I was driving.*
>
> — CAPTAIN PRESTON V. MCMURRY III, 432ND CIVIL AFFAIRS COMPANY.

Far to the west, 700 helicopters, the largest concentration of such aircraft seen in a combat situation, ferried the 101st Air Assault Division 80 miles into Iraqi territory and this airlift immediately created an enormous threat against Saddam's right flank. As Hussein attempted to push reinforcements toward this newly vulnerable point, American and Coalition air units simply pulverized the Iraqis and destroyed dozens of tanks and trucks. By nightfall of the first day of the war, 13,000 enemy soldiers had been captured at a cost of only four American dead, and the carefully prepared Iraqi positions were often being outflanked before they could even be employed.

The next day, February 25, the already impressive American and Coalition advance continued to gain momentum. In the eastern sector of the battle, the 24th Mechanized Division linked up with the 101st Air Assault Division and the combined force began overrunning airfields and setting up roadblocks to cut off enemy retreat. Meanwhile, along the coast, Kuwait and other Arab units began liberating towns in southern Kuwait

Smoke from a burning oil well outlines an LVTP-7 of the 2nd Marine Division on the Saudi-Kuwaiti border at the start of the ground war against Iraqi forces. Although the LVTP-7 was lightly armored and intended for amphibious landings, the "Amtrac" proved useful for desert operations.

while in the center, the highly mobile American VII Corps began deploying in positions to challenge Saddam's most elite unit, the Republican Guard.

The third day of the war opened with an American offensive toward the Euphrates River which could trap enormous Iraqi forces who would be cut off from resupply, while Marines and Coalition Arab forces closed in on Kuwait City from two directions. At Kuwait International Airport, the 1st Marine Division and the Tiger Brigade of the 2nd Armored Division engaged in one of the largest tank battles of the war as they confronted a powerful force of Iraqi tanks around the perimeter of the airfield. At this point Saddam began to realize that a threat to his rear was developing and in the center of the battlefield major Iraqi units began to launch a last, desperate offensive to throw the American drive off balance. In one of the most dramatic episodes of the day, a single unit, G Troop of the 2nd Armored Cavalry, found itself face to face with an entire brigade of the Republican Guard and for six hours the two mismatched forces dueled over the sand dunes. The small American unit held off the Iraqis long enough for reinforcements and supporting artillery units to arrive, and by nightfall, the elite Tawakalma Division of the Republican Guard was in a state of near collapse and the overall prisoner count had passed the 40,000 mark.

The final full day of the Gulf War, February 27, saw a general advance on all fronts as most of the Iraqi army was now merely interested in getting back to friendly lines in one piece. American and Coalition planes flew unchallenged over the desert highways and strafed and bombed long columns of Iraqi vehicles which were now being abandoned rapidly by

The short week of the 432nd's stay at Khobar Village began and ended with surprises. The first was being awakened at 0200, Thursday, February 7, by an air raid siren and sound of a loudspeaker calling out, "SCUD launch . . . . SCUD launch." A new experience now for the main body: being down range from an enemy attempting to kill our people.

The first reaction after the initial shock wore off was to don gas masks and assemble in the commons areas of each of the apartments. After about seven minutes, members heard the welcome words, "All clear . . . All clear." They later learned the voice on the loudspeaker was appropiately named, "Dr. Death."

There would be more SCUD alerts, and all but one were regarded as a joke because of what the troops regarded as the uncanny accuracy of American Patriot missiles . . . .

The tragic exception to this comedy of missiles errors was the failure to intercept one SCUD that fell on a reserve quartermaster unit's quarters in Dhahran on Sunday, February 24, after the 432nd had left for Al Jubayl. Twenty-eight reservists died in the freak hit and one hundred were wounded, the largest total loss during the entire conflict.

— A MEMBER OF THE 432ND CIVIL AFFAIRS COMPANY FROM GREEN BAY, WISCONSIN.

———— ★ ★ ★ ————

Near the end of Desert Storm, a soldier of the 24th Mechanized Infantry Division weeps when he learns that a wounded buddy has died. Less than 150 Americans were killed in the Persian Gulf during active operations; about a quarter of these were from friendly fire.

Saddam's disheartened troops. By the time that President Bush announced that a cease-fire would take effect at 8 A.M. the next morning, 33 Iraqi divisions were listed as destroyed. Yet during the night Allied forces kept up the pressure with powerful thrusts further into Saddam's country. By the time the cease-fire took effect, the Iraqi casualty toll was approaching astronomical proportions, including 29,000 dead, 85,000 captured, and 100,000 deserted, compared to 148 Americans killed in action along with about 100 Allied troops. The United Nations had authorized the use of force to eject the Iraqis from Kuwait, and by the morning of February 28, that mission had been fully accomplished. While considerable debate followed the war as to whether American and Coalition forces should have driven for Baghdad itself, the fact remains that the United States had scored a stunningly one-sided victory in a remarkably short span of time. An enormous number of new technologies had proven effective, female personnel had played a significant role in key aspects of the overall operation, and National Guard and Reserve units fought with distinction. The American Armed Forces came out of the Gulf War with their prestige at the highest point since the end of World War II, with servicemen and servicewomen better educated and trained with more sophisticated methods than at any point in the nation's history.

CHAPTER IX

America the Brave and the Free

A short time before the opening of the American Revolution, Major John Pitcairn, the man who would command the redcoats on Lexington Green, wrote to the Earl of Sandwich explaining why the colonists would never defeat His Majesty's forces. He insisted that these deluded "country people" were so obsessed with money and physical comfort that they could never endure the agony of a long conflict with Britain. He was certain that when the British army actually went into action, "they will soon be convinced that they are very insignificant when opposed to regular troops . . . I am satisfied that a smart action and burning two or three of their towns will set everything to rights." A few weeks later this Royal Marine major discovered that he made a fatal error. He and dozens of his fellow officers were mortally wounded by a small but determined band of patriot militiamen defending a hastily built fort in front of Bunker Hill.

Over two centuries later, a far more powerful adversary, Iraqi dictator Saddam Hussein, made the same error. He told his advisors that the Americans would not fight to defend newly-conquered Kuwait. Saddam was convinced that a combination of obsession with luxury and the trauma of Vietnam had left the United States incapable of sacrificing blood to liberate a distant desert kingdom. Yet during the early morning hours of January 16, 1991, as cruise missiles and war planes pounded Baghdad, the Iraqi leader began to realize that the United States was a far more formidable adversary than he ever imagined. Major Pitcairn, President Hussein, and a large number of adversaries in the intervening two centuries failed to understand that while the United States was essentially a peace-loving society, the American people were capable of enormous sacrifice, bravery, and energy when called upon to protect the ideals upon which their nation was founded.

In the last two centuries, American men and women have defended the principles of liberty and democracy at home and abroad—from New England village greens to desert dunes. Despite the many different battlefields that have challenged American warriors, common characteristics are readily apparent. First, Americans have entered most conflicts relatively unprepared to fight. We have seldom shown much enthusiasm for the European tradition of turning the country into an armed camp. Because of this we have been forced as a nation to hit the ground running in most wars. Second, American warriors have demonstrated a combination of ferocity and humanity in conflict. After the battle of Lexington and Concord, the same rebel militiamen who had launched such a deadly fire on the redcoats treated their British prisoners with such compassion that a number of His Majesty's soldiers wrote letters to their relatives describing the humanity of their colonial adversaries. And a century later, within moments after American sailors had obliterated the Spanish fleet at Santiago in the summer of 1898, those same men were risking their lives to rescue the seamen of the vanquished navy. Finally, Americans have always been creative on the battlefield—exhibiting more individual initiative and intelligence in combat than most of their adversaries. Our society has historically recognized the individuality of each citizen, and so our soldiers have been willing to make vital decisions in the heat of battle—and that has frequently meant the difference between victory and defeat.

The United States enters the 21st century as the freest, most prosperous society in the history of the planet and at least one significant reason for this enviable status is that from Concord to Kuwait City, American citizens have sacrificed comfort, security, and their lives to defend a unique experiment in the story of mankind: the premise that each and every person in a society has value and importance. While the challenges of the next century are still far from certain, this spirit of sacrifice seems likely to ensure America's status as a continuing beacon of liberty in a still very perilous world.

INDEX

Photo Credits